The Economic and Social Environment for Tax Reform

The Fair Tax Commission was established in 1991 by the Treasurer of Ontario to provide the government with advice on how to design and implement a more equitable tax system in the province. The commission developed a research program, hoping to inform the public debate on taxation issues while leaving a legacy of studies, data, and other information. A series of publications has been undertaken by University of Toronto Press in cooperation with the Fair Tax Commission to make the research studies available to tax professionals, academics, interest groups, and the general public.

The Economic and Social Environment for Tax Reform Papers by David Conklin and John Whalley; Bruce Campbell; Peter Dungan; and Brian B. Murphy and Michael C. Wolf son

Major economic and social developments that will determine the context for tax reforms in the 1990s are the subject of this volume. They include the globalization of markets, free-trade arrangements, changing technology and production processes, macroeconomic policies and conditions in Canada, and population growth and changes in demographic structure.

The Economic and Social Environment for Tax Reform

DAVID CONKLIN and JOHN WHALLEY

BRUCE CAMPBELL

PETER DUNGAN

BRIAN B. MURPHY and MICHAEL C. WOLFSON

Edited by

ALLAN M. MASLOVE

Published by University of Toronto Press in cooperation with the
Fair Tax Commission of the Government of Ontario

UNIVERSITY OF TORONTO PRESS
Toronto Buffalo London

Reprinted in paperback 2014

ISBN 978-0-8020-7629-8 (paper)

∞

Printed on recycled paper

Canadian Cataloguing in Publication Data

Main entry under title:

The economic and social environment for tax reform

(Research studies of the Fair Taxation Commission of Ontario)
Includes bibliographical references.
ISBN 978-0-8020-7629-8 (pbk.)

1. Tax incidence – Ontario.   2. Taxation – Ontario.
3. Canada – Economic conditions – 1991–   .*
4. Ontario – Economic conditions – 1991–   .*
I. Con lin, David W.   II. Maslove, Allan M., 1946–   .
III. Ontario.   Fair Tax Commission.   IV. Series.

HJ2323.C2E3 1995   336.2'00971   C94-932340-3

Contents

Foreword

The Ontario Fair Tax Commission was established to examine the province's tax system as an integrated whole and, in conjunction with its working groups, to analyse individual components of the system in detail.

It has been many years since the Ontario tax system was subjected to a comprehensive examination. However, a great deal of research on taxation has been undertaken over the past two decades. This work, based in several disciplines, has been both theoretical and applied, and in this context the research program of the Fair Tax Commission was formulated.

The research program has two broad purposes. The first is, of course, to support the deliberations of the commissioners. The second, more novel objective is to inform public discussions of tax matters so that the commission's formal and informal public consultations can be of maximum value. For this reason we have opted to publish volumes in the series of studies as they are ready, rather than holding them all until the commission has completed its work. While our approach is more difficult from a technical and administrative perspective, we believe that the benefits will justify our decision.

The research program seeks to synthesize the existing published work on taxation; to investigate the implications for Ontario of the general research work; and, where required, to conduct original research on the context and principles for tax reform and on specific tax questions. We thus hope to add to the existing body of knowledge without duplicating it. The studies included in these publications are those that we believe make a contribution to the literature on taxation.

I would like to extend my thanks to my fellow commissioners and to the members of the FTC secretariat. I also thank the many members of the working groups and the advisory groups who have contributed to the research program and to the overall work of the commission.

Monica Townson, Chair

Introduction

Tax reform cannot be contemplated without consideration of the economic and social context in which it will occur. A good deal of recent discussion of international economic trends is summarized by the term 'globalization.' For purposes of tax policy, this term implies the diminishing significance of national and sub-national borders in the operation of important goods and resources (including financial capital) markets. Stated in other terms, the cross-border mobility of capital, goods, and, to a lesser extent, people is increasing. The impacts of these developments on the ability of governments to raise revenues and on the manner in which they do so are potentially profound. At the same time, in the coming years, Canada and Ontario will experience changes in demographic structure, including a major increase in the absolute and relative number of people over the age of 65, and a likely continuation of the increase in the participation rate of women in the formal labour force.

The Fair Tax Commission engaged several researchers to examine economic and demographic trends in Canada and Ontario. The commission also asked how these trends might affect the current tax system and shape or constrain reform options. Four of these studies constitute the present volume.

David Conklin and John Whalley argue that the developments in the global economy impact more significantly on Ontario than on any other province in Canada. Ontario's close linkages with the United States make the province especially vulnerable to shocks emanating from the United States, in part because its exports to them are heavily concentrated in manufacturing (especially automobiles).

Further, they argue that Ontario is more susceptible than other provinces to business disinvestment as a result of trade agreements such as the North American Free Trade Agreement (NAFTA) and the recent General Agreement on Trade and Tariffs (GATT). As a result, the Ontario government is heavily constrained in its ability to tax mobile bases, especially financial capital. In the authors' view, greater reliance will have to be placed on sales taxes and taxes on labour income.

Bruce Campbell also examines the significance of globalization for tax policy. He argues that fundamental changes have come about and continue to occur, *inter alia*, in regulatory regimes, the organization of production, financial markets, labour markets, and income distribution. Campbell argues that while global and regional trade developments have worked to limit the "policy space" of governments, one need not conclude that Canadian governments have lost all discretion and are limited to harmonizing taxes with other countries, primarily the United States. He concludes that if there is a consensus on the maintenance of public programs and the role of government in society, there is still room for Canadian taxes to diverge from those of our trading partners in order to support these programs.

The paper by Peter Dungan identifies eight sets of factors affecting the economic futures of the Canadian and Ontario economies, and the fiscal positions of their governments. The paper provides quantitative estimates of key parameters in the national and provincial economies along with "downside" projections that might occur as a result of developments in the key factors. Dungan's analysis indicates that, in the shorter term, there will be strong pressure on the tax system resulting from high deficits, but that towards the end of the 1990s the federal deficit and, later, the provincial deficit situations will ease significantly. Pressures for indirect tax measures, for environmental or other purposes, can exert inflationary influences unless offset by reductions in other indirect taxes. Finally, because consumption spending is likely to be a lagging sector for some time, he predicts that revenues from consumption-based taxes are likely to grow relatively slowly.

The Brian Murphy and Michael Wolfson paper focuses on demographic change scenarios and their potential interaction with government finances. Using SPSD/M simulations, their analysis, projected to the year 2011, suggests that the ageing of the population will put some pressures on public finances, particularly through health-care and pension spending. However, modest economic growth would generate additional tax revenues, possibly enough to more than offset the higher public costs. The Murphy and Wolfson analysis indicates that straightforward projections of demographic trends are not sufficient to determine impacts on government budgets in the future. It is necessary to factor in economic growth and revenue as well as expenditure impacts, and to consider changes in program structures.

Taken together, the papers in this volume suggest that Canada and Ontario will face major economic and demographic challenges as we move into the next century, and that these challenges will be reflected in the fiscal positions of governments. However, unlike much of the current "conventional wisdom" about these trends, these papers convey an optimistic tone and suggest that fiscal options remain open to governments – there will continue to be room to move.

Allan M. Maslove

The Economic and Social Environment for Tax Reform

1 The Ontario Tax System in the Global Economy of the 1990s

DAVID CONKLIN and JOHN WHALLEY

Introduction

For many decades, Ontario's economy has been closely linked to the economies of other jurisdictions, especially that of the United States. Ontario's exports and imports have formed a major portion of its aggregate economic activities, and foreign investment in Ontario has made an important contribution to the aggregate capital stock. This "open" nature of Ontario's economy and its heavy dependence on the United States, together with the large role of manufacturing in the Ontario economy, have important implications for tax design. While the economies of Canada's other provinces are also exposed to developments abroad, a central argument of this paper is that Ontario's situation is different from the rest of Canada's, and so Ontario's tax design should be developed independently in the context of Ontario's economy. This paper also evaluates key developments in the global economy of the 1990s that may significantly affect Ontario's tax system and assesses their implications for tax design. A central focus is the possibility of further growth in global interdependence and the implication of heightened international mobility, particularly of capital.

Close links with the United States expose the Ontario economy to the likelihood that tax bases, and hence revenues, will be susceptible to shocks emanating from the U.S. economy. In some circumstances these shocks may originate outside the United States, and their impact may be felt by way of Ontario's U.S. linkages, and also by way of Ontario's ties with other provinces. In its 1992 "Trade Policy Review" of Canada, the General Agreement on Tariffs and Trade (GATT) pointed to the Canada–U.S. Free Trade Agreement (FTA) as having "further increased [Canada's] dependence on economic developments in the United States."[1] The post-1989 recession has demonstrated the degree to which Canada's economy, and Ontario's economy and tax revenues, can be affected by a Canadian recession that is linked closely to a U.S. recession. The GATT review further noted that "both the prominent role of resource-based products in Canada's export basket and the Canada–US links in the industrial sector have contributed to the length and severity of the recent recession. Important primary commodity markets slumped, reflecting, *inter alia*, a global overcapacity in the pulp and paper industries, substantial sales of ores and metals from eastern and central Europe and intense competition in subsidized exports between major grains traders. The US recession, affecting in particular the large North American car producers, spilled over to discourage an earlier and stronger recovery."[2]

Apart from the dependence of Ontario's tax revenues on U.S. business cycles, there will likely be a series of externally generated shocks in the 1990s that will also impact on Ontario revenues, namely, the implementation and adjustments to new trade agreements; the impacts of new regulations and taxes designed to respond to environmental, labour, and social policy issues; and the implications of tax reforms of other jurisdictions. Import surges will likely occur in a wide variety of manufactured products, increases in some cases related to a relocation of manufacturing processes to low-wage newly industrialized countries (NICs). Commodity and resource price swings affecting extractive and other industries, particularly as they relate to energy prices, are other sources of shocks. Changes in international exchange rates may also be significant. These shocks are discussed in this paper. The focus is the possible relocation of businesses and corporate financing, and consequent changes in Ontario tax bases.

Ontario is particularly vulnerable to externally generated shocks for two reasons: first, its trade, dominated by automobile manufacturing, is concentrated sectorally; and second, trade is also concentrated geographically, owing to its dependence on the United States, in particular a few of the northern states. Therefore, these externally generated shocks should be considered in designing Ontario's tax system, both for making revenue forecasts and for maintaining Ontario's competitiveness as an investment location. This paper assesses these developments in light of international considerations that seem likely to both guide and constrain Ontario's tax policy in the decade ahead. On the one hand is the desire to use tax policy, in part, to insulate the economy from unanticipated shocks and adverse external developments. On the other hand is the danger that the revenue loss to Ontario's treasury as a result of insulating Ontario's economy may be so high as to limit this role.

The potential for an exodus of business activities is being increased by new trade agreements. The GATT–Uruguay round negotiations seem (at time of writing) likely to conclude at last. Implementation of the FTA will continue, as will the new North American Free Trade Agreement (NAFTA), which introduces an element of additional competition from Mexico. To the extent that these developments amplify the vulnerability of Ontario's economy and its potential revenue instability, they also impact on tax design. A central concern is the degree to which Ontario businesses will be encouraged to shift their activities to other countries as a result of these trade agreements. Ontario's dependence on manufacturing – in particular on automobile production – means that generalizations for Canada cannot be applied automatically to Ontario. Ontario is made much more susceptible than other provinces to business disinvestment as a result of these agreements.

The implications of Ontario's global interdependence for tax design also relate to environmental, labour, and social policy issues. Businesses may choose to relocate in jurisdictions whose government regulations are less cost-enhancing than Ontario's, or simply different. Consequently, Ontario's economy would be exposed to policy-generated capital outflow and revenue instability. Environmental, labour, and social policy concerns will lead also to changes in tax design both in Ontario and elsewhere, with the introduction of new kinds of taxes related to these issues. Tax design, for example, will be used to encourage businesses to adopt more environmentally friendly production processes. Payroll taxes will be modified in response to concerns about the funding of such programs as unemployment insurance, workers compensation, and health care. Consequently, these issues by themselves will cause differences in tax systems among jurisdictions. A general tax problem of the 1990s will be the possibility that regulatory and tax differences between Ontario and other jurisdictions – owing to differences in political responses to these issues – may cause a shift of investment and jobs out of Ontario.

Recent literature has emphasized the role that tax regimes are now playing in determining where businesses decide to locate. While this literature has focused on comparisons among federal tax systems, this paper also emphasizes the importance of comparisons among the tax systems of sub-national governments. For Ontario, more than for other provinces, relevant comparisons are those with governments in the United States where state and local governments are taking an aggressive position in offering tax concessions to entice investments. For Ontario, the 1990s will be a time of intense competition for investments, with tax provisions being a central weapon in this competition. At the national level, President Clinton is likely to implement significant general tax reforms that will alter the structure of this competition. Consequently, Ontario's tax design should be flexible and adaptable, allowing continual study of differences between Ontario's tax system and those in the United States.

In recent years, it appears that Canadians have increased the percentage of their consumer purchases made in the United States. Some have argued that differences in tax structures have been a significant factor in this increased cross-border shopping. Travel and time costs may limit this phenomenon to some degree, and it is also likely to be concentrated geographically in areas close to the Ontario–U.S. border. Nevertheless, mail-order catalogue shopping extends the potential scope of cross-border shopping to other areas of Ontario.[3] By the fall of 1992, numbers for cross-border shopping had begun to decrease, and this was related by some observers to changes in the Canada–U.S. exchange rate. Cross-border shopping provides a concrete illustration of the susceptibility of Ontario's economy to developments outside of Ontario, and shows the importance of comparisons – in this case, comparisons of consumer after-tax prices – between Ontario and nearby U.S. states.

This paper does not address the subject of deficits, debt, and Ontario fiscal policy. Nevertheless, the importance of tax design would be heightened by the possibility of an Ontario "debt crisis" and by a political desire to restrain Ontario's deficits. A debt crisis can occur precipitously. A theme of this paper is that economic relationships can exhibit discontinuities: the impact of certain developments may involve a period of gradual change followed by a rather sudden shock. New knowledge of fiscal realities, for example, could lead abruptly to a decision to raise taxes. This paper addresses the question of which kinds of taxes should be raised, given the current structure and circumstances of Ontario's economy. In particular, if taxes on capital were to be increased, outward flows of capital could minimize the potential revenue gain, and perhaps could even reduce aggregate tax revenue. Some capital outflows could entail job losses, leading to further negative revenue and expenditure impacts.

The picture for the 1990s in Ontario is of a tax system slowly becoming more constrained in its design by international factors, and vulnerable to major external shocks. A central issue is how to design Ontario's tax policies in light of varying degrees of mobility of tax bases. Financial capital is clearly highly mobile, with debt financing moving to the highest tax jurisdiction for cross-border integrated activities. The potential shift of manufacturing facilities in response to tax differentials is of primary importance. With sales taxes and taxes on labour income, concern about the mobility of tax bases seems to be less serious than concern with capital mobility. Autonomy in tax policy will not disappear entirely, but the constraints it faces will become more severe.

Increasingly, Ontario will be competing with other jurisdictions to retain and strengthen its existing businesses and to attract new economic activities. Several elements in tax design will be important in this interjurisdictional competition. If the Ontario government decides that it has to raise taxes, the perspective presented in this paper encourages a greater reliance on sales and labour income taxes rather than capital and capital income taxes.

Analytical Issues Underpinning Tax Design in an Open Economy

Mobility of Tax Bases in Response to Tax Design

Recent literature emphasizes that the increasing global interdependencies place new restrictions on tax design. Joel Slemrod (1990), for example, argues that tax differences between jurisdictions can be a cause of the mobility of tax bases. He discusses the design of the tax structure as a competition among jurisdictions for the pursuit of tax revenue. By reducing a certain tax, a jurisdiction may attract the migration of the relevant tax base in a way that increases aggregate tax revenue. He points out that "the internationalization of economic activities has profound implications for tax systems ... Factors, goods and other potential bases for taxation can flee a country in response to taxation or other regulatory restrictions, or be attracted to a country by relatively light taxation or regulation" (11).

In their paper, "The Cost of Capital in Canada, the United States and Japan," John Shoven and Michael Topper (1992) note that the tax systems of all three countries magnify "risk premia"; that is, they cause the extra return required to initiate risky undertakings to be larger than it would be in the absence of the tax system. They conclude that the cost of capital in Canada and the United States today is similar. However, both Canada and the United States are currently experiencing a large cost of capital disadvantage relative to Japan, owing, in part, to features of the Japanese tax system. Their conclusions support the view that Ontario will have to consider the tax structures of a larger number of foreign jurisdictions – not just that of the United States – in anticipating the impact of alternative tax designs on Ontario's capital base.

Many business surveys have included taxes as a possible location determinant. These surveys often conclude that taxes, when compared with other factors, particularly labour costs, have played a relatively minor role. Furthermore, analyses of business costs indicate that taxes often form a small component of total costs. Why, then, should taxes be designed from the perspective of potential impacts on business location decisions? Surveys and analyses generally report on the average past experience of diverse businesses. However, the focus of this paper is not on average experience; neither is it on the past. Rather, the concern is whether taxes can play a role in some, though not all, current and future business decisions to locate in one region rather than in another. The focus here is on the businesses that may shift capital and jobs into or out of Ontario in the coming years, and on the businesses that may base new investments upon a consideration of Ontario as a location in comparison with other regions. While many factors influence these decisions, it is clear that tax design can also play a role, particularly in manufacturing businesses.[4] Furthermore, tax design is one of the few location determinants that can be influenced in the short term by the Ontario government. Programs, for example, that are designed to improve education and retraining and to stimulate innovation require considerably more time to be effective.

Federal Tax Structures

Ontario's tax structure is an important feature of its interjurisdictional competitiveness. In deciding among potential investment sites, businesses compare Ontario's corporate income tax rates with those of other jurisdictions, particularly in the United States. While discussions often focus on tax structures at the federal level, it is necessary for Ontario's tax design to compare tax structures at the state, provincial, and municipal levels as well. Also relevant is the design of taxes in other provinces that may serve as alternative sites for business locations.

While Canadian tax literature has focused on the federal government's corporate profits tax in comparisons between Canada and other countries, it is the U.S. state and municipal governments that have offered a wide array of tax concessions for the purpose of attracting new investment. These include various exemptions from the payment of sales and property taxes as well as exemptions from the payment of corporate income taxes, or special provisions such as accelerated depreciation on tax-exempt bonds. In many cases, these exemptions are "tax holidays" for a stipulated number of years. Often these exemptions are combined with other incentives such as city- or county-revenue bond financing, employee training programs, industrial parks, and R & D assistance.[5] In the 1990s, many Ontario corporations will be examining these state and municipal tax provisions – and comparing them with Ontario's tax structure – as an element in their decisions concerning possible relocation to the United States.

Tax Incidence

Within this theme of an open economy with capital mobility, the possibility of tax shifting is an important analytical issue. However, the economics literature provides little conclusive evidence about tax shifting. Various types of taxes imposed on a corporation may be passed forward to customers through higher prices, or pushed backwards to employees through lower wages. Hence, the economic incidence may not be the same as the legal incidence of taxes on corporations.[6] The degree to which a corporation may shift taxes that are legally imposed upon it can vary significantly among business sectors. Consequently, the imposition of corporate taxes carries with it the disadvantage of horizontal inequity: corporations and shareholders are treated differently even though they are in the same economic circumstances.

The development of global markets and world prices may have reduced the ability of some corporations to shift taxes forward, restricting the shifting of taxes to the wage negotiation process. Today, a number of unions face the prospect of reducing their demands because an employer is threatening to close its Ontario operation and move to the United States. Taxes and wages can each form large components of the corporate cost comparisons involved in the relocation threat. To the degree that employees accept lower wages than they would in the absence of this threat, corporate taxes may be borne, at least partially, by the employees. Hence, the mobility of capital in response to various taxes may be limited by the degree that wages absorb part of those taxes.

Profit Shifting of Multinational Enterprises

The ability of multinational enterprises (MNEs) to credit taxes paid in one country against taxes owing in other countries adds a complicating feature to tax design. Ontario corporate taxes can be raised, without an impact on mobility, to the level that can be credited against taxes elsewhere. After this level is reached, the impact on MNE location decisions may be considerable. It introduces a discontinuity into the reaction of MNEs to increases in taxes on capital and income from capital. With increasing globalization, the tax laws of other jurisdictions will become of greater importance to Ontario MNEs.

A special feature of MNEs is their ability to shift profits, as reported for tax purposes, among countries. If faced with Canadian taxes that are higher than taxes in other jurisdictions where they operate, the MNE can place a greater reliance on Canadian debt financing as a way of reducing Canadian profits and hence taxes payable at the higher Canadian rates. Alternatively, or in combination with this rearrangement of corporate financing, the MNE can alter the transfer prices that it uses internally. By charging higher prices for the goods and services it provides to its Canadian business, and by paying lower prices for its purchases from its Canadian business, the MNE is able to reduce its Canadian profits as reported for tax purposes. These techniques mean that the MNE's tax base is highly mobile in response to Ontario's tax rates, compared with tax rates in other jurisdictions.

For Ontario, a particular concern is the potential for a shift of earnings from Ontario-located subsidiaries to U.S. parent companies. While it is not possible to predict how much shifting will occur or what the consequent revenue loss will be, analyses by Neil Bruce (1989, 208) led him to believe that there was considerable room for shifting, even after Canada's corporate tax reforms of the 1980s.

However, Bruce believes that this shift of earnings need not be accompanied by a large-scale shift of production operations to the United States on the basis of these tax considerations alone. To the degree that an MNE can avoid paying the higher tax rates of some jurisdictions, the MNE's location decisions will not be affected by interjurisdictional tax differentials. This may offer some support for the concept of Ontario's autonomy in tax design. Nevertheless, the potential loss of MNE corporate tax revenue will constrain the additional revenue to be gained through any imposition of higher tax rates than those of other jurisdictions, particularly those in the United States.

The Mobility of Manufacturing Jobs

For Ontario in the 1990s, a central concern will be that manufacturing activities can be undertaken today in a very wide range of regions and countries around the world. (This new global interdependence, which places Ontario's economy increasingly at risk, is explored in detail later on in this study.) In particular, the practice of automatically shifting standard production processes to low-wage countries may present Ontario with a continual threat of job loss, and a consequent need to create new job opportunities and to retrain the unemployed.

How dependent are jobs in other sectors on the strength of the manufacturing sector? How readily can new jobs be created to replace those jobs lost if manufacturing businesses leave Ontario? Will the new jobs provide incomes and tax bases as high as the jobs they are replacing? The section dealing with trade practices and agreements in the 1990s discusses regions in other countries that have endured rapid deindustrialization, and these experiences add concreteness to the threat of the mobility of manufacturing jobs.

Dependence of Personal Income and Expenditures on Business Investments

Closely related to the issue of capital mobility is the general question of the dependence of personal income and expenditures on business investment. Capital mobility, in response to interjurisdictional tax differentials, may not only alter the base for capital taxes but may also alter the base for sales taxes and personal income taxes, through its impact on jobs and incomes. This adds to the possibility that an increase in business taxes could actually decrease aggregate gov-

ernment revenues. Of central concern is the degree to which Ontario's economy as a whole will be damaged by the shift of certain
activities out of Ontario. The experience of deindustrialization in
other regions illustrates this threat, and many authors have emphasized these relationships. A report by the U.S. office of technology assessment points to what it terms "ripple effects in the
community."[7] As John Portz (1990) discusses in relation to the U.S.
Midwest, "At the local level, reports of plant closings often add
broader social and economic costs to the list of consequences. The
closing of a major plant has a ripple effect throughout the local
economy. As blue-collar jobs are lost in auto communities in Michigan, steel-mill towns in Pennsylvania, and other "company towns,"
the entire community feels the economic pinch ... In addition, such
losses are often accompanied by an increased incidence of crime,
mental health problems, divorce, and other family troubles" (vii, viii).

   Britain has also experienced this cumulative and integrated collapse of certain regions. In the years immediately following 1979,
a substantial loss of manufacturing jobs occurred in Britain's northern regions. Here too, authors have pointed to the impact of this
deindustrialization on businesses that supplied the manufacturing
sector, on average household incomes, and, consequently, on consumer spending.[8]

Benefit Taxation

Increased factor mobility in the 1990s will likely cause jurisdictions
to rely more heavily on benefit taxation. If people and businesses
must pay a level of taxation that is not commensurate with the
benefit they receive from the government, then they will be motivated to consider alternative location possibilities. It is generally
expected that these mobility pressures will be greatest for capital.
From this perspective, the analytical issue of significance is how
to relate provincial and municipal taxes to specific benefits provided
by Ontario and its municipalities, and how to relate taxes paid by
a business to the benefits received by that business. The most visible
connection may be established by reliance on user taxes, and so
it may be advisable to consider extending this principle beyond current practice. While user taxes are most common at the level of
municipal services, recent implementation of the employer health
tax and recent public discussion of highway tolls illustrate possibilities at the provincial level.

   Yet, for a wide range of government services, user taxes may not be feasible. The international competitiveness of Ontario businesses will depend on the quality of Ontario's labour force in terms of education and retraining. And it will depend upon the society's innovative capacity, with technological progress being built on such factors as university-corporate linkages and research parks. Much of Ontario's vital infrastructure and social overhead capital cannot be directly related to business success in a way that would permit funding through user fees. Furthermore, many of these factors, such as education and retraining, are provided to individuals rather than businesses, and the concept of equity would prohibit complete reliance on user fees. Nevertheless, when a business is considering the advantages and disadvantages of Ontario as a location site, it is important for the Ontario government to be able to present an analysis of the overall taxes and benefits as they relate to that business. Differences between Ontario and the United States in payment for health care illustrate the importance of such an analysis to the corporation. When capital mobility is the subject, taxes and tax design cannot be considered in isolation from government expenditures.

Subsidies as an Alternative to Tax Design

While a government can also influence business location decisions through a wide range of expenditure programs, subsidies may be the most direct and immediate enticement. A government's objective to retain and attract investment and jobs may be achieved through the design of a tax system that is competitive with those of other jurisdictions. Alternatively, a government may offer business subsidies of various kinds that may also make its jurisdiction attractive as an investment location. As discussed later in this paper, states and municipalities in the southern United States have made extensive use of subsidies as a way of attracting businesses. Some authors suggest that the expenditure approach has the advantage of making government support transparent or explicit. On the other hand, subsidy programs generally involve government decisions on a case-by-case basis in ways that may involve administrative difficulties. Reliance on tax design may be more simple administratively.

Personal Income Tax Design

Personal income tax provisions may encourage the individual taxpayer to invest in certain types of corporations and thus may play a role in business location decisions. In the 1980s, several provinces introduced provisions to direct private sector equity capital to provincial industry. Plans typically provided partial relief to the personal income tax liability of taxpayers who purchased the equity of designated corporations. However, the impact of such provisions on the aggregate capital stock within the province is unclear, and depends to some degree on the "openness" of the capital market. Potential impacts may be reduced to the degree that the provincial capital market is integrated with capital markets outside the province. Higher provincial personal savings may not reduce the market rate of interest, and so may not stimulate investment within the province. The economics literature is inconclusive on the extent to which higher domestic savings simply alter international capital flows.

In analysing the advantages Ontario might gain in this regard if it established a separate personal income tax (PIT) system, Robin Boadway and Neil Bruce (1984, 73, 76) have emphasized the importance of the openness of Ontario's economy as follows:

Imagine the extreme case in which both debt and equity capital are perfectly mobile internationally and the economy under consideration (e.g., Ontario's) is small. In this case, world capital markets determine some exogenous interest rate (or return on equity), i, at which non-residents are willing to lend or borrow. The rate of return on domestic financial assets is set so as to yield to non-residents the same net-of-tax return they can receive abroad. It will depend upon the domestic tax system only to the extent that the domestic authorities withhold taxes against capital-income payments to non-residents and that the non-residents cannot credit the withheld taxes against taxes they owe in another jurisdiction. These conditions seem unlikely to be satisfied since most jurisdictions give tax credits for foreign taxes paid. Therefore, it seems legitimate to treat i as independent of domestic taxes on capital income ... A change in personal taxes on capital income will shift the savings supply and thus the amount of savings forthcoming; it will have no effect on the amount of investment ... If the financial capital is free to flow into and out of the economy, if the economy is small, and if the taxes levied on capital income are fully credited in other jurisdictions, the PIT has no effect on the cost of capital and hence on corporate investment.

The Quebec stock savings plan (QSSP) was introduced by the

Parti Québécois government in 1979 to stimulate private sector investment in the province and to strengthen and increase the autonomy of the provincial financial system. The QSSP provided an incentive for citizens of Quebec to purchase new issues of voting stock of Quebec-based corporations by allowing a deduction from taxable income equal to the value of the new shares bought. Similar plans in Alberta and Saskatchewan restrict eligibility to Canadian-controlled companies that have a minimum of 25 per cent of their salaries and wages paid within the respective province.

Ontario introduced its employee share ownership plan in 1986. Under this plan, the province provided employees of small- and medium-sized Ontario businesses with a 15 per cent tax credit of up to $2000 of annual stock purchases. These shares had to be newly issued by their employers' corporations. As an inducement for corporations to issue new shares for this program, the province would compensate them for one-third of the cost of setting up the plan to a maximum of $10,000. In 1991, Ontario also proposed an Ontario investment and worker ownership program (OIWOP), modelled after the labour-sponsored venture capital corporations (LSVCC) in several provinces. This program enables employee groups to establish labour-sponsored investment funds to invest in small- and medium-sized businesses. Ontario residents who purchase certain shares in these funds are eligible for Ontario tax credits of 20 per cent on the first $3500 invested in any year, and in some cases a credit of up to 30 per cent on the next $11,500.

Such personal income tax provisions have introduced a new element in interjurisdictional tax comparisons, albeit an element whose impact is unclear. Some believe that such provisions can indeed have a major impact. Peter McQuillan (1989, 188) has suggested that the nature of a province's capital market may be dramatically affected by such provisions in the personal income tax. He observed that "We have recently seen the Quebec stock savings plans completely revitalize a dying capital market – the Montreal Stock Exchange – by creating an incentive to offer shares to the public. Companies responded, the investors responded, and the Montreal Stock Exchange has regained a vitality that it had not possessed for 20 years."

Insulating the Economy versus Insulating Tax Revenue

A related subject, apart from these design features, is the extent to which Ontario's tax system will be structured to insulate the provincial economy from external shocks such as changes in energy prices and exchange rates. A considerable body of literature examines tax features that automatically stabilize after-tax incomes in the context of business cycles. Tax provisions may reduce aggregate tax revenues in times of recession and raise them in expansionary periods. Should Ontario's tax system be designed to further reduce aggregate revenues automatically when negative external shocks occur? The tax system's existing stabilization features do absorb some portion of these shocks on incomes and profits. Is this current partial absorption appropriate, or should additional explicit provisions seek to insulate the private sector to a greater degree? The answer to this question rests upon a political judgement involving the acceptable level of deficit financing, and the choice between tax design and expenditure programs as mechanisms of adjustment assistance.

Table 1 presents a summary of these 10 analytical issues important to the design of Ontario's tax system from the perspective of the global economy. Several of these issues, while important, involve elements of uncertainty concerning the extent to which tax revenues will be affected. It will be helpful to clarify these relationships and impacts in order to improve Ontario's tax design in the global economy of the 1990s.

Global Interdependence

Ontario has an exceptionally "open" economy. Its merchandise trade as a percentage of its gross domestic product (GDP) has remained high through the 1980s. In 1980, Ontario's merchandise exports and imports totalled $66 billion, or 57 per cent of its $115 billion GDP. In 1990, Ontario's merchandise exports and imports totalled $153 billion, or 54 per cent of its $281 billion GDP.

Ontario's trade is concentrated in manufactured goods to a far greater degree than is the trade of other provinces. In 1992, fully 93 per cent of Ontario's international exports were in the form of fabricated materials or end-products, while only 60 per cent of the exports of the rest of Canada were in these categories. For end-products alone the difference is even more dramatic; 70 per cent of Ontario's international exports in 1992 were in end-products, as compared with only 9 per cent of the exports of the rest of Canada.

Not only is Ontario's trade concentrated in manufactured prod-

TABLE 1
Analytical Issues

Issue	Potential impacts	Implications for Ontario's tax design
1. mobility of tax bases in response to interjurisdictional tax differences	may reduce potential revenue gain of tax rate increases	constrains Ontario's tax design
2. federal tax structures	role of state and local tax structures is important, as well as national tax structures	need to compare integrated rate structures rather than just national structures
3. tax incidence	higher taxes may be shifted to customers or employees	uncertain incidence of business taxes; may mitigate mobility of tax bases in response to interjurisdictional differences
4. MNE profit shifting	higher taxes may be avoided by shifting profits to other jurisdictions	higher tax rates may not result in higher revenue; but profit shifting may mitigate mobility of tax bases
5. degree to which manufacturing activities are most mobile in response to tax differences	capital mobility in manufacturing will impact other sectors	taxation of manufacturing may be a particularly important feature of the tax system, more so than overall taxes on capital or income from capital
6. dependence of personal income and expenditures on business investment	impact of capital mobility on employment and personal income	differences in business taxes may impact other tax bases as well
7. benefit taxation	links taxes with benefits received	can reduce mobility of tax bases; need to consider tax design in context of expenditures
8. subsidies as alternative to tax design	subsidies may influence business location decisions	need interjurisdictional comparisons of subsidies
9. personal income tax design	saving incentives may affect investment in Ontario	need to consider personal income tax design
10. insulating the economy versus insulating tax revenue	trade-off between economy absorbing external shocks and tax revenue absorbing external shocks	political judgement concerning trade-off

ucts, it is further concentrated in the automobile industry. In 1990, of Ontario's $74 billion in international exports, $30 billion, or 40 per cent, were related to the motor vehicle industry, while of Ontario's $79 billion in imports from other countries, $20 billion or 25 per cent were so related. Ontario's trade is also concentrated geographically; 86.5 per cent of its 1990 international exports went to the United States, and 76.3 per cent of its international imports came from the United States. Of exports to the United States in 1990, 56.4 per cent went to Michigan or New York, and 43.1 per cent of its imports came from Michigan, New York, or Ohio.

This sectoral and geographic concentration in Ontario's international trade makes Ontario's exposure to certain external shocks relatively high, compared with the exposure of other provinces. This exposure may be most threatening in the automobile industry, which is undergoing major global change. Of particular importance to Ontario is the surging transplant production in the United States by non-North American firms, and also the expanding automobile production in Mexico's *maquiladoras*. Plant relocation and rationalization involving Ontario operations in autos and other sectors is likely to accelerate in the 1990s.

Foreign investment has been a much more important factor in Ontario's economy than in the economies of other provinces. Between 30 June 1985 and 30 September 1992, Ontario received 57.7 per cent of all foreign investments in Canada, by number of investments – 52 per cent in terms of aggregate value. Foreign investment in Ontario totalled $61 billion over this seven-year period.[10] As a result of this investment influx, the Ontario economy has a much greater degree of international business capital linkages than do other provinces, and it is uniquely vulnerable to any future changes in the level of foreign investment in Canada. For this reason as well, future differences in tax design between Canadian and foreign jurisdictions will be a more important issue for Ontario than for other provinces.

It is likely that manufacturing activities will be more mobile than activities in other business sectors, and this poses a special problem for Ontario because manufacturing plays a larger role in Ontario's economy than it does for other provinces. In 1990, 20 per cent of Ontario's jobs were in manufacturing, while for the rest of Canada only 14 per cent of employment was in manufacturing. Consequently, the potential shift of manufacturing businesses from Canada to other countries poses an especially significant threat to Ontario's tax bases. The dependence of Ontario's employment, personal income, and retail sales on the viability of Ontario's manufacturing sector means that all of Ontario's tax bases face the threat of long-term erosion because of capital mobility and potential "deindustrialization." However, this increasing capital mobility presents opportunities as well as threats, since Ontario may be able to compete successfully against other jurisdictions as the site for future investments.

An important aspect of capital mobility in the manufacturing sector is discussed in the "product-cycle" literature, which suggests that for much of the manufacturing sector there will be an ongoing shift of production activities to low-wage countries. The corporate structure of the MNE provides for a nearly automatic shift of business activities out of developed jurisdictions like Ontario into less developed countries that have lower wage rates. Consequently, for Ontario's MNE branches, the development of global mandates for new products and components will be a continual necessity. This product-cycle process adds to the potential volatility of profits and mobility of capital.

In international product-cycle theory, MNE production and trade are linked to innovation and the international diffusion of new technology. In the first stage, a new product is developed and produced exclusively for the market where the innovation has been introduced. If the product is successful, it is exported and foreign direct investment is required to establish distribution and service facilities abroad. Rationalized production and global mandates have been "prompted mainly by growing differences in labour costs between the advanced industrial and the developing countries and [it] tends to be concentrated in labour-intensive industries."[11] The interjurisdictional interdependencies discussed in this paper are facilitating this process more and more. Rationalized product or process investments "flourish in conditions of free trade and low transport costs."[12] In the final stage, when the product has become standardized, production will be carried out where production costs are lowest. At this stage, the MNEs home market may be served from abroad. According to findings by E. Mansfield (1984), it appears that the product cycle has been compressed in recent years, with the initial export stage being truncated and sometimes eliminated.

F.T. Knickerbocker (1983) has added the concept "oligopolistic reaction" to this product-cycle literature. He posits that the more highly concentrated an industry is, the more likely it is that rival corporations will decide to establish foreign subsidiaries once the leading firm has pursued that option. This suggests that if one firm shifts certain activities out of Ontario, it may quickly be followed by competitors. Consequently, the shift of industrial jobs to less developed countries may be abrupt and substantial for each sector.

There has been concern, especially in the United States, over the employment impact of MNE rationalization and product-cycle trends. Allegations from American labour unions, for example, have claimed that through their expansion of manufacturing facilities abroad, MNEs have been a vehicle for exporting U.S. jobs.[13] This will likely also be of increasing concern to Ontario labour unions. Adhip Chaudhuri's studies have indicated that at the end of each product cycle, domestic employment for that product will have dropped even though there might be gains in white-collar employment. High-tech personnel will have to move to new products, as will blue-collar and eventually some white-collar workers. He notes further (1983, 266) that "the stability of employment due to the foreign sector in the U.S. economy would then depend on two things: steady "waves" of new products, and similar market successes for each product to generate stable employment." For Ontario, this phenomenon will likely be an ever-present reality emanating from global interdependence.

These fundamental changes reflect a dramatic increase in global competition.[14] It is not possible to distinguish clearly between the elements that cause this trend and those that occur as a result of it. Trade negotiations have reduced tariffs to such a degree that new international agreements are undoubtedly an important factor in the trend toward increased global competition. However, the distinction is not so clear for other elements, such as the adjustment of corporate investment strategies in favour of global mandates and intra-firm trade, and the erosion of technological leadership in North America.

Business Location Decisions and Externally Generated Shocks

Faced with a greater international competitiveness owing to increasing global interdependence and to trade agreements, Ontario businesses appear to be adopting new strategies concerning the location of their investments. The potential shift of Ontario businesses to other jurisdictions is especially important in terms of the Ontario tax base. In his book *Multinationals and Canada–United States Free Trade,*

Rugman (1989) has summarized several studies conducted in the 1980s on the determinants of Canadian investment in the United States. These studies found that the most important location determinants were various aspects of the U.S. market that acted as "pull" factors. Relatively few firms pointed to "push" factors that led them to leave Canada. Firms decided to invest in the United States for positive reasons, rather than choosing to disinvest in Canada for negative reasons. Much of the pre-1990 literature based on surveys such as Rugman's found Canadian direct investment abroad to be an extension of, and an addition to, existing domestic investment.

Recent developments, however, include the reduction or even closure of Canadian businesses and their replacement with alternative facilities in the United States. This phenomenon may occur to an increasing degree in Mexico. This type of capital mobility has direct implications for Ontario tax bases that earlier investment strategies did not entail. Prem Gandhi (1986, 213–14) did perceive the beginnings of this trend as early as the 1970s. He observed: "In the 1960s Canadian resource-based firms invested abroad to overcome the barrier of small markets in Canada and to diversify. In the 1970s the usual reasons for investing abroad have been supplemented by Canadian concerns about high inflation, profits, labour-management relations, frequent strikes, union militancy and fear of expropriation, and general economic and political uncertainties surrounding Quebec."

John R. Baldwin and Paul K. Gorecki (1990) have examined the pace of change in Canadian corporate location decisions in the 1970s through an analysis of births, deaths, and job turnover within various sectors. Their studies demonstrated that manufacturing capital, especially, was highly mobile and that businesses do open and close their facilities at a surprisingly rapid rate. They note that "the results show that over the period from 1970 to 1979, the cumulative effects of entry and exit over the decade were large: new firms in manufacturing operating in 1979 that did not exist in 1970 accounted for 33 per cent of all firms and 29 per cent of employment. On the other hand, 43 per cent of the firms existing in 1970, accounting for 32 per cent of employment then, had disappeared by 1979" (xvi, 79). These trends suggest that Ontario could experience rapid deindustrialization in the 1990s. Other regions in other countries have already experienced such a situation, and their difficulties illustrate the seriousness of the deindustrialization threat. Tony Dickson and

David Judge (1987) have edited a selection of articles that examine this phenomenon in post-1979 Britain and analyse the collapse of manufacturing in particular. Lloyd Rodwin and Hidehiko Sazanami (1989) have edited a book that examines the recent deindustrialization of certain U.S. regions, and they emphasize the way in which a recession can intensify and accelerate this process. They note: "Then the situation is extremely serious and in some respects economically and socially disastrous. Unemployment and migration rates are far higher, and the entire complex of manufacturing industries is apt to disappear, not just decline" (17).

Michael Storper and Richard Walker (1989) have also written about several regions where structural disinvestment has occurred. They conclude that regions that have been extremely successful for many decades may suddenly and abruptly experience economic devastation. They stress that structural disinvestment can develop very rapidly. One of the more interesting aspects of structural disinvestment is that the previously prosperous region usually has not experienced any noteworthy changes within itself that might cause disinvestment. Rather, the cause of disinvestment lies with economic developments in other jurisdictions. They point out that the most dramatic paradox of industrial location is the way industries centred for decades in "optimal" spots with strong agglomeration economies, enormous sunk capital, and a stable labour force suddenly melt away (90–91). This has occurred, for instance, throughout the U.S. rustbelt, and in northern Britain and northern France. (See Bluestone and Harrison 1982; Martin and Rowthorn 1986.)

In the 1970s the Midwest was the industrial heartland of the United States. Suddenly, many of the industrial sectors that provided employment and a regional tax base began to close, leaving large numbers of people unemployed and causing economic devastation in many cities. This substantial decline of the Midwest has been one of the most significant economic developments in U.S. history. Many people relate this recent decline to the growth of the South, referring to a movement of industry from the "rustbelt" to the "sunbelt." Since the 1930s, the South, partially as a result of its tax incentives and labour policies, has been an increasingly attractive investment location for many activities.

A dramatic lesson to be drawn from the experiences of others is the special vulnerability of regions that have come to depend on a single type of industry. Studies indicate that people who lose their jobs are more readily absorbed if they can find new employment in firms in the same industry where they previously worked. To transfer to a different economic sector involves more difficult adjustments. Retraining, for example, need not be as extensive if the person is hired by another firm in the same industry. Ontario's heavy reliance on the automobile industry has placed Ontario at a special risk from this point of view. If Ontario's automobile firms were to widely shift investment out of Ontario, the employees who would lose their jobs would not find an easy transition to employment alternatives.[15]

Following an economic decline from 1975 to 1985, many municipalities in the U.S. Midwest experienced an economic revival, with growth occurring in sectors different from those that had previously provided employment. The Midwest has experienced a particularly substantial growth in the service sectors. From the perspective of total employment, it appears that the Midwest has enjoyed a strong recovery. However, the new jobs offer lower wages than did earlier manufacturing jobs. The expanding services include personal services that were once performed within the home, especially food preparation. Thus, the expansion of service jobs may not reflect an increase in economic activity, but merely a transfer of economic activity from the home to the marketplace. The U.S. Midwest example illustrates that job creation to replace jobs lost through deindustrialization may involve a deterioration in the economic well-being of the people in the region.

The Midwest recovery has involved a significant restructuring that has left many people worse off than they were previously. For example, writing about Buffalo, New York, Robert Kraushaar and David Perry (1988) state:

> Service sectors that have exhibited consistent growth in Buffalo are the least well linked to manufacturing, that is, they grew in spite of the decline in manufacturing. While this trend may appear, at first blush, to be quite healthy, it should be pointed out that these sectors also recorded the lowest levels of earnings, less security, and fewer opportunities for advancement. This pattern of consistent growth in economic sectors supplying the lowest earnings has driven this once "high wage" area's overall average earnings below the national average. The illusion of Buffalo's transforming itself into a producer service region replete with high-power and high-paying jobs has not materialized. Buffalo is metamorphosing from a high-wage manufacturing town to a low-wage service town (74).

Lawrence Rothstein (1986) has examined lay-offs and plant clo-
sures that have resulted from the shifting of manufacturing jobs
from the United States to less developed countries. His book, entitled *Plant Closings: Power, Politics, and Workers*, discusses capital mobility as a conflict between business and labour, with businesses
shifting to jurisdictions where labour is not as powerful politically.
He, too, points to the difference between the quality of jobs lost
and the quality of jobs that have been created to replace them, em-
phasizing that "the new jobs are more likely to be less well paid,
less skilled, less unionized, only part-time, and located in regions
of the country other than those suffering most from job destruction
and unemployment" (14). For Ontario in the 1990s, design of the
tax system must be guided, at least to some degree, by the desire
to avoid this kind of structural adjustment.

A survey mailed to Ontario companies in 1991 asked if the company had any plans to invest in Ontario in the next five years and
what the critical investment factors were.[16] For the 37 per cent of
respondents with no plans to invest in Ontario, the most important
reasons were as follows: Ontario's wage protection policies; the government of Ontario deficit; levels of Canadian and Ontario productivity; Ontario's employment equity legislation; and the corporate income tax. For the 40 per cent who had plans to invest outside
of Ontario in the next five years, the factors cited as most significant
in their decision were these: the value of the Canadian dollar; interest rates; Ontario's wage protection policies; the government of
Ontario deficit; levels of Canadian and Ontario productivity; capacity utilization; and Ontario's employment equity legislation. Most
companies planning to invest outside of Ontario cited the United
States as their likely future location.

This evidence of potential capital mobility is supported by a 1990
survey conducted by the Canadian Manufacturers' Association. The
survey asked its members for their opinions concerning the cost
of doing business in the United States compared with doing business
in Ontario. The majority of responses indicated that the United
States is significantly more attractive as a business location.[17]

Most of the U.S. literature concerning business location decisions
consists of many surveys that have been directed at newly arrived
corporations in the U.S. South. These surveys ask respondents why
they chose a southern state for their investment. A wide variety
of factors seem to bear on these decisions. Many factors are similar
to the determinants found in the Ontario survey. For example, tax-

ation is often mentioned explicitly as an important location determinant. Social policies that impact on wage costs also received frequent mention.[18]

Ontario's tax revenue will be susceptible to a large number of
potentially strong shocks from the global economy in the 1990s,
both as a result of their direct impacts on Ontario tax bases and
also through their impacts on business location decisions. This susceptibility adds great uncertainty to revenue forecasts. It also means
that it may be necessary to modify Ontario's tax system frequently
in the 1990s in continual response to these externally generated
shocks. A central issue will be the degree to which Ontario chooses
to insulate economic activities from these shocks by allowing tax
revenues to fluctuate, thereby increasing budget deficits in times
of negative shocks and increasing budget surpluses in times of positive shocks. An important political judgement will have to be made
concerning this trade-off between insulating economic activities and
attempting to balance the budget.

Within the past two decades, a growing number of newly industrialized countries (NICs) have dramatically expanded their manufacturing sectors and are increasingly capable of exporting to Europe and North America. Paying extremely low wage rates, they
are now able to compete within the markets of the developed nations
in a substantial range of manufactured goods. Apart from the ongoing threat related to the product cycle, this new competitiveness
will lead to repeated import surges in specific products. These import surges, based upon changes in consumer preferences as well
as technological developments within the NICs, will be largely un-
predictable as to types of products.

For generations, Canada, like Great Britain and the United States,
maintained a competitive advantage in international trade through
technological superiority. In the 1990s, this lead will be challenged
in many types of production. Japan's dramatic success in developing
new manufacturing techniques and new forms of business organization will likely be copied by the lower-wage NICs. This will expose Ontario manufacturing to a continual threat of new competition and a sudden loss of markets.

Changes in exchange rates in the 1990s will likely be rapid, frequent, and substantial, and they too will alter the international competitiveness of many of Ontario's business activities. Ontario's agriculture and natural resource industries, for example, have long been
affected by changes in exchange rates, since they have generally faced

"world prices." A higher Canadian dollar value has automatically reduced their export receipts denominated in Canadian dollars, while a decrease in value of the Canadian dollar has increased them.

The impact of fluctuating exchange rates has become increasingly important for businesses in the manufacturing sector as well. Manufactured products take up an increasing share of total world trade and many are now being sold at a relatively uniform world price. For Ontario manufacturers, exchange rate fluctuations can alter the domestic prices of their exports and also the domestic prices of the imports against which they compete. For Ontario retailers as well, exchange rate fluctuations can dramatically affect the extent of cross-border shopping. Consequently, changes in Canada's exchange rate will have direct impacts on many of Ontario's tax bases related to profits, sales volumes, and employment income.

For Ontario, it is the value of the Canadian dollar vis-à-vis the U.S. dollar that will be most important, and experiences of the past 20 years indicate that wide swings can be expected in this exchange rate. Within the 1977 calendar year, for example, the Canadian dollar fell from parity with the U.S. dollar to a value of 90 cents U.S. and reached 69 cents U.S. in 1986. It climbed to 89 cents in 1990 and it fell to less than 80 cents by the end of 1992.[19] In light of these fluctuations, the most significant development affecting Ontario business in the post-1992 period may be the 1992 decline in the U.S.-denominated value of the Canadian dollar. Combined with business-cycle recovery, this may revive Ontario's tax bases and revenue in a dramatic fashion, although the corporate profits tax base will be constrained for several years owing to tax provisions for carrying forward losses. For those Ontario businesses that now operate on the basis of U.S.-priced goods, this volatility will directly affect international competitiveness, profitability, and tax payments.

Ontario's heavy dependence on imported energy sources also exposes Ontario's economy to external shocks related to the supply and price of energy. Experiences of the past 20 years indicate the potential volatility of energy prices. (For example, the U.S. price of oil per barrel rose from $5.38 in 1973 to $33.59 in 1981 and fell to $14.67 in 1986.)[20] Current low oil prices could quickly skyrocket in the 1990s in the event of unfortunate Middle East political developments. Many Ontario businesses will be particularly affected by the investment and pricing policies of Ontario Hydro, which, in turn, will be affected by externally generated changes in energy prices as well.

The concentration of Canadian manufacturing in Ontario makes it more vulnerable to these shocks than other provinces. The automobile industry, in particular, is undergoing a major global restructuring, with increasing North American involvement in Mexico. Plant relocation in this and other sectors and the further rationalization of Ontario's automobile production are of central concern to Ontario's future economic prospects. Aggregate world employment in manufacturing has remained relatively stable in industrial countries, and so any shifts in location decisions may mean that a gain for one jurisdiction occurs at the expense of another. Ontario will increasingly be subject to an interjurisdictional competitiveness for business investments and a potential volatility of business-related tax revenues.

Trade Practices and Trade Agreements in the 1990s

This paper has indicated various relationships between globalization and the growth of MNEs on the one hand, and the volatility and mobility of Ontario's tax bases on the other. A major impetus for these economic trends has been the growth of new trade relationships. New trade agreements have added to the threat of relocation and job loss for certain activities. Among these agreements, the FTA, with its extension through NAFTA to include Mexico, deserves special attention.

The post-1989 recession appears to have combined with the FTA to form an important stimulus for Canadian companies to develop new North American strategies. The recession has meant that decisions to close operations or to downsize can swiftly alter previous production and distribution patterns. In the discussions leading up to the FTA negotiations, economists pointed to the economies of scale that would result from specialization within a larger market. Canadian businesses, it was anticipated, would be able to reduce costs on the basis of serving the United States as well as Canada. However, the post-1989 period has not witnessed a smooth or easy transition. Many companies have found that they can compete only with significant structural adjustment, which may require a shift of some production facilities to other countries where costs are lower. It appears that manufacturing activities can be shifted more readily than can businesses in the service sector, which have to remain close to their customers, and those dependent upon natural resources, which must remain close to their supply sources. Communities heavily dependent on manufacturing have suffered severely because manufacturing is now the most mobile sector. Consequently, the concentration of Canadian manufacturing in Ontario means that Ontario is more exposed to these potential losses than are other provinces.

In corporations experiencing adjustment costs, there is a division of losses between employees and shareholders. In some cases, the corporation may be better off than previously, from the shareholders' perspective, while the employees, or at least those laid off, may be in a worse position. During the post-1989 recession, for example, the lay-offs referred to as permanent appear to exceed greatly the lay-offs referred to as temporary. This is the case, in particular, where corporations are shifting production facilities from Ontario to other jurisdictions. Consequently, the impact may not be uniformly felt by Ontario's tax bases. This restructuring of Ontario businesses is likely to continue throughout the 1990s, with the ongoing adjustment to new trade agreements.

Some recent studies have presented a sanguine view of NAFTA's impacts on Canadian employment. Leonard Waverman (1991, 58), for example, has concluded that "Opposition to a NAFTA will come from blue-collar unionized and non-unionized labour who feel that they will bear the brunt of increased Mexican competition. And they will. However, the job losses due to increased Mexican competition in Canadian markets are, in my calculations, more than offset by the job gains to Canada due to penetration of Mexican markets."

However, several points should be understood in considering such analyses. First, job losses will be real, while job gains will depend upon the problematical attractiveness of Ontario for future investment. Second, the long-term net benefits of NAFTA will be small consolation for those who lose their jobs in the short run. Third, as argued elsewhere in this paper, generalizations about Canada as a whole are not necessarily valid for Ontario, due to its uniquely heavy reliance on manufacturing. Even for predictions concerning Canada as a whole, Waverman has noted that "A sector-by-sector analysis of Mexican and Canadian industry is required but unavailable" (48). Fourth, the low average productivity in Mexico is not the relevant focus in Ontario-Mexico comparisons. Rather, it is the competitiveness and investment of specific Mexican businesses that employ specific workers whose productivity is much higher than the Mexican average. Non-North American firms, for example, may increase their investments in Mexican businesses in ways that could quickly alter previous trade patterns. Fifth, NAFTA opens up a new era of trade and investment between Canada and Mexico. These relationships were negligible in the past, and so the past, and analyses based on the past, may be of little guidance for the future. Sixth, NAFTA provides for admission of other countries to the agreement, and so may automatically create additional low-wage competition in the future. These points do not, by themselves, support a negative view of NAFTA's impact on Ontario, but they do argue for an Ontario tax system that is much more responsive to the changing realities of Ontario business, if Ontario business is to be successful in the more intensely competitive markets of the 1990s.

The Uruguay round of GATT negotiations has focused on several issues other than tariffs. The global protection of intellectual property is necessary to prevent the flooding of world markets by counterfeit products. The recent growth of services has resulted in demands for freer access by MNE personnel to foreign markets. The export of services requires a local presence, and so investment policies have acquired a new significance. Limitations on subsidy programs, procurement policies, and non-tariff barriers have also been receiving increasing attention. Many government activities other than tariffs result in a distortion of prices from what would exist without such government intervention. Businesses in other jurisdictions often regard these as "unfair" competition, and support trade negotiations that will create "a level playing field."

In recent decades, Ontario has expanded these kinds of government activities considerably.[21] Instead of tariffs, businesses often seek alternative types of assistance from government. For example, the growing significance of technology as the basis for international competitiveness leads more firms to seek R & D assistance.[22] Whether, and to what degree, these sub-national government assistance programs for businesses can or should be limited by international agreements may be an important issue of the 1990s for Ontario. Among commentators on this subject, Richard Simeon (1986, 189) has expressed the view that "to achieve its minimal objectives, a trade agreement must constrain provincial and state, as well as federal, activities."

Special tax provisions to assist businesses may not be subject to the same negotiation and possible limitation as the more direct forms of government intervention. Since they are available to a wide range of businesses, tax provisions are generally not viewed as providing specific firms with an unfair competitive advantage. Consequently, the design of Ontario's tax system and its role in maintaining and attracting investments may become more significant in the 1990s, to the degree that other types of government assistance may be constrained by trade agreements.

From Ontario's perspective, another important subject of the 1990s concerns the provisions trade agreements make regarding retaliation by one jurisdiction against another jurisdiction that offers subsidies. Ontario's tax bases are vulnerable to erosion to the degree that U.S. state and local governments, in particular, offer financial inducements for firms to locate there. The enforcement provisions are an important aspect of agreements to limit such investment incentives. Countervail measures and the dispute settlement procedures under the FTA will be of continuing importance for Ontario.

Despite the broad provisions of the FTA, its tariff reductions by themselves will not likely dramatically change much of the U.S.-Canada trade flows. Before the agreement, trade between Canada and the United States was already largely duty-free or at low duty. Non-tariff barriers in key sectoral areas such as textiles, steel, agriculture, and energy were largely untouched by the agreement. And while there had been growth in the use of anti-dumping and countervailing duties, their coverage of trade was relatively small. On the other hand, the FTA has provided confidence to business that the relatively free cross-border trade flows will not, in the future, be impeded by the imposition of new tariffs. In this sense, the FTA has placed a stamp of authority on the concept of an integrated North American market. At the same time, the FTA has alerted Canadian business managers to the opportunity to shift their facilities to the United States and serve both nations from a U.S. location. The NAFTA has now extended this geographical scope for investment to include Mexico. In fact, a central Mexican objective has been to stimulate foreign investment and, consequently, employment. For Mexico, NAFTA can be seen as much more than a trade agreement.

Sectors where NAFTA negotiations seem to have been the most intense include autos, textiles, agriculture, and petrochemicals. In these sectors, labour organizations have voiced concerns over threats to their domestic market share from low-wage Mexican imports. Fears have also focused on the possibility that new investment in Mexico from non-North American countries would add to potential U.S. job losses. Ontario should share these concerns. One protective mechanism has been the rules-of-origin. In the automobile sector, NAFTA has increased content provisions above the FTA levels. An objective has been to restrict shipment through Mexico. The textile and clothing sectors are also relying upon rules-of-origin for this purpose.

While protecting Ontario manufacturers from competition originating outside North America, these rules-of-origin do little to restrain the shift of Ontario production facilities to Mexico. It is this shift that could quickly and substantially reduce Ontario tax bases. Once again, it is important to note that generalizations about impacts of NAFTA on Canadian trade and production do not hold automatically for Ontario's trade and production, owing to Ontario's unique industrial structure. A Statistics Canada report (1991) on "Canada's and Mexico's trade position in the United States market" illustrates the necessity of questioning such generalizations.[23] This report concludes that, "With the exception of automobiles, crude petroleum and to some extent tele-electronic products, Canada and Mexico export a complementary rather than a competitive mix of commodities to the United States" and that for Canada as a whole, "[a] trilateral Free Trade Agreement may not present any immediate threats to either country's exports to the United States." For Ontario, of course, it is exceptions such as automobiles and tele-electronic products that are essential to Ontario's tax bases.

New Interjurisdictional Environmental Labour and Social Policy Issues

The 1990s will likely see a continued and perhaps intensified concern in many countries about environmental, labour, and social policy issues. Within North America, the individual provinces and states have significant jurisdictional responsibility for these matters, and each jurisdiction has been implementing unique regulations. A lack of harmony is creating differences in production costs, which threaten to alter trade and investment patterns. In many jurisdictions, legislation is less restrictive than Ontario's and is not as stringently enforced. Consequently, in the 1990s, other jurisdictions will appear to be corporate havens, attracting investors who wish to avoid the costs imposed by Ontario's regulations.

Some policy advocates are now looking towards trade agreements as a way of strengthening legislation and enforcement in other countries. Whether and how this can be achieved will affect business location decisions. An article by Ebba Dohlman (1990), entitled "The Trade Effects of Environmental Regulation," has emphasized the international impacts of each jurisdiction's automobile emission standards, and has suggested that higher standards in one or a few jurisdictions may automatically lead to their adoption elsewhere. It is uncertain, however, whether this harmonization of standards will occur in other regulatory areas, and how quickly it will develop. Many would disagree with the sanguine view presented by Ebba Dohlman that "[standards, whether imposed on product or production, may introduce distortions in the conditions of international competition ... [and that] the adoption of strict standards in one country clearly puts pressure on others to modify the nature or composition of their exports or even to adopt the standards themselves" (30).

Financial analyses rely heavily on corporate accounting practices, and the rapid changes in environmental laws are creating interjurisdictional differences in the reporting requirements for financial statements. Corporate obligations arising from new environmental laws are not being presented consistently among countries. Accounting standards in Canada and the United States have long required disclosure, and in certain situations expense recognition of contingencies. However, they are much less stringent in many other countries.

In Canada, accounting rules were changed in 1990 so that financial statements would explicitly reflect the costs imposed by some elements of new environmental legislation. In particular, in those jurisdictions that now have rules requiring clean-up and site restoration, public accountants must ensure that corporate management has properly accrued those costs and included them annually in current profit and balance sheet reporting. For some sectors, the accounting treatment of resource depletion has also become a serious issue.

Some jurisdictions have also placed new responsibilities on lending institutions for the clean-up costs connected with their borrowers, in the event of loan default. The act of taking over a mortgaged property can make a bank responsible for the clean-up cost. Hence, both equity and debt elements of financial markets are being affected. The rapid pace of change in environmental law and accounting practices and the discontinuous nature of these changes mean that trade, investment, and financial markets will be affected abruptly in the 1990s in ways that may be unanticipated.

A number of significant differences have developed among jurisdictions in regard to various aspects of corporate liability. These include the size of fines, the administrative authority of public servants to negotiate with industry, the responsibilities of corporate boards of directors, and the requirements in regard to environmental impact statements.[24] In many North American jurisdictions, real estate carries with it a future legal obligation for clean-up and site restoration. Consequently, investors now have to consider potential future costs that may be connected with a specific piece of property because of environmental concerns. For mergers and acquisitions, these obligations now take a prominent position in the negotiation process. In the United States, New Jersey and California require that an environmental assessment be conducted for property prior to any purchase or sale. This is not yet a legal requirement in some other states, or in Ontario.

For Ontario, an important illustration of these developments is the recent passage in many U.S. states of legislation requiring that newspapers contain a certain percentage of recycled material. Suddenly, Ontario pulp and paper mills may no longer be able to supply these markets as they have in the past. Should Ontario mills transport recycled material from the U.S. markets to Northern Ontario, so as to create the appropriate mix of new and recycled newsprint? Transportation costs could be prohibitive. Should they build new mills near the U.S. cities? How can management anticipate its future competitive position when much of the U.S. public is advocating the passage of such legislation in other states? For businesses in this sector, trade, investment, and capital markets may all be affected.

Environmental, labour, and social policy issues entered the NAFTA negotiations, more directly than in the FTA. Key areas included workers' rights, drug enforcement, and labour mobility. In the environmental area, the concerns of environmental groups in the United States propelled the process. They documented cross-border environmental problems associated with *maquiladora* production, such as ground water contamination, effluent discharge into border rivers, high incidence of hepatitis and other diseases in U.S. border towns, and other problems. In the United States, fears arose that increased U.S.-Mexico trade resulting from NAFTA will worsen these problems, and many advocated that Mexican environmental standards be made more stringent. They also sought stronger enforcement of Mexican environmental regulations, perhaps involving some form of a new trilateral environmental commission, and, if necessary, cross-border inspections. They feared that a cross-border trade agreement might even result in a lowering of U.S. environmental standards in some areas. These groups also wanted environmental impact statements to be prepared in the United States to accompany the NAFTA agreement.

While not formally a NAFTA issue, tuna imports from Mexico have also attracted the attention of environmental groups, since Mexicans use fishing methods that capture dolphins as well as tuna. Nonetheless, a 1991 GATT dispute panel ruled in favour of Mexico against U.S. import bans on tuna, despite the documented support of a 1988 act to protect marine mammals. Such disagreements in the environmental arena have created global tension over American extraterritorial rights and actions.

Weak labour laws may give Mexico an unfair advantage in attracting businesses and jobs. Linkage between workers' rights and trade in the NAFTA negotiations has also focused on alleged use of child labour in production for export in Mexico.[25] As well, drug enforcement issues have arisen in the context of proposals linking trade concessions by the United States to an agreement by Mexico to allow stronger cross-border enforcement. Labour mobility has been another issue linked to NAFTA negotiations, with Mexico arguing for liberalization of immigration restrictions against both Mexican permanent and temporary residents in the United States. Some Mexicans have suggested the choice for the United States is one of either taking more Mexican goods or suffering more illegal Mexican immigration. This wide range of regulatory issues now bears on trade and investment agreements in ways that cannot be ignored.

The 1990s will witness extensive changes in the content and enforcement of many of these regulations. For the focus of this paper, what is important is that differences between jurisdictions will stimulate capital mobility, thereby posing another ongoing threat to Ontario's tax bases. Particularly important are the regulatory differences between Ontario and Mexico. Ontario wants higher standards and the ability to strengthen enforcement. However, this points up, once more, the importance of using the design of Ontario's business taxes as an attractive feature to offset the cost advantages otherwise promised by locations in other jurisdictions.

Tax Reforms in Other Countries

A considerable body of recent tax literature emphasizes the need to consider tax reforms in other jurisdictions in the process of reforming the Canadian tax structure. In an article by Robin Boadway and Neil Bruce (1992), entitled "Pressures for the Harmonization of Income Taxation between Canada and the United States," they conclude that the two countries' corporate tax systems are more alike than are the personal income tax structures. They see this similarity as a result of stronger pressures for harmonization in the taxation of highly mobile capital. An illustration of these pressures is found in the discussion by Jack Mintz and John Whalley of the federal government's decision in the late 1980s to reduce statutory corporate tax rates. Mintz and Whalley (1989, 3) see this as, in part, a response to U.S. corporate tax rate reductions. They note that "left uncorrected, this situation could lead to a substantial erosion of the tax base in Canada. The proposal to reduce Canadian statutory rates reflects the influence of tax changes abroad in another sense as well: the Canadian rates must be reduced, the argument runs, in order to prevent Canadian taxes from becoming a deterrent to foreign investment, since with the reduction in rates in the United States, the U.S. foreign tax credit is no longer large enough to offset Canadian taxes."

In designing Canada's tax system, the federal government appears to have been influenced by these tax reforms in other countries. There is less evidence that Ontario has been motivated in the past by such considerations. A central thrust of this paper is that Ontario will also have to focus carefully on foreign tax systems in its future tax reforms. As a result of Ontario's global interdependencies and capital mobility, particularly within its manufacturing sector, Ontario has to show greater concern than other provinces in this regard. For Ontario, this concern will focus on the tax systems of the United States at the federal, state, and local levels. Future tax reforms at any of these levels could affect the competitiveness of Ontario businesses, and Ontario's relative attractiveness as a potential location site.

François Vaillancourt (1992, 325) has analysed tax differences between Canadian and U.S. sub-national governments and he has noted that:

> Subnational taxes are almost twice as high in Canada as in the United States, when their importance is measured as their share of GDP. This differential is highest when direct, indirect, and payroll taxes ... are used for this measurement and smallest when property taxes are also used ... The disparity is thus greater at the state/provincial level ... while the three main sources of subnational government rev-

enues are the same – personal income tax, retail sales tax, and property tax – their relative importance is not the same. In Canada the main source of revenue for both provinces and all subnational (including local) governments is the personal income tax, while in the United States the main source for states is the retail sales tax and for all subnational governments it is the property tax.

Prior to the U.S. 1986 tax reform, property and sales taxes were deductible in calculating federal taxes. Individual states and municipalities were thus limited in the degree to which tax concessions or lower tax rates could impact after-tax profits. Any reduction in tax payments at the sub-national level was offset to some degree by consequently higher tax payments at the federal level. The 1986 reform eliminated these sales tax deductions and it made deductions for income and property taxes less valuable due to lower marginal tax rates. As a result, state and local tax rates and tax concessions are now more significant determinants of business location decisions.

It is likely that President Clinton will attempt to modify the U.S. tax system. His reform plans may well affect the competitiveness and location determinants discussed in this paper. During his election campaign, Clinton emphasized a desire to increase the effective taxation of foreign companies. This focus could affect the choice of North American subsidiary locations by some foreign MNEs, and Ontario could conceivably be the recipient of such investment diverted from the United States.

Clinton's desire to reduce the deficit and, at the same time, improve the health care system could also lead to an increase in tax rates, perhaps including those related to businesses. Yet in his election campaign, he often suggested the need to provide new investment incentives in the tax system. Imposition of a value added tax is another possibility that has been discussed in U.S. political circles, as well as by U.S. economists. The likelihood of significant tax reforms within the United States means that the prospects presented in this paper will remain a central force in future Ontario tax design, and that tax reform in Ontario will be an ongoing process.

Conclusion

The following table indicates a number of trends likely to impact on Ontario's tax system in the 1990s, and it suggests some implications for tax design. These implications are presented as issues to be considered in tax design rather than recommendations for specific tax provisions, and the focus of most issues is interjurisdictional comparisons.

Ontario's tax system will play a significant role in future business location decisions. Capital has become increasingly mobile in recent years, particularly in the manufacturing sector. Businesses are more willing to change the location of their activities in response to their assessment of economic realities, and it is likely that capital will continue to become more mobile in the years ahead. Of special importance in this regard is the impact of capital mobility on employment and labour income. Capital mobility, in response to interjurisdictional tax differentials, may not only alter the base for capital taxes, but may also alter the base for sales taxes and labour income taxes through its impacts on jobs and incomes. The greater potential for cross-border shopping as a result of the FTA adds further constraints to the design of Ontario's tax system.

Decisions about Ontario's tax system will increasingly have to include estimates concerning the likely impacts of alternative tax provisions on business location decisions, and the further impacts of these location decisions on Ontario's tax revenues. If Ontario's taxes on capital and income from capital were to deviate significantly from those in other jurisdictions, then Ontario's total tax revenue could be substantially affected by changes in its tax bases. For the 1990s, this places a new emphasis on comparisons between Ontario's tax system and the tax systems of other jurisdictions. Consequently, the trends of tax reforms in other countries, particularly U.S. tax reforms, will be increasingly important for Ontario's economy and for the design of Ontario's tax system. With Bill Clinton as president, it is likely that the United States will adopt a number of significant tax reforms.

Decisions by individuals and families to move physically to another jurisdiction are motivated by many factors other than personal income taxes or sales taxes. In addition, the costs of moving to another jurisdiction, the difficulties of finding suitable employment, and the legal requirements concerning employment in other countries all tend to restrict the mobility of people in response to tax differentials.

Many of the shocks or trends discussed in this study are increasing the potential mobility of the Ontario tax bases that relate to business activities. The increase in global interdependence, the var-

TABLE 2
External Trends Impacting Ontario's Tax System in the 1990s

Trends	Implications for tax bases	Issues for tax design
1. more extensive globalization and MNEs	threat of long-term erosion, particularly in the manufacturing sector	corporate taxes that are competitive with other jurisdictions that are likely alternatives for corporate locations
2. new trade agreements	threat of relocation and job loss for certain activities	provisions to assist corporate and employee adjustment
3. higher costs imposed by new labour, social, and environmental policies	erosion of tax base	tax concessions to offset higher costs of certain policies; policy harmonization through trade agreements
4. tax reforms in other jurisdictions, particularly in the United States	abrupt changes in net advantage of locating in certain jurisdictions	continual adjustment in response to tax reforms elsewhere
5. rapid changes in skill requirements and job descriptions	quality of labour a new determinant of business location decisions	provisions to stimulate retraining
6. greater technological intensity, innovation, and labour skills	urban agglomeration; greater differences in tax bases among regions within Ontario	provisions concerning land price escalation and speculation; property tax reforms; municipal finance reforms
7. competing jurisdictions, with states and municipalities offering special tax provisions designed for each new investment	loss of potential tax base on a case-by-case basis	flexibility to offer special tax provisions to new investments in competition with other jurisdictions, particularly manufacturing investments; right of municipalities to offer property and business tax concessions
8. devolution of federal powers to provincial governments	greater competition within Canada for investments	maintaining corporate tax competitiveness with other provinces
9. overall, greater capital mobility	greater sensitivity of corporate tax bases to interjurisdictional tax differences	greater reliance on PIT and RST, less reliance on corporate taxes (profits, property, capital, and business levies); stock purchase incentives

ious potential shocks to the global economy, the trade practices and agreements of the 1990s, tax reforms in other countries, and differences in legislation and regulations are making Ontario's tax system increasingly sensitive to developments abroad.

The increasing mobility of capital leads to the recommendation that less reliance should be placed on business taxes (profits, capital, property, and various business levies) and more reliance should be placed on taxes borne by individuals (personal income, sales taxes, and residential property). The possibility that some businesses may shift some of their taxes backwards onto their employees in the form of lower wages deserves special consideration at a time when businesses are confronting unions with threats to relocate unless wage concessions are made. The uncertain incidence of corporate taxes, particularly in this environment of increased capital mobility, adds another argument for this shift towards a greater reliance on other tax bases.

New trade agreements have accompanied these trends towards globalization and multinational enterprises, and the negotiation and implementation of additional trade agreements of various kinds will continue to be of importance for Ontario. The globalization process will continue to create international economic issues and disputes that will require resolution. The forces behind globalization and multinational enterprises have also created interests in favour of such agreements. The past emphasis on tariff reduction is now expanding to include agreements concerning non-tariff barriers, and tax provisions could become more important as location determinants if subsidies and other investment incentives are constrained by these agreements.

Many regions within the industrialized world have experienced very rapid and substantial deindustrialization, and these are examples Ontario can learn from. In particular, the experience of the U.S. Midwest is relevant, where the 1975–82 loss of high-paying manufacturing jobs has been accompanied by the growth of low-paying service sector jobs. This kind of development is obviously one that Ontario should attempt to avoid, or at least limit, in the design of its tax system.

The corporate location decision is influenced by many factors. Two of the most important factors for the future will be the quality of the labour force and the environment for innovation. Here, the Ontario government can play a very important role. It is possible that tax reforms can be used to strengthen these important location determinants. However, such objectives may also be achieved through government expenditures. In considering tax reforms, it is important to consider alternative expenditure measures that could achieve the same objectives.

Ontario is now involved in a new permanent competition with other jurisdictions to attract investment, and the jobs and local purchases that come with that investment. The tax structure is an important weapon in this competition. American states and municipalities are offering special tax concessions as an investment enticement. American municipalities have the right to offer special tax concessions, while Ontario municipalities are forbidden by the provincial government to do so. Whether Ontario municipalities should be allowed to follow the American practice deserves consideration. Of greater general concern are the nature and extent of municipal taxes and their impact on business location decisions.

The interjurisdictional competition for new investment is both a threat and an opportunity. To focus only on the threat of deindustrialization is to miss the opportunity. The greater mobility of capital means that the Ontario government can attract investment from other jurisdictions. A central issue for tax design is the degree to which the Ontario tax structure should be used for this purpose.

Notes

The authors would like to thank Allan M. Maslove and an anonymous reviewer for helpful suggestions; the Donner Canadian Foundation and the Institute for Research and Public Policy for providing core funding to the Centre for the Study of International Economic Relations; and the National Centre for Management Research and Development for research concerning Canada's international trade and investment.

1 See GATT (1992, vol. 2, 4).

2 See ibid. (1992, vol. 1, 2).

3 See "Standing Committee on Finance and Economic Affairs: Report on Cross-Border Shopping" (1991). In 1991, Ontario's Standing Committee on Finance and Economic Affairs submitted its "Report on Cross-Border Shopping." They discussed a range of estimates of lost retail sales. The Ontario Ministry of Industry, Trade and Technology estimated these to be $340-$360 million in 1989, with losses of tax revenues in the range of $40-$50 million. The retail Council of Canada estimated lost retail sales of over $600 million in 1990, while John Winter estimated losses of $1 billion in 1991. A later study by the Ontario Min-

istry of Industry, Trade and Technology estimated the loss of retail sales to be $2.2 billion.

4 Ernst and Young have prepared a paper for the Ontario Fair Tax Commission entitled "The Impact of Taxes on Business Locations" (1994). Their literature survey suggests that tax differences at the provincial or state level may not have played a major role in new location decisions, but that the generation of corporate earnings from existing businesses and the local investment of those earnings may have been influenced to a greater degree by taxes. Furthermore, their paper points out that if tax differentials were greater than those during the periods studied, then business location decisions might be much more sensitive to tax considerations.

5 See James C. Cobb (1982; 1984).

6 See Robin W. Boadway and Harry M. Kitchen (1984). In *Canadian Tax Policy*, they present a survey of the literature on the incidence of the corporate tax. For example, they refer to the study by Richard Dusansky and J. Ernest Tanner entitled "The Shifting of the Profits Tax in Canadian Manufacturing, 1935–65." This study concluded that the corporate tax was approximately 75 per cent shifted. Other authors have reached a wide variety of conclusions, depending upon the variables included and the statistical techniques used.

7 Carolyn C. Perrucci et al. (1988).

8 See Stephen Fothergill and Nigel Guy (1990, 15).

9 Data in this section have been drawn from *Business Facts: Ontario Canada* (Ontario 1992) and various publications by Statistics Canada (1991; 1992; 1993).

10 Canada, Annual Reports (1989–1990; 1990–1991).

11 See J.M. Stopford and J.H. Dunning (1983, 31).

12 Ibid.

13 See I.A. Litvak (1981) and Adhip Chaudhuri (1983).

14 See, for example, Martha Chandler and Michael Trebilcock (1986, 188).

15 See, for example, Marie Howland (1988, 1, 115–16, 151–53).

16 Paul Bergman (1991). It should be noted that respondents to such surveys may, in fact, identify factors other than those that actually drive their decisions. In particular, respondents may be reacting to recent political pronouncements, and, over time, these reactions may be tempered by the realization that fears may have been unduly exaggerated, and that compliance may not be as costly as originally thought.

17 See Ian Allaby (1990, 43–44).

18 James C. Cobb (1982 and 1984).

19 See *Global Press* (1992, 629).

20 Wilfrid L. Kohl (1991, 69).
21 Paul Davenport et al. (1982).
22 See Paul R. Krugman (1987, 131–44) and James Brander and Barbara
    Spender (1983, 225–355).
23 Statistics Canada (1991), Catalogue No. 65-001.
24 See Mary W. Walsh (1990) "Environmental Law in Canada Comes of
    Age."
25 For a detailed discussion, see S. Charnovitz (1986, 61–78).

Bibliography

Allaby, Ian. 1990. "Free Trade, Why Everybody's Flying South." *Canadian Business*, December: 42–49

Baldwin, John R., and Paul K. Gorecki. 1990. *Structural Change and the Adjustment Process, Perspectives on Firm Growth and Worker Turnover*. A study prepared for Statistics Canada and the Economic Council of Canada

Bergman, Paul. 1991. "National Centre for Management Research and Development." University of Western Ontario

Boadway, Robin, and Neil Bruce. 1984. "A Personal Income Tax: Implications for Investments." In *A Separate Personal Income Tax for Ontario: Background Studies*, ed. David W. Conklin, 30–58. Toronto: Ontario Economic Council Special Research Report

Boadway, Robin, and Neil Bruce. 1992. "Pressures for the Harmonization of Income Taxation between Canada and the United States." In *Canada–U.S. Tax Comparisons*, ed. John B. Shoven and John Whalley, 25–74. Chicago: University of Chicago Press

Boadway, Robin W., and Harry M. Kitchen. 1984. *Canadian Tax Policy.* 2d ed. Toronto: Canadian Tax Foundation

Brander, James, and Barbara Spender. 1983. "Strategic Commitment with R & D: The Symmetric Case." *Bell Journal of Economics*, 4: 225–355

Bruce, Neil. 1989. "The Impact of Tax Reform on International Capital Flows and Investment." In *The Economic Impacts of Tax Reform*, ed. Jack Mintz and John Whalley, 193–217. Toronto: Canadian Tax Foundation

Canada. Annual Reports, 1989–90, 1990–91. *Investment Canada*. Government of Canada

Chandler, Martha, and Michael Trebilcock. 1986. "Comparative Survey of Industrial Policies in Selected OECD Countries." In *Economics of Industrial Policy and Strategy*, ed. Donald G. McFetridge, 85–224. Toronto: University of Toronto Press

Charnovitz, S. 1986. "Fair Labour Standards and International Trade." *Journal of World Trade Law*, 20: 61–78

Chaudhuri, Adhip. 1983. "American Multinationals and American Employment." In *The Multinational Corporation in the 1980s*, ed. Charles B. Kindleberger and David B. Audretsch, 263–77. Cambridge, MA: MIT Press

Cobb, James C. 1982. *The Selling of the South*. Baton Rouge: Louisiana State University Press

Cobb, James C. 1984. *Industrialization and Southern Society 1877–1984*. Lexington, KY: The University Press of Kentucky

Congressional Quarterly. May 4, 1991. Weekly Report, 49 (10): 1121

Davenport, Paul, et al. 1983. *Industrial Policy in Ontario and Quebec, 1982*. Toronto: Ontario Economic Council

Dickson, Tony, ed., and David Judge. 1987. *The Politics of Industrial Closure*. London: The MacMillan Press Ltd

Dohlman, Ebba. 1990. "The Trade Effects of Environmental Regulation." *The OECD Observer*, 162: 28–32

Ernst and Young. 1993. "The Impact of Taxes on Business Locations." In *Business Taxation in Ontario*, ed. Allan M. Maslove. Fair Tax Commission, Research Studies. Toronto: University of Toronto Press

Fothergill, Stephen, and Nigel Guy. 1990. *Retreat from the Regions: Corporate Change and the Closure of Factories*. London: Jessica Kingsley Publishers Ltd

Gandhi, Prem. 1986. "Foreign Direct Investment and Regional Development: The Case of Canadian Investment in New York State." In *Reindustrializing New York State, Strategies, Implications, Challenges*, ed. Morton Schoolman and Alvin Magid, 205–27. Albany: State University of New York Press

General Agreement on Tariffs and Trade (GATT). 1992. *Trade Policy Review: Canada 1992*. Vols. 1 and 2. Geneva

Global Press. *The Canadian Global Almanac, 1992*. 1992. Toronto: Global Press

Howland, Marie. 1988. *Plant Closings and Worker Displacement: The Regional Issues*. Kalamazoo, MI: W.E. Upjohn Institute for Employment Research

Kelly, M.E., and D. Kamp. (n.d.) "Mexico–U.S. Free Trade Negotiations and the Environment: Exploring the Issues." Austin, TX: Texas Center for Policy Studies, Discussion Paper

Knickerbocker, F.T. 1983. *Oligopolistic Reaction and Multinational Enterprises*. Cambridge, MA: MIT Press

Kohl, Wilfrid L., ed. 1991. *After the Oil Price Collapse, OPEC, the United States, and the World Oil Market*. Baltimore: The Johns Hopkins University Press

Kraushaar, Robert, and David Perry. 1990. "Buffalo, New York: Region of No Illusions." In *Economic Restructuring of the American Midwest*, ed. Richard D. Bingham and Randall W. Eberts. Boston: Kluwer Academic Publishers

Krugman, Paul R. 1987. "Is Free Trade Passé?" *Economic Perspectives*, 1: 225–355

Leonard, R.E., and E. Christensen. 1992. "Economic Effects of a Free Trade
  Agreement Between Mexico and the United States." Testimony on be-
  half of Community Nutrition Institute before the International Trade
  Commission Hearing on Docket No. 302-307. Washington, DC. April
Lester, J., and T. Morehen. 1989. "Trade Barriers Between Canada and the
  United States.' Working Paper No. 88-3. Ottawa: Department of Finance
Litvak, I.A. 1981. *The Canadian Multinationals.* Toronto: Butterworths
Low, P. 1991. "Trade Measures and Environmental Quality: The Implica-
  tions for Mexico's Exports." Washington, DC: International Trade
  Division
Mansfield, E. 1984. "R & D Innovation: Some Empirical Findings." In *R &
  D, Patents and Productivity,* ed. Z. Griliches, 127-54. Chicago: University of
  Chicago Press
McQuillan, Peter. 1989. "Comment: Tax Reform - Some Unfinished Busi-
  ness with Respect to the Cost of Capital and Return on Investment." In
  The Economic Impacts of Tax Reform, ed. Jack Mintz and John Whalley,
  185-92. Toronto: Canadian Tax Foundation
Mintz, Jack, and John Whalley, eds. 1989. *The Economic Impacts of Tax Reform.*
  Toronto: Canadian Tax Foundation
National Wildlife Federation. 1990. "Environmental Concerns Related to a
  United States-Mexico-Canada Free Trade Agreement." Background
  Paper. Washington, DC. November
Ontario. 1991. "Standing Committee on Finance and Economic Affairs: Re-
  port on Cross-Border Shopping." 1st Session 35th Parliament 40 Eliza-
  beth II
Ontario. 1992. *Business Facts: Ontario Canada.* Toronto: Queen's Printer
Perrucci, Carolyn C., et al. 1988. *Plant Closings: International Context and Social
  Costs.* New York: Aldine de Gruyter
Portz, John. 1990. *The Politics of Plant Closings.* Lawrence, KS: University
  Press of Kansas
Rodwin, Lloyd, ed., and Hidehiko Sazanami. 1989. *Deindustrialization and Re-
  gional Economic Transformation: The Experience of the United States.* Boston:
  Unwin Hyman, Inc.
Rothstein, Lawrence E. 1986. *Plant Closings: Power, Politics, and Workers.* Dover,
  MA: Auburn House Publishing Company
Rugman, Alan. 1989. *Multinationals and Canada-United States Free Trade.* Co-
  lumbia, SC: University of South Carolina Press
Shoven, John B., and Michael Topper. 1992. "The Cost of Capital in Can-
  ada, the United States, and Japan." In *Canada-U.S. Tax Comparisons,* ed.
  John B. Shoven and John Whalley, 217-35. Chicago: University of Chi-
  cago Press

Shoven, John B., and John Whalley, eds. 1992. *Canada–U.S. Tax Comparisons.* Chicago: University of Chicago Press

Simeon, Richard. 1986. "Federalism and Free Trade." In *The Free Trade Papers,* ed. Duncan Cameron, 187–92. Toronto: Lorimer

Slemrod, Joel. 1990. "Tax Principles in an International Economy." In *World Tax Reform: Case Studies of Developed and Developing Countries,* ed. Michael J. Boskin and Charles E. McLure, 11–23. San Francisco: ICS Press

Statistics Canada. 1991. *Summary of Canadian International Trade.* Catalogue 65-001, December 1991, lxiii

Statistics Canada. 1991. "Summary of Canadian International Trade." Ministry of Industry, Science and Technology. December

Statistics Canada. 1992. "Summary of Canadian International Trade." Ministry of Industry, Science and Technology. December

Statistics Canada. 1993. "Historical Labour Force Statistics." Ministry of Industry, Science and Technology. February

Stopford, J.M., and J.H. Dunning. 1983. *The World Directory of Multinational Enterprises 1982–1983: Company Performance and Global Trends.* Detroit: Gale Research

Storper M., and R. Walker. 1989. *The Capitalist Imperative: Territory, Technology and Industrial Growth.* Oxford, UK: Basil Blackwell Inc.

Vaillancourt, François. 1992. "Subnational Tax Harmonization, Canada and the United States: Intent, Results, and Consequences." In *Canada–U.S. Tax Comparisons,* ed. John B. Shoven and John Whalley, 323–57. Chicago: University of Chicago Press

Uimonen, P., and John Whalley. 1991. "Trade and Environment." Draft. Washington, DC: Institute for International Economics

United States International Trade Commission. 1990. *Review of Trade and Investment Liberalization Measures by Mexico and Prospects for Future United States–Mexican Relations.* Washington, DC: USITC No. 2275

Walsh, Mary W. "Environmental Law in Canada Comes of Age." *Los Angeles Times* 8 April 1990, 109, 126, 1(D)

Waverman, Leonard. 1991. "A Canadian Vision of North American Economic Integration." In *Continental Accord: North American Economic Integration,* ed. Steven Globerman, 31–64. Vancouver: The Fraser Institute

Whalley, John. 1990. "Now That the Deal Is Over: Canadian Trade Policy Options in the 1990s." *Public Policy,* June: XVI No. 2. 121–36

2 Changes in the World Economy and Fiscal Implications for Canada and Ontario

BRUCE CAMPBELL

Introduction

The goal of this paper is to sketch out major forces at work in the world economy, how they affect the Canadian and Ontario economies, and specifically the fiscal capacity of governments. Fiscal capacity implies the ability to tax and/or borrow. This paper focuses on tax.

An exercise of this nature deals with issues and phenomena that are complex and in flux, and whose nature and consequences, often ambiguous, are the subject of much disagreement. However, in public policy analysis, to deal only in certain or complete knowledge is to stay within the realm of the trivial, and to leave out what is most important in terms of providing guidance to makers of public policy.

What happens as a result of the interaction between the international and the national economy depends not only on developments in the international arena, but also on the structures, institutions, and policies that exist within Canada and Ontario and their ability to change in response to external stimuli. It also depends on the configuration of domestic social forces, the extent to which it is possible to articulate a consensus of values about the kind of society we want, and unanimity around policy goals and how to achieve them.

Policy goals include full employment, universal social programs, economic growth, equitable distribution of income, price stability, and environmental sustainability. However, there are major differences within our society about what these goals mean, how to prioritize them, and how to achieve them. There are also different perceptions of the roles of government and markets in achieving these goals, and of the roles of various levels of government, and of labour and management.

The differences can, for simplicity, be grouped into two broad camps, or two paradigms, each with its own agenda (though neither is without internal differences and there is substantial fuzziness at the edges between the two). Each paradigm defines and orders values and goals differently, and advocates different strategies for achieving its goals. The first agenda starts from the position that markets can do most everything best, while the best government governs least (but with some notable exceptions such as defence, universal bank insurance, and intellectual property protection). The conservative federal government espouses the first agenda. That agenda was articulated concisely in the document "Agenda for Change" (Canada 1984).

The second agenda, while recognizing the value of markets as a mechanism for providing signals and incentives to producers and consumers, also sees their limitations: many instances of market failure, the maldistribution of power that unregulated markets tend to engender, and their inability to supply public goods, such as education or a clean environment. While acknowledging that the question of balance is critical, it sees an activist role for governments in regulating markets and shaping economic development.

The agenda of the government of Ontario, as articulated in Budget Paper E Ontario in the 1990s (Ontario 1991), falls into the second camp. However, there are many (see, for example, Gindin, 1992) who think that Budget Paper E's framing of economic challenges facing Ontario in terms of "how to become competitive" – the overriding preoccupation of the first paradigm – blurs the distinction between approaches and has led to confusion and weakness when translated into concrete policies.

It is worth mentioning some of the goals for sustainable prosperity in the 1990s, as outlined in Budget Paper E. The goals include high levels of employment in well-paying, high-quality jobs; prosperity that is environmentally and socially sustainable; fairly shared costs for economic changes; and a public sector that provides the services necessary to promoting the health, education, and social well-being of its citizens. It further notes that sustainable prosperity is best achieved on the basis of increased equity and social cooperation. Social cooperation, however, means partnerships among the key participants: government, labour, business, and community groups.

Budget Paper E distinguishes the Ontario government's economic strategy as a proactive strategy as opposed to the federal strategy, which is *laissez faire*, that is, let the market do it. Ontario's alternative approach is for government to play a facilitating role for structural change, not only to minimize the costs of transition and to distribute them more fairly, but to actively promote the development of value added, high-wage jobs through strategic partnerships (87). The paper further notes that success will depend on the ability of business, labour, and government working together to increase the flexibility of the Ontario economy, its supporting institutions, and society in general (88). Success will also depend on enhancing productivity growth through new investment, innovation, research and development, and on enhanced managerial and workforce skills (101).

Major Developments in the World Economy

This paper identifies and analyses the following key structures and processes in the world economy: regulatory regimes; production, investment and trade; finance; knowledge and information; and employment and income distribution.

The term most often used by analysts to describe and simplify these complex changes is "globalization." Business spokespersons, neoclassical economists, and journalists associate globalization with a worldwide "freeing of market forces," that is, liberalization, deregulation, privatization, integration, enhanced capital mobility, and a reduced role for government. Often blurred is the distinction between the normative (what they want to happen), and the positive (what is actually happening). What is desired is often presented as reality or political inevitability. To the extent that powerful forces pushing political agendas nationally and internationally achieve their goals, the desired becomes the actual and, once entrenched in law and practice, proves difficult if not impossible to reverse.

On the other hand, the world is still a diverse patchwork of national and regional regulatory regimes that reflects different degrees of "freeing of market forces." Moreover, the winds of change within societies have, over time, blown in different directions.

The term globalization does have analytical value in describing what is going on in the world and, at the risk of oversimplification, this paper will use that term and will begin by outlining three interrelated manifestations.

The first is the generalized opening since the Second World War of national economies (ratio of trade to output), and the emergence of the global marketplace. It should be noted, however, that the past two centuries have been marked by periods of economic openness followed by periods of protectionism. Moreover, throughout those periods European empires imported resources from their colonies in exchange for manufactured goods. Market openness within an empire was, from the beginning, an essential feature of the colonial economic relationship.

What is new, particularly in the past 25 years, is the internationalization of goods production or global sourcing. (This process is also becoming evident in services such as data processing.) For an élite group of transnational corporations (TNCs), decisions about how and where to locate and combine the various elements or steps in production processes are global in scope and take place more and more as if national boundaries did not exist. (This is not to imply, however, that corporations are not without national loyalties.) Knowledge and information have become the critical new input in the globalized production process.

The second manifestation of globalization is the emergence of what is, in many respects, a global financial market – privatized and greatly deregulated – coexisting with national currencies, but through which disturbances can be more readily transmitted from country to country. However, the cost of credit in various countries, adjusted for exchange rates, differential inflation rates, risk, and so on, did not converge as was expected in the 1980s, the decade of integrated financial markets (Fieleke 1988). Although there was convergence in 1990–91, this may just be an aberration in short-term monetary policies. Will the gaps open up once again when current government policies in Germany and Japan are reversed? That, as Thurow (1992, 45) states, remains a mystery.

The last manifestation of globalization is the ascendance of the transnational corporation as the principal agent of globalization, which has become the principal economic and political driving force in the world economy. One hundred transnational banks account for the vast majority of global financial flows. A relatively small group of 600 TNCs account for roughly one-quarter of global output, both inside and outside their home countries (United Nations 1988). Transnationals control 70 per cent of global trade. The 350 largest account for almost 40 per cent of the world's merchandise trade (Daly 1992, 23). Commodity trade is even more concentrated.

For example, from three to six transnationals control 85–90 per cent of global wheat trade, 75 per cent of crude oil trade, and 90–95 per cent of iron ore trade (United Nations UNCTAD Statistical Pocket book 1989, Table 4b). Transnationals operate mainly through foreign direct investment (FDI) and global networks of affiliates and subsidiaries through which they have internalized markets, but also through joint ventures, strategic alliances, and other arrangements. Besides conducting the bulk of international trade, they hold proprietary rights over most of the world's technology.

Structures of Regulation

The globalization process has been driven by simultaneous technological revolutions in computers, telecommunications, and transportation, but it is also driven by corporate strategies and government policies, both domestic and foreign, especially those of the dominant states: Europe, Japan, and the United States. The process has been entrenched and advanced by agreements arrived at in multilateral forums such as the Group of Seven (G-7), the International Monetary Fund (IMF), the World Bank, the Organization for Economic Cooperation and Development (OECD) and the General Agreement on Tariffs and Trade (GATT), as well as regional arrangements such as the European Community (EC) and the Canada–U.S. Free Trade Agreement (FTA).

Transnationals have reshaped and restructured the world economy, not only through their enormous technological, productive, and financial power, but also through their awesome political power. They have succeeded in shaping political agendas and structures, both nationally and internationally, and in securing tax regimes, protective intellectual property codes, and other regulatory systems supportive of their needs. They have had great success in blocking or dismantling trade barriers, investment regulations, labour, social, and environmental legislation that impaired their activities and interests.

The role of the state is shifting, as Cox (1991, 337) observes, from protecting their societies, or at least mitigating the adverse effects of external pressures, to adjusting their economies to the needs of the global economy, as agreed to in such international forums as the OECD, GATT, the IMF, the World Economic Forum, and private financial markets.

In the 1970s, industrial economies began to slow down. As inflation grew and as profit levels fell, corporate élites saw an opportunity to advance their interest by aligning with neoclassical economic theorists and right-wing political parties to undermine the Keynesian economic management structures and the welfare state, and to promote their *laissez-faire* agenda encapsulated in the triad of deregulation, privatization, and liberalization (Marchak 1991). Neoconservative political ideology had, by 1980, established its dominance within key centres of political power, notably in the United States and Britain.

The Reagan administration's tight Friedman-style monetary policy, combined with supply-side tax cuts for the wealthy and a surge of military spending, plunged the world into recession, pushed Third World debtor countries towards collapse, and produced huge fiscal and trade deficits in the United States.

Throughout the 1980s, international financial institutions – the IMF and the World Bank – ensured that new lending was conditioned on the debtor governments of less-developed countries (LDCs) restructuring their economic policies in accordance with the new economic orthodoxy, namely, credit rationing, price deregulation, wage controls, removal of trade and investment barriers, and privatization. In industrial countries, key sectors such as banking, securities, airlines, trucking, and telecommunications were deregulated and public enterprises were sold off.

The GATT–Uruguay round of negotiations began in 1986 with an agenda to expand the scope of and liberalize the global rules of economic exchange to include investment, intellectual property, services, and industrial policy tools. These negotiations, although close to completion, have stalled. However, ambitious regional integration initiatives have proceeded more quickly, resulting in agreements in Europe, the 1992 single market and the Maastricht treaty, and in North America, the FTA and the North American Free Trade Agreement (NAFTA).

Production, Investment, and Trade

What are the major dimensions of structural change in world production, investment, and trade? Since 1947, world trade volumes have grown by 500 per cent, more than double the 200 per cent growth of world output. Trade has become a more important component of the economies of many countries. For example, U.S. trade more than doubled, from 4.5 per cent of the gross domestic product

(GDP) in 1950 to 10.7 per cent of the gross domestic product (GDP) in 1990, and Germany's trade soared from 13.5 per cent to 33.2 per cent of GDP during this period. In other countries, such as Britain and Canada, trade was a major component of their economies throughout this period and its share of GDP remained relatively stable. Britain's trade was 25.5 per cent of GDP in 1950 and was the same in 1990. Canada's trade was 22.1 per cent of GDP in 1950. After rising to 27 per cent in 1980, it settled down to 25 per cent in 1990. Japan's trade jumped from 10.9 per cent of GDP in 1960 to 15.7 per cent in 1980, but dropped back down to 10.4 per cent by 1990 (Fieleke 1988, 198; International Monetary Fund 1992a).

It should be recalled that this postwar opening of national economies followed an extended period during which national economies became progressively more protectionist. Thus, it was only in 1970 that the ratio of world trade to output regained its 1913 level.

World output and trade growth were most rapid in the first two postwar decades. Thereafter, the world economy slowed markedly, especially during the 1980s (see Table 1). In the industrial world, the annual GDP growth dropped from 3.7 per cent during the period 1967 to 1976 to 2.5 per cent during the 1980–91 period. More dramatic was the situation in the Third World, where annual GDP growth fell from 6 per cent during the years 1967 to 1976 to 2.5 per cent during the 1980–91 period. The growth of trade volumes also slowed considerably in the industrial world, from an annual rate of 7.8 per cent during the 1967–76 period, to 4.4 per cent during the years 1980 to 1991; and in the Third World from 6.8 per cent in 1967–76 to 3.2 per cent during the 1980–91 period.

Accompanying the economic slowdown in industrial countries was a decline in the growth of gross fixed capital formation, from an annual 3.2 per cent in 1967–76 to 2.6 per cent during the 1980–91 years; and a drop in annual productivity growth from 4.3 per cent to 2.9 per cent during the same period (International Monetary Fund 1985, 1992a). In Canada during this period, capital formation growth slowed from 4.4 per cent to 2.7 per cent per annum, and productivity growth slowed from 4.4 per cent to 3.5 per cent per annum.

Since 1970, global capital flows (short- and long-term debt capital) have grown at a faster pace than global trade. They now exceed annual global trade flows by a ratio of 25:1. Moreover, capital flows continue to grow much faster than trade – 20 per cent per annum during the years 1983 to 1988 as compared with trade growth, which was 5 per cent per annum. Foreign direct investment by TNCs (which involves ownership and control) grew three times faster than the growth of exports and four times faster than the growth of world output in the 1980s. In 1989, the FDI flows totalled $196 billion, pushing the global stock of FDI to $1.5 trillion (United Nations Centre on Transnational Corporations 1991).

More than four-fifths of the world's FDI stock and flows (outflows and inflows) takes place among the developed countries. The LDCs' share of FDI flows dropped from 25 per cent during the 1980–84 period to 17 per cent in 1988–89.

During the 1985–89 period, 77 per cent of the outflow of FDI (denoting the home base of corporations undertaking the foreign investment) and 65 per cent of the inward flow of FDI (denoting the destination of that investment) occurred within the triad of Europe, Japan, and the United States. This is much higher than their share of world trade, which is roughly one-half. Five countries – Britain, France, Germany, Japan, and the United States – are the home bases for 70 per cent of the global outflow of FDI.

Most significant is the emergence of Japan in the second half of the 1980s as the fastest growing source of FDI outflows. From 1985 to 1989 these outflows increased at an annual rate of 62 per cent, accounting for 23 per cent of world FDI outflows in this period. Concomitantly, the EC supplanted the United States as the largest source of FDI outflows (37 per cent); the United States accounted for 18 per cent of FDI outflows. Although Japan's share of home-country FDI is currently about one-third of the share of the United States and the EC, it is projected to reach parity by the turn of the century and, thereafter, surpass the others and become home to the largest share of foreign direct investment. The vast majority of Japanese FDI went to the EC and the United States. (By the end of the 1980s, flows to the EC exceeded those to the United States, indicating that the EC could emerge in the future as the largest host region.)

The patterns of foreign investment suggest that Japanese transnationals are pursuing regionalization strategies, that is, building self-contained, regionally sustainable networks of affiliates in each of the triad members. The components of their strategy include market share, volume, cost reduction, and competitiveness. These strategies are being applied not only to other members of the triad, but also in their own backyard. East Asia, a dynamic area stretching from Tokyo to Jakarta, and including some parts of China, will have 600 million consumers by the year 2000. Japanese investment, which originally located in East Asia to exploit low-cost labour in production that was largely for export, is now locating to ensure control of a share of an expanding domestic market. For example, two-thirds of the growth in the world's car market in the 1990s is projected to be in East Asia (Courtis 1992, 20–21).

As a host country to FDI, Japan's stocks and flows are extremely low (less than 1 per cent of all productive assets), reflecting a structure that discourages foreign investment by means of informal barriers to takeovers such as the system of cross-ownership and complementary business strategies called *keritsu*, as well as procedures of administrative guidance that informally screen unwanted investment. If anything, Japan's economy became more closed in the 1980s. The share of foreign corporate control of Japanese manufacturing assets dropped from 2 per cent in 1977 to 1 per cent in 1986, and its share of gross sales dropped from 5 per cent to 2 per cent during the same period (Julius 1991, 13). The United States, while declining in importance as a home country, has become the largest host country for FDI, accounting for 46 per cent of the world's FDI inflows during the years 1985 to 1989, with its resulting rise as host of 31 per cent of the world's FDI stocks.

These changes in investment patterns mirror the emergence of European and especially Japanese transnationals to rival the traditional dominance of U.S. transnationals. In 1970, there were 64 of the world's 100 largest industrial corporations located in the United States, 26 in Europe, and 8 in Japan. By 1988, there were 42 located in the United States, 33 in Europe, and 16 in Japan. In 1970, of the 50 largest banks in the world, 19 were North American, 16 were European, and 11 were Japanese. By 1988, only 5 were North American, 17 were European, and 24 were Japanese (Thurow 1992, 30).

The figures also reflect the emergence of Japan as an economic superpower. It accounted for 3 per cent of the world's output in 1960. Thirty years later its share of global output had climbed to 16 per cent. In 1950, per capita income of the United States was 15 times higher than Japan's. It is now roughly equal. The Japanese economy, currently 60 per cent of the size of the U.S. economy, will equal the U.S. economy in size by about the year 2000 at present growth rates.

Another major structural change in foreign direct investment has been the shift from resource-based and manufacturing industries to services. In 1970, one-quarter of the global stock of FDI was in services. By the late 1980s that share had increased to 50 per cent (United Nations 1991). This shift accelerated in the 1980s. Between 1975 and 1989, the services sector share of Japan's home FDI outflows increased from 40 per cent to 67 per cent, the services share of U.S. FDI outflows rose from 29 per cent to 40 per cent, and that of Canada's FDI outflows rose from 28 per cent to 44 per cent.

Several reasons account for this trend, beyond the fact that the limited tradeability of most services has made foreign direct investment the logical vehicle for the globalization of services provision, even more so than it has for the globalization of goods production. They include technological changes such as the increased knowledge component of most services; government policy changes such as the deregulation of many services, notably banking, telecommunications, and transportation; changes in corporate strategy that are designed to internalize corporate functions, such as the establishment by TNCs of service affiliates, particularly in finance and the wholesale and retail sectors.

The 1991 *World Investment Report* of the UN Centre on Transnational Corporations predicts that technological developments could increase the tradeability of services and thereby change the nature of FDI in certain services. The advent of trans-border data flows through the convergence of computer and communications technology, permitting instantaneous interactive transactions, is making it possible for information-intensive services to be produced in one place and consumed in another. In some cases, this could make a range of services tradeable, reducing the need for FDI in certain areas. It could also increase FDI in other areas, allowing service TNCs, like their manufacturing counterparts, to split their production into parts, sourcing certain operations with foreign affiliates where, for example, wages are lower. The realization of these changes, however, would require the further dismantling of national regulatory regimes.

The rapid expansion of FDI in the 1980s is almost certainly increasing the proportion of world trade accounted for by intra-corporate trade, that is, transfers across borders of goods and services between affiliates of the same corporation. Data deficiencies make the share of world trade that is intra-corporate difficult to determine. Estimates have placed it at 25 per cent of world trade

(International Monetary Fund 1992b, 227–30). However, in the United States, intra-corporate trade accounts for 35–40 per cent of trade (UN Centre on Transnational Corporations 1991, 46) and in Canada it accounts for fully one-half of all trade (Mersereau 1992). Unlike arm's length or open-market transactions, the prices of these transfers are internal accounting entries determined by the management. A growing proportion of intra-corporate trade in the world suggests that transnationals have greater capacity to use internal transfer price accounting to evade taxes in jurisdictions where taxes are high and declare profits where taxes are low. In the absence of international regulation of these practices, transferring pricing puts downward pressure on corporate taxes everywhere. Furthermore, the local sales of TNCs' subsidiaries based in host countries typically have exceeded exports from the home country to the host country by a wide margin.

These factors, among others, have led Julius (1990) to propose an alternative form of balance-of-trade accounting. In the case of Canada–U.S. trade, for example, to U.S. exports to Canada one would add the sales in Canada by U.S.–owned subsidiaries that are twice as large as that of the United States to exports (1986 figures). On the other hand, one would subtract the equivalent of two-thirds of U.S. exports to Canada that go to U.S.–owned subsidiaries. Thus, in this example, $100 billion of U.S. exports to Canada would become $233 billion. On the other side of the equation, one would subtract from Canadian exports an amount equivalent to 43 per cent of Canadian exports to the United States which are by U.S.–owned corporations (1986 figures), but add 60 per cent (estimate) to exports representing the Canadian content of U.S.–owned subsidiaries' Canadian sales. Thus, $110 billion of Canadian exports to the United States would become $129 billion. A similar calculation would have to be done for Canadian-owned corporations in the United States.

Such an accounting procedure would greatly enhance the overall American balance-of-trade picture, given the continuing dominance of U.S. transnationals. In the Canadian case, it is obvious from this rough and incomplete example that a Canadian merchandise surplus under current trade accounting would turn into a huge deficit.

Globalization has changed not only relations of power among nations, but also relations of power within nations. The growth in the power of the transnational corporation has constrained the power of nation states, as well as the power of labour and other social organizations.

Wilkinson (1993, 39) pinpoints the power of TNCs to frustrate national economic policy objectives. "The TNCs can borrow abroad and shift profits via transfer pricing to evade monetary and fiscal policies ... and even alter international production patterns as may be appropriate in the light of exchange rate changes. Similarly, microeconomic policies relating to performance requirements of firms, industry taxation, or subsidy policies, anti-pollution measures, anti-combines regulations, and the like may be of limited effectiveness owing to the flexibility of TNCs's operations and their ability to play one nation off against another to maximize their own advantage."

Similarly, a country that internalizes environmental costs into its prices is disadvantaged vis-à-vis a country that does not internalize its environmental costs, according to World Bank environmental economist Herman Daly. "International capital mobility, coupled with free trade of products, stimulates an international competition to lower standards and attract (or retain) capital. Wages, health insurance, worker safety standards, and environmental standards, etc., can all be lowered in the name of reducing costs" (Daly 1992, 11).

TNCs can frustrate and undermine the fiscal capacity of governments, either through evasion, or by raising revenue in the form of tax deductions, or subsidies. One measure to challenge the TNCs and reverse the erosion of government taxing power is a unitary tax which was introduced in California. It taxes corporations operating within its boundaries on the basis of the estimated ratio of state-to-worldwide operations. This was designed to offset the TNCs' practice of transfer pricing. However, the unitary tax was abandoned in California when the Thatcher government put pressure on the Reagan administration by threatening to retaliate in kind against U.S. corporations in England. Nevertheless, it does remain, in principle, an option for a government determined to bring in an effective corporate tax (see, for example, Gordon 1984).

Globalization, in altering the relative power between workers and corporations, has weakened industrial relations systems. There is a tendency for corporations operating especially in countries that do not restrain or regulate the market to adopt low-wage strategies as a substitute for technology-driven, high-wage competitiveness strategies, with the consequence being widening income disparities, and a decline in wages and living standards in these countries (Marshall 1991). Labour's gains, achieved painstakingly over time, quickly dissipate as plants close in their countries or communities and reopen where unions are weak or nonexistent.

One of the seemingly paradoxical trends in the globalization process is a regionalization of the world economy into three blocs: East Asia, Europe, and North America. This is evidenced both in trade and FDI trends, as well as in integration arrangements such as the EC and the Canada–U.S. (and now Mexico) Free Trade Agreement. (The value of trade among the three spheres or blocs is currently about the same size as trade within these regional economic blocs.)

These arrangements have some disturbing national political sovereignty implications according to the United Nations 1991 *World Investment Report*, which states that "A country with policies of high taxation and extensive social benefits may find its fiscal base eroded, if businesses shift to neighbouring countries with lower taxes following regional integration ... A whole range of policies, including industrial, environmental and social policies, may face increasing pressures to change as a result of integration with countries with different policy frameworks" (85).

The UN report (86) continues: "No single country can effectively regulate the activities of transnational corporations, and the boundaries between national and international issues of governance are becoming increasingly blurred with the increasing globalization of business activities." It cautions: "Competition among countries for more foreign direct investment, if free from any rules, may lead to a beggar-thy-neighbour policy and detract from the bargaining power of governments vis-à-vis transnational corporations." What is required, according to the report, are multilateral instruments of governance. It notes that such a multilateral framework is lacking and that attempts at coordination have been episodic and often limited in the context of regional economic blocs. What it does not say is that existing agreements on rules and regulations governing the activities of transnationals, which are negotiated in forums such as the GATT, reflect the interests of the dominant triad nations, specifically those of their home-based transnationals.

Finance

The international financial system is the sum of all arrangements governing the availability and terms of credit and the determinants of currency exchange rates. The way in which the supply of credit is managed is vital to the health of national economies and the global economy. Immense power accrues to those who control the creation of credit. Likewise, those who have ready access to credit also have great power.

Susan Strange (1988, 180) asserts that "the instability and uneven growth recorded in trade statistics over the century have been a reflection of the uneven creation and availability of credit in the world market economy. All the boom times in world trade have been times when credit was being freely created by banks or by governments, or by both, and made available internationally, either directly or through international capital markets. All the slumps have followed a drying up of credit, capital, sometimes due to the drying up of credit, sometimes due to the diversion of credit flows from international to domestic capital markets ... protectionist responses made by governments in such situations were the symptoms of financial disorder, not the cause of depressed trade."

Changes in the international financial system in the past 20 years such as the abandonment of fixed currency exchange rates, the de-linking of the dollar from gold, and the expansion of international credit driven by the explosive growth of the Eurodollar market that transcended national systems of regulation and control, have had major impacts on national economies and have placed perhaps the greatest constraints on national sovereignty and, according to many analysts, have been a central factor in the greater instability in the world economy. This has been evident in exchange rate volatility, chronic balance of payments disequilibria, inflation/deflation swings, interest rate swings, financial crises, and severe recessions.

The LDCs and Eastern European debtor countries paid dearly for their participation in the new unregulated system of credit creation when bank finance dried up in the early 1980s. The unwillingness of bank creditors and their creditor governments, led by the United States, to accept any default or write-off on loans led to the forced adjustment of their economies to meet debt service payments. This procedure was supervised by the IMF and the World Bank. These forced austerity programs have typically involved strict control of money and credit creation, wage controls and price deregulation, public spending cuts and privatization, removal of trade and exchange controls, and currency devaluation. The consequences have been extraordinary social and economic hardship among the populations of these countries whose debt burdens are as high as ever.

Although the debtor countries were shut out, the expansion of credit continued after the recession at its staggering growth rate throughout the 1980s. This rate was far in excess of the growth in production and trade, with governments and corporations of industrial countries being the main borrowers.

The explosive growth of the world financial market has led, according to Bienefeld (1990, 30), to a situation in which market mechanisms have been largely deprived of their capacity to provide meaningful signals to producers, consumers, and investors. As a result, their capacity to regulate the real economy has been effectively undermined. In other words, exchange rates no longer reflect the supply and demand for traded commodities. The result is that large disequilibria remain and these are financed by the issue of new credits that merely add to the problem.

The U.S. dollar is the main currency of international exchange and credit. Roughly three-quarters of the lending in international financial markets is denominated in dollars. As the *hegemon* of the world financial system, the United States, with the tacit acceptance of the other dominant powers, facilitated the privatization of global credit creation. The U.S. government simultaneously undertook policies of spending hikes, tax cuts, and high interest rates that, combined with falling savings rates, produced huge domestic fiscal and trade deficits financed by sucking in capital from around the world. Consequently, the United States became a net debtor by 1985, maintaining upward pressure on interest rates worldwide.

Deregulated financial markets have perversely injected an inflationary bias to interest rate policies in the 1980s. Raising interest rates, instead of reducing borrowing, attracted high-risk, shorter-term speculative borrowers, which, in turn, required higher interest rates that were then transmitted to all borrowers, including those who were obliged to continue borrowing to meet interest payments on existing debt. So the credit boom continued, and borrowing continued, although it hurt economies by discouraging productive investment by reducing income and aggregate demand and by increasing inflation. The rash of junk-bond–financed, leveraged corporate buy-outs, real estate booms, and the like in the 1980s – followed by a cycle of bankruptcies, savings and loan collapses, bail-outs, historically high levels of corporate and government debt, and severe economic recession – are the legacy of increasingly unstable and unmanageable international financial markets (Bienefeld 1990).

The fact that countries such as Canada have allowed their own financial systems to become increasingly integrated with unregulated global markets has encouraged an increase in net foreign indebtedness, and an increased portion of this debt of a short-term nature, which is thus highly sensitive to changed expectations on the part of foreign money managers. Ballooning current-account deficits are not corrected by currency devaluation, but are propped up by the inflow of credit. Once hooked, governments become increasingly hostage to the logic and imperatives of these markets. Both their monetary and fiscal polices are constrained. Political accountability to the electorate becomes less important than accountability to foreign creditors. Should they defy market expectations – for example, by increasing government spending or lowering interest rates – they risk large-scale capital flight and reductions in their credit ratings, along with those of public and private corporations who also depend on global financial markets.

Knowledge and Information

Since "knowledge is power" (who controls it, for what purposes, and for whose benefit remain the key questions), changes in the structure of knowledge in the world have far-reaching social, political, and economic implications for nation states and societies. And knowledge structures have perhaps undergone the greatest change of all, profoundly altering the structures of production, investment, trade, and finance.

The technological revolutions driving change have been the computer, which has permitted a vast increase in the ability (and lowered the cost) of gathering, storing, and processing information; and satellites, which have vastly increased the ability and speed (and lowered the cost) of transporting information around the globe. They have permitted and accelerated the expansion of global financial markets. They have brought a profound shift in the production process that is referred to as knowledge-based and time-based production. Production has become dematerialized and deterritorialized. Knowledge has become critical to the production process. It has allowed the globalization of markets, the global sourcing of inputs in manufacturing, and, increasingly, the global sourcing of services, including knowledge inputs into the production process. Knowledge/information has become the major focus of competition among nations. Being at the leading edge of advanced technology has become the source of economic and military dominance.

Twenty years ago 80 per cent of the cost of an IBM computer was in its direct manufacture. Today 90 per cent of the computer's cost and 95 per cent of the production is comprised of software and other services. In the mid-1980s, 18 per cent of IBM's profits came from designing software; five years later that share had risen to one-third. Another example is the pharmaceutical industry, which has only a minute portion of its costs in manufacturing.

A key consequence of changes in the knowledge structure has

been the concentration of the power of TNCs within global production and financial structures. Also, it has centralized power in
national economies (and governments) – home to these corporations
and where the bulk of knowledge classes and other knowledge resources reside – that purchase and finance knowledge and education,
and regulate the terms and conditions under which knowledge is
generated, transmitted, and owned.

One of the reasons that the production of knowledge has become
increasingly concentrated is its heavy financial cost. However, transnationals have strengthened their control over the production of
knowledge by successfully achieving, through national legislation
and international agreements, long periods of monopoly protection
for their patents and other intellectual property instruments. This
control is further enhanced as the life cycle of products diminishes.
For example, in the informatics industry more than half the products
are less than five years old. In the chemical and pharmaceutical industries half the products are less than 10 years old (Mytelka 1987,
50).

TNCs have tended to keep the production of knowledge under
tight control and concentrated in the home country, which explains
the preference for FDI and particularly for wholly owned subsidiaries. Globalization of markets was part of the corporate strategy
to recoup the costs of knowledge production. There has recently
been a modest decentralization or delocalization of knowledge production within subsidiaries located in areas where the markets are
large and the supply of knowledge workers is "high" (Mytelka 1987,
53). These have become technology suppliers to the parent corporation. Another development has been increased inter-corporate
cooperation, because of the complexity, risks, and costs, in knowledge production. These arrangements, which include joint ventures
and strategic alliances, are creating worldwide knowledge-based
webs or oligopolies of corporations. According to Sylvia Ostry, the
number of intercorporate strategic alliances increased from 80 to
4700 during the period from 1980 to 1989 (R. Laxer 1991).

Employment and Income Distribution

Changes in global structures of knowledge, production, trade, and
finance have had major implications for employment and distribution of income between and within nations.

One consequence of the changing structure of knowledge has

been the increasing automation of production. This is further decreasing the share of labour costs in the production process and may affect future corporate strategies regarding the internationalization of production.

Generally, the "growth of high technology industries on one hand, and the growth of electronic devices in almost all industries on the other, leads to small increases in the number of technology-oriented workers and high-tech occupations, and to a large increase of workers with little experience and education required, such as building custodians, cashiers, secretaries and clerks" (Junne 1987, 77).

Furthermore, it is now possible to transfer technologically sophisticated, highly capitalized production processes to low-wage countries, resulting in productivity levels that are the equivalent to those of industrial country facilities. This broadens the low-wage competitive threat beyond the traditional labour-intensive, low, value-added sectors. This is not to say that this will lead to a wholesale transfer of investment and production to the LDCs. There are other important investment determinants besides wages. Indeed, the trends discussed earlier suggest that, overall, the LDCs now account for a proportionally smaller share of trade and direct investment than they did 20 years ago. However, where low wages exist in conjunction with other favourable conditions, large-scale, productive investment transfers are growing.

Mexico, especially in the northern border region, is a good example of this and with the FTA/NAFTA in place it becomes even more attractive. When combined with a stable, regulatory environment, with few barriers to the movement of capital, few border restrictions, weak labour and environmental standards, proximity to U.S. markets, and relative political stability, low wages are powerful magnets. Shaiken (1990, 16) in an in-depth study of five Mexican-based, TNC–owned, high-tech plants in the electronics, computer, and auto sectors, found that "all five plants had comparable or better productivity and quality than similar U.S. plants operated by the same parent."

Of the hundred wealthiest entities in the world, in terms of output, 47 are now corporations and 53 are countries. The 1992 United Nations *Human Development Report* found that the gap between the rich and poor countries has doubled since 1960. The countries that make up the richest 20 per cent of the world's population now have an average per capita income 60 times greater than the countries that comprise the poorest 20 per cent (1992, 36). With domestic inequalities factored in, the income gap rises to 150 times. Third World debtor countries have been squeezed extra hard in the 1980s by northern banks and their governments who work through the IMF and the World Bank. Debtor countries made net financial transfers to the industrialized countries of U.S. $22 billion per annum during the 1983–90 years, a dramatic reversal from the net financial transfer into the LDCs of U.S. $21 billion per annum during the period from 1972 to 1982 (1992, 52).

The polarization of income – the gap between the rich and the poor, and the shrinking of the middle-income strata – has been accelerating; not only is this pattern evident between nations, but also within nations. For example, in the 1980s, in Latin American countries, where the distribution of income is already more severely skewed than in the industrialized countries of North America, these imbalances have worsened at a much faster rate than in the North. In Mexico, for example, the real minimum wage dropped 58 per cent from 1981 to 1988 (Barkin 1991, 31) and the wages share in national income dropped from 37.4 per cent to 20.3 per cent (Ecumenical Coalition for Economic Justice 1991, 4).

Nevertheless, the United States also experienced a polarization of incomes that had not occurred since the 1920s. In the United States, real wages of non-supervisory employees dropped 20 per cent between 1972 and 1991 (Mead 1992, 41). The share of family income held by the one-fifth with highest incomes jumped from 41.7 per cent in 1979 to 44.6 per cent in 1989, with the top 5 per cent accounting for almost three-quarters of this increase. Conversely, the bottom four-fifths of families all lost income share, with that of the lowest fifth dropping from 5.2 per cent to 4.6 per cent of the national income pie (Mishel and Frankel 1991, 21). In Canada, the deterioration in income distribution has been slight. However, real wages, which had grown 4.9 per cent annually during the 1968–76 period, fell 2.1 per cent during the years from 1977 to 1990 (Crane 1992, 5).

Robert Reich (1991) is explicit in linking wage polarization to globalization. What he calls "symbolic analytic services," based on the manipulation of information (e.g., lawyers, accountants, and management consultants), accounted for the roughly 20 per cent whose wages are rising, while the wages of routine production and clerical workers are falling. The so-called good jobs, according to Betcherman (1992), which derive from skills in technology and information, are concentrated in a few countries and are characterized by rising wages. Bad jobs, that is, routine lower-skill jobs, can increasingly originate anywhere, and therefore wages are being bid downward.

Thurow (1992, 52) reinforces the point: "In a global economy a worker has two things to offer – skills or the willingness to work for low wages. Since products can be built anywhere, the unskilled who live in rich societies must work for the wages of the unskilled who live in poor societies. If they won't work for such wages, the unskilled jobs simply move to poor countries."

Many observers see a cumulative trend toward de-skilled jobs and therefore project that the requirements will be for a small highly skilled élite segment of the workforce, but workforce requirements overall will be for a less skilled and less educated workforce in the future. Others project a process of market-driven, creative destruction, of substitution of new jobs for old jobs; new jobs that are higher value added, higher skilled, and higher waged. They project a future economy that requires a more educated workforce.

The empirical evidence – certainly the Canadian and American experience in the past 15 to 20 years – tends to support the former perspective. It suggests that displaced workers, when or if re-employed, have found jobs at lower skill and lower wage levels. Moreover, the record of job creation in the 1980s, as well as predictions for job creation in the 1990s, are predominantly in low-value-added, low-skill service occupations (Economic Council of Canada 1990).

The problems of growing inequality and poverty between and within nations that have accompanied globalization not only raise issues of social justice, but are also directly linked to problems of chronically weak aggregate demand and economic stagnation, as well as to ecologically reckless resource depletion, and environmental pollution.

Summary

It is useful to draw out the inferences from the analysis thus far that are most relevant to the Canadian and Ontario economies.

• In the past 40 years, world trade growth has outpaced world output growth. Foreign direct investment (internationalization of production through TNCs) has outpaced growth in world trade. And growth in international credit through private financial markets has, since 1970, far outstripped all the other economic aggregates.

• However, this growth must be seen in the context of a slowing down of world economic expansion (of output, investment, productivity, and trade) in the 1970s and 1980s as compared with the two previous decades. This situation, with few exceptions, is most pronounced among the developing countries and seems likely to continue in the 1990s.

- Services becoming more tradeable (world services trade and FDI grew faster than world goods trade and FDI in the 1980s) and, increasingly, the globalization of production of services could have major consequences for national economies and tax regimes.
- Four-fifths of FDI flows emanate from TNCs headquartered in three countries: Europe, Japan, and the United States (which James Laxer describes as the first post-national state). The foreign policy actions of these dominant powers generally reflect, or are consistent with, the interests and strategies of home-based TNCs.
- Japan has emerged as a full-fledged economic superpower and East Asia has become the most dynamic economic area going into the 21st century. The western hemisphere, with the United States at its centre, is lagging. Without idealizing the Japanese experience, we can discover in its achievement important lessons that contradict the conventional economic wisdom, specifically regarding the relationship of government and market, the role of foreign direct investment, and the relationship of the national to the world economy.
- Commensurate with globalization has been a regionalization of the world economy, with three basic spheres of regional integration: Japan and East Asia, the European Community and peripheral southern and eastern Europe; and the United States and the Americas. The latter two regions are establishing formal integration arrangements. In the case of Europe, formal political union is the explicit goal. In the Americas, the direct and indirect harmonization of key policies in line with those of the United States under the free trade initiatives is reducing the sovereignty of its partners and leading towards de facto political union. Trade and other economic relations between regions will continue to be governed by multilateral arrangements such as the GATT, while new rules will likely supersede the GATT in governing relations within regions.
- The formidable power of TNCs as central agents of the globalization process - for example, their mobility, their power over knowledge and information, and their political power - has major consequences for national societies and their governments. In the

absence of a proper regulatory structure, nationally and internationally, TNCs weaken public treasuries by their ability to evade taxes and by their power to extract tax incentives. They foster downward cycles of competitive bidding among governments, weakening tax regimes, social, environmental, and other regulatory regimes, and generally narrow the parameters of public-policy options. They weaken the power of labour, exacerbate imbalances in the distribution of income, and destabilize social contracts. They bankroll political parties coming to power with accommodative policies that facilitate the kind of regulatory regimes that heighten these tendencies.

- Knowledge/information has become a key input into the production of goods and services, a key factor driving the global production process. This power is increasingly centralized and guarded within TNCs. What are the implications for governments that want to ensure that their citizens and businesses, research and educational institutions can access this knowledge, transform it into products and processes, and appropriate a sufficient share of the value it creates?

- The bulk of knowledge-intensive (high-skill, high-wage) jobs have been created in countries that are home to TNCs. Changes in the knowledge structure are generating a transnational re-stratification of employment, creating a relatively small number of knowledge-intensive jobs and a relatively greater number of low-skill, low-value-added jobs, for which workers in industrialized countries and workers in LDCs are increasingly in direct competition. The demand for the former group of workers, coupled with accommodating legislative changes such as those in the FTA/NAFTA, make jobs more mobile internationally.

- Changes in structures of production, investment, trade, finance, and regulation have been forcing changes in the structure of employment and income distribution. Average levels of unemployment in the industrial world have risen. Income disparities with nations and between nations of the North and South have widened dramatically. The changing structure of employment and income distribution has adverse implications for macoeconomic stability for the fiscal capacity of governments, for aggregate demand, investment, and for environmental sustainability.

- The private, largely unregulated, global financial market – to which national financial markets have become increasingly linked – is unstable. To the extent that this global market has a structural bias towards pushing up interest rates; to the extent that short-term capital flows cause greater exchange rate instability; to the extent that such a market frustrates the ability of the exchange rate to equilibrate trade imbalances; to the extent that countries (public- and private-sector borrowers) have become net debtors; to the extent that this globalization has contributed to a huge overhang of debt (public and private) in their economies with no apparent political will to reduce this debt, these countries have become increasingly vulnerable to external disturbances and, perhaps more important, have lost major control over monetary and fiscal and other economic policy levers.

The Domestic Impact

External forces do not affect nations in a homogeneous or uniform manner; neither do nations receive stimuli passively. The process is a dialectical one – action and reaction. The process is complex and, as indicated at the outset, is a function of internal structures, institutions, and policies, and the extent to which they change over time in response to external stimuli.

The questions I now turn to are: What shape are the Canadian and Ontario economies in, in terms of their ability to cope with and ride the formidable wave of global forces into the 21st century? How do their structural characteristics, their institutions, and their policy environments position them to adapt, adjust and/or insulate themselves from external pressures in the coming decade?

First it should be said that Canada, at present, fares well when compared with other nations on the basis of aggregate indicators of economic well-being. Canada is second in the world in output (GDP) per capita; third in output per employed worker; first in the world on the UN Human Development Index, a broader measure of economic and social well-being that includes literacy, life span, and income purchasing power. This is said not to encourage complacency, but rather to acknowledge that, despite the major economic, social, environmental, and political problems that now confront us, we have achieved, over many years, high income and living standards and a comparatively fair distribution of income; and we have done reasonably well in meeting the basic needs of our citizens in terms of housing, health care, and education, despite the damage done by neoconservative governments in the past decade.

It is important to realize that our current position is the result of a long, cumulative process of economic development. There is no guarantee that in the next hundred years we will be as well off as we are now. Nations rise and nations decline. History is littered with examples of rich societies that have become poor and poor societies that have become rich. Sweden was one of the poorest societies in Europe at the turn of the century. Many contend that it has now become the most advanced society in the world in terms of the broadest measures of human well-being. Argentina was the third richest nation in the world in 1913; it has now become a relatively poor nation. The Chiapas region in southern Mexico, an independent country in the 18th century, was a flourishing society – one of the most prosperous in the Americas; it is now one of the poorest regions in Mexico. The relative decline of Scotland within the United Kingdom, or Nova Scotia within Canada are further examples.

Decline, if it happens, is likely to be gradual, barely perceptible on a year-to-year basis. Deterioration can be mistaken for cyclical swings in the economy. On the other hand, the hurricane force and pervasiveness of globalization may well make decline much more rapid than the historical record would suggest.

Production, Investment, and Trade

Canada's output growth in the 1980s slowed in line with the decline in the industrial world compared to earlier decades (see Table 4) and, according to the major Canadian forecasting entities, will continue this way in the 1990s (Canadian Labour Market Productivity Centre 1992). Compared with the eleven major industrialized countries (the G-7 countries plus Switzerland, Austria, Norway, Sweden, the Netherlands, and Australia), Canada's output growth was second highest in the 1980s, although it dropped to last in 1990–91. Its unemployment record was the third worst in the 1980s and fell to last place in 1990–91. In terms of labour productivity growth (output per person employed), during the 1979–88 period Canada ranked third last among all 24 OECD countries (ahead only of Australia and the United States) at 1.6 per cent a year; this was half the annual rate of productivity growth of Japan, the top performer. In manufacturing (1980–89), Canada had the lowest rate of labour productivity growth among the seven largest industrialized countries (the G-7) – less than half the G-7 average. Between 1985 and 1990, the manufacturing sector experienced virtually no productivity growth (Canadian Labour Market Productivity Centre 1991, 26–29).

The gap between actual and potential output in Canada, which averaged 2 per cent during the 1980s, widened dramatically during the years from 1990 to 1992 and reached 9 per cent in 1992. (See Dungan 1994, this volume.) This is by far the biggest gap among the major industrialized countries, bigger than during the 1982 recession, and at least the biggest gap ever recorded by any G-7 nation since 1960 (Canadian Labour Market Productivity Centre, 1992).

Until now, an abundance of natural resources has been key to Canada's prosperity, but is not likely to remain as important in the future, given changes in global structures of production. Resources are declining as a source of both wealth accumulation and competitive advantage. The development of manufactured substitutes and new lower-cost sources of supply has resulted in the general erosion of resource prices compared with other traded goods. The real price index of natural resources, taken as a whole (including oil) in 1990, was 30 per cent below its 1980 level and 40 per cent below its 1970 level (Thurow 1992). Resource and semi-processed exports make up 33 per cent of all Canadian exports. It has, by far, the highest share of resource-based exports in the G-7. Moreover, its share of non–resource-based industrial exports is declining (Porter 1991).

Not only are we losing out on export markets with manufactured goods, but we are also losing out in our own domestic markets and becoming increasingly dependent on imports of manufactured goods. In 1980, 73 per cent of manufactured goods consumed in Canada were produced in Canada. By 1991 that figure had dropped to 56 per cent (Canadian Manufacturers' Association 1991). In the high-tech sectors – aerospace, office equipment, machinery, computers, electronic components, drugs, instruments, and electrical machinery – Canada has a large trade deficit. According to the National Advisory Board on Science and Technology 1991a (NABST), its performance, 17th out of 24, is among the worst in the OECD. These figures reflect a disturbing backsliding towards a hewer-of-wood, drawer-of-water status in the world economy.

There are further unsettling indications that the Canadian economy is not well positioned to cope with the knowledge shift. The National Advisory Board on Science and Technology (1991a) found that Canadian companies do significantly less research and development than their counterparts in other countries. On the GERD ratio (proportion of GDP accounted for by gross expenditures on research and development), Canada ranks 17th out of 24 OECD countries. Moreover, this ratio has been dropping in the past five years. This is reflected in the low proportion of the workforce employed in research and development activities, half the level of Japan, Sweden, and the United States. Major reasons for weak performance, according to the National Advisory Board on Science and Technology 1991, include a preponderance of firms in manufacturing sectors where typically little research and development is done (for example, resource extraction and processing), a plethora of foreign-owned corporations, and the high cost of borrowing.

High capital costs are part of the reason that, during the period from 1980 to 1989, Canada's machinery and equipment investment as a proportion of GDP was only 6.5 per cent, the lowest in the G-7. The U.S. ratio was 8.1 per cent and Japan's was 14.9 per cent, more than twice the Canadian rate. The cost of capital in Canada was 6.5 per cent in 1990, compared with 4.8 per cent in the United States and 2 per cent in Germany and Japan (OECD 1991b). But, as well, Canada has a very small domestic machinery sector. At just 9.8 per cent of value added in manufacturing, it occupies the lowest level in the OECD.

Canada's weak overall research and development performance is magnified by the lower levels of research and development done by Canadian corporations. Twenty-five firms in Canada perform more than 50 per cent of all industrial research and development in Canada. Part of the problem, as noted, is the negligible research and development in the resource-based sector, but it is also related to weak linkages and transfer mechanisms with public sector research and development facilities.

Thus the former head of the Science Council, Geraldine Kenney-Wallace (1992), attributes the non-replacement of jobs lost in response to economic restructuring to the weakness of the technological capacity of the small/medium Canadian business sector, which is the predominant source of job creation in Canada. According to Kenney-Wallace, Canada lacks an umbrella framework of innovation policies to build not only research and development capability, but also increase the capability of the workforce to transform scientific results into high-quality, tradeable goods and services.

Further evidence of Canada's weakness in this important area is found in the fact that Canadians hold less than 2 per cent of the world's patents, and 95 per cent of patents registered in Canada are owned abroad (Davidson 1992). Canada ranks 15th out of 24 OECD countries in terms of applications for patents on new products and processes, 50 per 100,000 population, compared with 490 in Switzerland, 340 in Japan, and 110 in the United States.

A necessary corollary to high levels of research and development in knowledge-based production is education and training. Here, too, Canada is poorly positioned. Canadian employers invest in formal worker training and retraining at one-half the U.S. rate. Three out of four Canadian employers invest nothing at all (Marshall 1991). According to the NABST, the average Canadian adult receives 7 hours formal training a year, compared with the average Japanese adult who receives 200 hours a year, and the average Swede who receives 170 hours a year. The World Economic Forum rated Canada 20th out of 23 countries in terms of the effectiveness of in-company training. Canada does reasonably well in the area of post-secondary education; however, the proportion of high school graduates, as well as the proportion of university students enrolled in science and engineering, has fallen since 1985.

The Canadian economy has an extraordinarily high level of foreign ownership and control through foreign direct investment, far beyond that of any other industrialized country. Some U.S. analysts, notably Reich (1991), downplay the importance of the nationality of investment, while for others, like Thurow (1992), nationality does matter.

Currently, 52 per cent of Canadian manufacturing capital (assets) is under foreign control. After declining from 1970 to 1986, foreign control is on the rise again (Crane 1992). There is a rich Canadian political economy literature that suggests that foreign direct investment has not been automatically beneficial to Canada. Foreign-controlled corporations may destroy more jobs than they create, and may kill off Canadian competitors. They tend to import more, export less, do less research and development, and are less likely to use local suppliers than Canadian-owned firms.

A recent Statistics Canada study (Mersereau 1992) made the following observations about the ownership structure of Canadian imports:

- Foreign-controlled corporations (of which 75 per cent are U.S.-controlled) accounted for between 67 per cent and 71 per cent of all of Canada's imports during the years 1978 to 1986.
- Almost three-quarters of Canada's imports were by a small group

of large corporations. The 50 largest of these accounted for almost half (47 per cent) of all Canada's imports (82 per cent of which were accounted for by the 35 foreign-controlled companies in this group).

- The import propensity (ratio of imports to sales) of foreign-controlled companies was three times higher than that of Canadian-controlled companies in 1979 and widened to four times by 1986.
- Despite globalization, U.S.- and Japanese-controlled corporations sourced a very high (90 per cent) and growing proportion of their imports from home.
- Though growing as well, European firms import a much lower proportion of imports from home (70 per cent).
- One-half of all imports in 1986 were between affiliates (intra-firm) and non-open market transactions. Two-thirds of foreign-controlled company imports were tied in this way.

Canada's export structure differs from that of other industrialized countries in that it has a much lower proportion of manufactured exports and a very large deficit in manufactured end-products. Williams (1983) demonstrated through analysis of the documents of federal Canadian trade officials that Canada's export impotence was due in large part to directives from American head offices to their Canadian subsidiaries blocking exports into the U.S. market. Rather than converting to export platforms under the FTA, branch manufacturing plants have been shutting down in large numbers. Ontario's Ministry of Labour records show 397 complete plant shutdowns from January 1989 to August 1992, almost half of which were in foreign-owned organizations. In the auto parts sector, for example, 51 plants (mostly U.S.-owned) have shut down in Ontario since 1989.

Michael Porter's 1991 study for the Business Council on National Issues and the federal government sheds light on the relation between the truncated nature of the Canadian manufacturing sector and foreign ownership. Porter found a lack of depth in the Canadian economy in key industrial sectors of related and supporting industries that are essential for upgrading competitive advantage. This deficiency, according to Porter, weakens the prospects for productivity growth in light of increasing globalization of trade and investment, accelerating technological changes, and rapidly evolving company and country strategies that confront Canadian-based industry.

Porter found that foreign-controlled corporations can be a substitute for home-owned corporations, but only if the subsidiary is really independent or is what he calls "home based" in Canada, that is, managed independently, doing its own research and development. Otherwise, it is just a passive recipient of directions from abroad, with the result that it creates low-value-added, low-wage jobs. Porter defines home base in a variety of ways: it is the place/ nation in which essential competitive advantages of the enterprise are created and sustained; it is where a firm's strategy is set and the core product and process technology are created and sustained; it is where the firm contributes the most to the local economy by providing the best jobs, investing in factor creation, and helping to create clusters of reinforcing activities. Porter observes that very few foreign-controlled TNCs in Canada have a home base here.

Finance

Among the most important but least understood impacts of changes in the global economy on the Canadian and Ontario economies are the changes in the structures of international finance. Federal monetary policy, coupled with federal and provincial deregulation of financial markets and their resulting exposure to world financial markets, has affected domestic economic activity and policy freedom at all levels of government.

The deregulation/globalization of financial markets has also meant that Canadians can put their savings (either directly or through intermediaries) into international markets and therefore make them unavailable to investment in Canada. Moreover, these earnings are less accessible to taxation by domestic authorities.

The deregulation and integration of Canadian financial markets with world markets, combined with the government's high interest rate policy, has allowed Canada's indebtedness, and especially its foreign indebtedness, to soar in the past decade.

The path of interest rate policy is clear. (See Table 3.) Real interest rates – that is, adjusted for inflation – soared in the 1980s, especially in the latter half, far above real economic growth (in fact suppressing growth), which increase accelerated debt levels throughout the economy. Moreover, Canadian monetary authorities pushed Canadian rates far above U.S. rates, especially in the past four years.

The most important component of foreign indebtedness has been the growth in external holdings of Canadian government and corporate bonds – up from $44 billion in 1978 to $179 billion in 1990 (Laliberté 1991). For example, foreigners held 38 per cent of Government of Canada marketable bonds in 1990, up from 15 per cent in 1978. Foreign holdings of Canadian bonds far exceeded external holdings of Canadian stocks ($21 billion) and money-market instruments such as treasury bills ($25 billion).

The deregulation of Canadian financial markets greatly increased the propensity of foreign investors to come directly to Canadian bond markets, rather than Canadians going to foreign or Euro-markets to issue bonds. In 1990, there were 28 per cent of foreign-held Canadian bonds obtained from Canadian markets, compared with 7 per cent in 1978. Still, only $76 billion, or 43 per cent, of bond debt was denominated in Canadian dollars in 1990. The other $103 billion was denominated in foreign currencies (mainly U.S. dollars) and any depreciation of the currency would increase its size.

Not only has this debt grown rapidly, but its maturity has shortened. In 1983, less than a quarter of these bonds matured in under five years, but by 1990 this share had risen to one-half. In 1990, $91 billion was repayable in five years or less, and $32 billion of this was repayable in foreign currency.

Little of this foreign debt is going to long-term productive investments that will increase our exports and therewith our ability to repay this debt. Much is going just to service existing debt. Still, we are forced to export more and more to acquire the foreign exchange needed to repay this debt. We now appear to be caught in both an export bind and a debt bind. To continue to attract the required flow of external financial capital, we have to set interest rates higher than the already high rates on world financial markets, but this discourages productive investments by Canadian business and keeps the exchange rate far too high, thereby damaging the competitiveness of Canadian exporters and squeezing the flow of exports. The pressure on exports, combined with the accompanying rise in interest outflows (which have grown from 7 per cent of the total revenue from exports of goods and services in 1970 to 15 per cent in 1990), increases our balance-of-payments deficit. This deficit is maintained for now by inflow of capital, which requires a high interest rate; this high interest rate, in turn, adversely affects the domestic economic investment, growth and exports; and so the cycle continues.

Canada has accumulated huge current account balance-of-payments deficits, especially in the past three years, creating a vulnerable and ultimately unsustainable economic situation. As Table 4 reveals, Canada's current account deficit has grown precariously high, both in absolute terms and in relation to the GDP; it was the highest among the industrialized countries in 1991.

The international deregulation/integration of financial markets has produced a kind of reversal of the relationship between the real and financial economies, rendering the exchange rate ineffective in equilibrating demand and supply of production between the Canadian and the global economy – finance rules. Any loss of "confidence" – a constitutional crisis, or a government (federal or provincial) that tries to defy the "logic of the market," as defined by the world money managers, to which it is now held hostage – will be punished by an increase in the cost of borrowing due to assessments of increased credit risk; or worse still, the contraction of new flows, a net financial outflow, a collapse in the exchange rate, and an increase in inflation.

The debate as to whether, for example, government debt or deficit is a problem and how it should be dealt with (and we have had periods in Canada, for example, just after the Second World War, when the debt was proportionately twice as high as it is today) becomes less relevant. The reality is that, if those who control large pools of financial capital think Canadian government debt policies or other economic policies are a problem, they can destabilize the economy.

Both public- and private-sector Canadian borrowers are vulnerable to the interruption of foreign capital inflows, as well as domestic capital flight, not only by changing perceptions of creditworthiness, but also by major disturbances in the system that are completely beyond our control, such as a European financial collapse.

Labour Markets

Global forces interacting in complex ways with internal structures, institutions, and policies have clearly influenced Canadian labour markets: the nature and composition of employment (and unemployment) and underemployment, wages and income distribution. Not only do these changes reflect changes in the foundations of future economic prosperity and the ability of the economy to meet the needs of its population, but these trends have important implications for the fiscal capacity of government and, consequently, its capacity as a key player to shape economic and social life.

Since the mid-1970s, Canada has been a high unemployment country. Unemployment in Ontario, on average, has been lower than that of the country as a whole. Although some Ontario regions have experienced high rates of job creation and low levels of unemployment through most of this period, others have experienced chronically high unemployment levels. Government labour market programs have been predominantly (75 per cent) passive, and have focused on income support (unemployment insurance) rather than on active programs that focus on training and job creation.

Key developments in labour markets since the mid-1970s include a virtual end to real-wage growth, and its subsequent decline in the 1980s; polarization of individual earnings; periods of rapid, low-wage job growth (1983–88) punctuated by periods of stagnation or decline (1981–82 and 1989–92); rapid growth of consumer-services jobs (for example, retail, food and accommodation, personal services); shrinking of manufacturing employment; polarization of skills and wage levels within industries, firms, and occupations; absolute and relative decline in the real wages of entry level jobs across the board, regardless of education.

Sixteen per cent of Canadians in 1990 either drew welfare, social assistance, or old-age income supplements (Battle 1992, 165). The figure for 1991 likely exceeds 20 per cent. Minimum wages have lost 30 per cent of their value since 1976. Nine out of every ten jobs created in Canada in the past 20 years have been in the service sector. One-half of all jobs created since 1980 have been "non-standard," that is, part-time, short-term, temporary and temporary help agency, and self-employed. One-third of all Canadian jobs now fall into this category (Betcherman 1992). From 1981 to 1986, fully 92 per cent of the jobs created in Ontario paid less than $6.76 an hour. By 1991, the percentage of all jobs that were part-time was 17.4 percent, up from 12.9 per cent in 1980 (Statistics Canada 1991). The changes in the labour market reflected in these figures have disturbing implications for the strength of the tax base.

Researchers at the Economic Council (Betcherman 1992) and Statistics Canada (Myles 1991) who have uncovered these trends have also found empirical evidence of a "declining middle" phenomenon in the shrinking relative numbers of middle-income earners as increasing numbers of workers drop down into the low-income categories, and an increasing share of the national income pie goes to the top 20 per cent of income earners. This is similar, if less acute, to the declining middle phenomenon discovered in the United States.

Myles's (1991) work gives empirical support to the claims of Reich and others of the emergence in Canada and the United States of a polarized labour market with a well-paid core, a large low-paid mass, and an underclass of state dependants. Betcherman (1992) sees the wage polarization implied by the declining middle phenomenon reflected in growing poverty, greater pressure on the transfer system, and on fiscal capacity. Moreover, the disappearing middle phenomenon of which he and others have found evidence, may, in his view, reflect the polarization of "good jobs/bad jobs," not only in the shift to service sector jobs, but polarization within industries and within firms that is driven by globalization, technological change, and the weakening role of unions. His analysis of 1000 Canadian companies shows that firms that were introducing computer-based technological change between 1980 and 1985 experienced a widening of the wage gap between high-skill and low-skill jobs, whereas firms that did not innovate showed no increase in the gap (132). He also notes that, where unions are absent, there tends to be greater concentration at the low and high ends of the income scale. Private sector unionization density rates have been falling since the mid-1970s, and in the fastest employment-growing service sectors they are below 10 per cent.

The rise of transnational corporate power, as discussed earlier, is changing the configuration of social forces within countries. It has put pressure on labour/management relations and on the social and political cohesion of societies. A key factor in the ability of countries to respond successfully to these pressures depends in large part on the extent to which they are able to achieve and maintain a social consensus around the nature of the problems and how to solve them.

The Canadian Labour Market Productivity Centre (1991) found that countries where a high degree of consensus exists among the social partners tend to have an economic performance superior to those of countries where the social consensus is low. The study develops a typology of international experience in consensus building. Canada, along with the United States and Britain, falls into a category of countries with a low success rate in consensus building, whether through formal or less formal institutional means between business and labour. Fortin (1991) confirms the importance of social consensus, pointing out, for example, that the top macroeconomic performers, such as Japan, Sweden, and Switzerland, have developed inflation norms that are accepted as fair by all elements of society, thereby precluding the need for deflationary macro policies.

There is a tendency for corporations operating in countries where social consensus is low, and where governments do not regulate the market, to adopt low-wage strategies as a substitute for technology-driven, high-wage competitiveness strategies, with the consequence being widening income disparities, and declines in wages and living standards in these countries. Marshall (1991) argues that under conditions of genuine (not superficial) worker participation in economic decision making, labour organizations do improve productivity. Moreover, they are essential in pressing governments to adopt high-wage competitiveness strategies. Workers with a stake in high-performance industry will support it. Unionized workplaces tend to be significantly more productive than non-unionized workplaces.

Continental Regulation: The Impact of FTA/NAFTA

The Canada–U.S. Free Trade Agreement is an economic integration agreement of sweeping dimensions. It covers trade in services as well as goods; capital mobility as well as labour mobility for professional and business groups; the regulation of corporations as well as the management of resources; the regulation of financial, transportation, telecommunications, and agricultural sectors, as well as the regulation of intellectual property; and the establishment of harmonization standards in areas such as professional qualifications, agricultural inspection, and health standards. It is as comprehensive as the integration of the European Community in many areas and, indeed, goes beyond it in some areas. Directly or indirectly, no part of Canadian economic and social policy has remained untouched by it.

The FTA has recently been extended, expanded, and superseded by the North American Free Trade Agreement (NAFTA), which could extend throughout the hemisphere by the year 2000. This is the explicit goal of the United States and Canadian governments and the transnational corporate community.

The FTA/NAFTA codifies, or entrenches in treaty, a continental integration process (and accompanying changes in national regulatory regimes) that has proceeded quite rapidly in the 1980s. Not only has it continentalized these regulatory regimes, but it has also introduced new regimes and has stimulated a major new round of economic integration and restructuring. Ultimately, the FTA/NAFTA represents a further shift in power in favour of capital, reinforcing the globalization trends already discussed, further constraining government policy and weakening the power of labour (with the exception of a small knowledgeable élite), and other social groups.

The Attorney General's (Ontario 1988, 9) legal analysis of the free trade agreement captured the magnitude of the deal in the following passage: "It will permanently alter the capacity to make economic and social policy in Canada, sometimes shifting it to the federal government, sometimes abandoning it for all governments. This dramatic change in the ability of governments to respond to the legitimate expectations of their populations amounts to a constitutional change."

Unlike the European Community, which transfers power from the national level to the supra-national level, the FTA/NAFTA transfers power to the market (that is, to those who have power in the market). The huge asymmetry between the countries, and the absence of truly supra-national decision-making structures to mitigate these asymmetries, means that the surrender of power has been one-sided. Moreover, unlike the European Community, the FTA/NAFTA has no social dimension, no set of minimum social, labour, and environmental standards placing limits on the competitiveness rules of the game. Consequently, lowest common denominator competition has become the rule de facto. In contrast, the European model, as James Laxer (1991) points out, puts greater pressure on the TNCs to adapt their behaviour to social and environmental legislation; forces technological advance to be the impetus behind their competitiveness strategies; and encourages the upward convergence of standards in the region.

This is not the place for a detailed analysis of the FTA/NAFTA (see for example: Ontario, Attorney General 1988; Cameron 1988; Gold and Leyton-Brown 1988; Campbell and Barlow 1991; Campbell 1992; Grinspun and Cameron 1993). Nevertheless, it does raise important questions that have a bearing on taxation. Is the reduced policy space that remains to both levels of government sufficient to meet the economic challenges facing Canada and Ontario? Does removing these powers produce a market-driven outcome that is superior for the economy and society? Will the painful restructuring process that FTA has set off or accelerated eventually make Canada and Ontario better off? Or will it prove to be a historical turning point marking the beginning of a period of prolonged economic and political decline and disintegration?

Tax Implications

Many questions, and some answers, emerge from this paper. How, and to what extent, has globalization, as it has evolved especially in the past two decades, constrained or circumscribed public policy tools and eroded fiscal capacity? Does globalization necessarily mean reduced fiscal capacity and a smaller role for governments? What tax space is left compared with 20 years ago and how will global forces affect what space is left by the year 2000 and beyond? What room is there for countervailing measures to reverse these trends? How mobile has capital really become? Are different forms of capital more mobile than others? What can governments do in the current environment to make capital less mobile? Is this desirable? How mobile in fact is so-called knowledge-intensive labour and how sensitive is it to income tax change? Are certain segments of it more mobile, and are its emigration patterns responsive to tax changes?

Clearly, the dynamism of the Canadian and Ontario economies are the most important determinants of the fiscal capacity of government. Elements of a thriving economy include output and productivity growth, high average levels of income relatively evenly distributed, low unemployment, a skilled workforce, a strong social and physical infrastructure, low real interest rates, high domestic savings and (productive) investment rates, and stable inflation (preferably low, but necessarily agreed to by the main social partners).

The central effects of globalization observed in this paper have been transmitted to, or reproduced within, the Canadian and Ontario economies: the slowdown in economic output, investment, and productivity; the growth of unemployment; the intensification of the struggle for income shares, resulting in the concentration of wealth and growing imbalances in income distribution; increased monetary and financial instability; and the growth of public and private indebtedness. These effects have clearly been the main factors responsible for the weakening fiscal capacity of the Canadian and Ontario governments.

Some nations have managed to buck global trends or mitigate their effects. However, given that the current Canadian situation is the culmination of structural weaknesses and government policies discussed earlier, the prospects for transcending or mitigating these global trends by the year 2000 are not promising. Moreover, many of the very policies that would address these weaknesses and retrieve some national governmental control are those that would meet resistance from the so-called mobile factors so influential within government circles.

Under the current conditions of globalization, Canadian advocates of massive public investments in physical infrastructure (for example, highways, airports, telecommunications) and social infrastructure (for example, education, training, research and development, health) as a way to lure corporate investment face a dilemma. A weak and deteriorating fiscal capacity does not, in the short term, permit the magnitude of investment expenditure necessary to stimulate the economic development that would, in the long run, strengthen the economy and the fiscal capacity of government.

What are the consequences of formally entrenching and expanding these patterns of globalization in a continental treaty such as the FTA/NAFTA? Clearly, it has formally and permanently reduced the powers of government, for example, the power to control access to the internal market as a potential counterweight to the ability of capital to leave. The enhanced ability of large corporations (foreign- and domestically owned) to move freely – either to transfer production facilities or to transfer profits through intra-corporate transfer pricing, interest, retained earnings dividends, and so on, within the continental economic space – imposes ceilings on corporate taxation and generates more pressure to keep them in line with the lowest common denominator regime in the region.

It is also likely that certain forms of corporate taxes such as payroll taxes, given the pressure on labour at the bargaining table, will be passed on in the form of lower wages. Similarly, it gives corporations increased power to play one jurisdiction off against another (since there is no common code of allowable and prohibited subsidy practices) in order to obtain generous tax incentives as a condition for locating new production or maintaining existing production. This could constitute a significant additional drain on provincial and federal resources.

On the other hand, new measures (including tax) to stimulate the provincial economy must respect the national treatment provisions; that is, they must not (with limited exceptions) discriminate against U.S. companies. These can have adverse tax implications that derive from a lower employment-creating propensity, higher import propensity, and weaker linkage effects of foreign-controlled sectors.

The temporary entry provisions of the FTA/NAFTA give new

freedom to the knowledge classes (entrepreneurs, executives, professionals, and certain technicians) to move across borders to sell their services and perhaps emigrate. This puts downward pressure on the upper personal income tax rates, although probably not nearly as great as on corporate taxes.

The FTA/NAFTA reinforces globalization trends, thereby weakening labour power, strengthening low-wage corporate competitiveness strategies, wage polarization, and high unemployment, skewing income distribution patterns, and diminishing both consumption and income tax bases obtainable from the bottom half to two-thirds of income earners whose mobility is not enhanced under the agreement.

The provisions on services reinforce and accommodate global trends to increased tradeability of services and heightened involvement of TNCs in this sector, especially in accounting, engineering, advertising, legal, software and other information services, financial management consultants, and other business services. This portends a wave of restructuring in the services sector, including much more external sourcing and intra-corporate trade. These developments would appear to increase the opportunities for tax evasion and avoidance, and would put greater pressure on tax regimes to be more sensitive in these sectors to taxes in other jurisdictions in the integration area.

There are constraints on the ability of governments to tax mobile factors of production, particularly capital, but their extent is unclear. Couzin (1991) cautions that raising taxes on income or capital moving freely across borders will not generally succeed. An OECD report (1991a, 12) asserts that under conditions of globalization "international capital flows may have become more sensitive to differences in the tax regimes as between countries" and are placing tax policy makers under greater pressure to consider international implications of national tax policies. It also suggests that international tax agreements need to be reviewed and perhaps modified in light of these trends (OECD 1991, 13–14).

According to a Coopers and Lybrand study, globalization has made international tax comparisons extremely important. It identifies the harmonization of tax structures as one of eight key requirements of competitiveness and warns that "Canada still has corporate, personal and property taxes that are higher than those in the United States and investment incentives that are less generous. The net result has been a shifting of corporate head offices and hence economic activity to more competitive jurisdictions" (Coopers and Lybrand 1991, 6).

Still, one of the most striking characteristics of the tax regimes of the OECD countries is, despite some convergence in some areas, the extent to which they differ in their levels and composition in the face of 15 years of intense globalization.

Tax revenue as a share of GDP ranges from a high of 57 per cent in Sweden to a low of 30 per cent in the United States (see Table 5). Canada, at 35 per cent, is below the average for the OECD. For most countries the share has been stable or growing modestly for the last decade. (Although these increases are going to meet debt charges and mask, in many cases, reductions in program expenditures.) Tax levels do not seem to be a barrier to productivity growth, since high tax countries such as Austria, Germany, and Norway experienced high productivity growth in the 1980s.

Nor, as Wilkins (OECD 1990, 33) found, are lower tax areas, per se, necessarily a magnet for capital: "To the extent that the United States may appear more like a tax haven to some relatively high tax countries, one might expect a post-reform increase in the share of direct investment in the United States coming from high tax countries relative to the share coming from low tax countries ... Contrary to expectations, the share of high tax country direct investment (EC countries) in the United States has decreased two percentage points." Obviously other factors outweigh tax considerations here.

There has been a trend towards lowering the highest personal income tax rates as well as reducing the number of tax brackets in many OECD countries. Nevertheless, big differences remain. This is so even within the European Community, where presumably the integration process has advanced the furthest. So, for example, Japan has a top tax rate of 50 per cent. The top rates in selected European countries are: the Netherlands 60 per cent, Germany 53 per cent, and the U.K. 40 per cent. The Canadian and U.S. top personal rates are 29 per cent and 28 per cent, respectively. Although Canada and the United States have reduced the number of tax categories to 3, Japan still has 5, France has 12, and Spain has 16.

The share of corporate income tax revenue varies widely among countries, from a high of 25 per cent in Japan to lows of 3 per cent in Austria and Sweden. In some countries corporate income tax revenue has maintained a stable share of total tax revenue, while in others (such as Canada and the United States), its share has dropped, and in still others (such as Japan) it has increased. There is wide variance among countries in the relative importance of employer social security contributions and of consumption taxes in overall revenue.

According to the OECD Fiscal Affairs Secretariat (1990), there is still much movement (in the treatment of corporate profits) and in different directions in OECD member countries. The extent to which the follow-the-leader reductions in personal and corporate income tax in Canada, the United Kingdom, the United States, and other countries were undertaken to prevent a possible outflow of capital in a globalized environment, and the extent to which they were motivated by the ideological dispositions of the governments in power, is not clear.

The OECD Fiscal Affairs Secretariat report (1990, 131) asserts that the continuation of these trends will "vary from country to country according to its present tax structure and its future economic situation and political preferences." It observes that, although the current trend is towards less government intervention and thus a smaller role for taxes, this trend may well reverse itself.

This would suggest that, despite the pressure of globalization, particularly the increased mobility of capital, there will remain room for differences among national tax policy makers in terms of the levels and mix of their tax policies.

It is also useful to recall the historical record of Canadian tax policy vis-à-vis the United States. Gillespie (1991) observes that Canadian governments since Confederation have shaped tax policies with a close eye to what the United States was doing. Fearing the consequences of emigration and capital flight, it was not until after the United States imposed a personal income tax in 1913 that a Canadian government followed suit with its own personal income tax. Declines in corporate tax rates in the United States in the past 40 years have been closely paralleled by declines in Canada.

The Liberal government in the early 1970s lowered Canadian corporate taxes in direct response to reductions in the United States. Finance Minister Walter Gordon was forced to rescind his 1963 tax on foreign take-overs and his increase in withholding tax on repatriation of dividends by foreign corporations.

In 1986, the conservative government lowered personal and corporate tax rates in direct response to reductions in U.S. personal and corporate income tax rates. Finance Minister Wilson warned in his 1987 budget speech that this was necessary, otherwise "significant income earning activities [production] would shift to the United States ... and firms with operations in both countries [would] allocate more of their tax income outside the country" (cited in Gillespie 1990, 203). Thus, economic and political élites in Canada have had a long-standing preoccupation with keeping income taxes in line with their American counterparts. Unlike Michael Wilson, Gillespie does not believe that globalization, per se, will pressure future Canadian governments to substantially increase tax harmonization with U.S. structures.

Perhaps the constraints on taxation are more the result of internal factors than they are external. Perhaps they are more related, for example, to issues of legitimacy, that is, popular consensus around public goals, the role of government in achieving them, the appropriate level of taxation, and whether taxes are being spent properly in pursuit of these goals. But to what extent is the "legitimacy" question defined by what Galbraith (1992) calls "the culture of contentment" (that is, the interests of the upper 30 or 40 per cent of the society, the corporate élite, the opinion makers, the knowledge classes, and so on) and how these groups perceive their lifestyles to be affected by changes in tax regimes and expenditure priorities?

If globalization is ultimately about the growth of corporate power and how it is expressed within and among nations; if it is about the mutuality of domestic and external corporate vested interests and the policy constraints they place on social democratic governments, then the question must be asked: What do governments do to strengthen their fiscal capacity? This question is, however, part of a much broader question: How do governments, individually and collectively, regain a measure of the control they have lost in order to achieve the economic policy objectives for which they were elected? In other words, how do governments re-regulate and mitigate the socially disintegrating and polarizing effects of these so-called mobile factors so that they are more accountable to the interests of society as a whole?

Power, once achieved and entrenched, is not easily relinquished. Unless government has the political will, unless the issues and the choices are crystal clear to the electorate, and unless the electorate supports the legitimacy of the political leadership and its choices, then the prospect for rolling back the constraints on public policy is limited.

TABLE 1
Total Tax Revenue as Percentage of GDP (to nearest percentage point)

	1980	1985	1987	1989[a]
Australia	29	30	31	n.a.
Austria	41	43	42	41
Belgium	43	46	46	n.a.
Canada	32	33	35	33
Denmark	45	49	52	51
Finland	33	37	36	38
France	42	44	45	44
Germany	38	38	38	38
Greece	29	35	37	n.a.
Iceland	30	28	28	n.a.
Ireland	34	38	40	39
Italy	30	34	36	38
Japan	25	28	30	n.a.
Luxembourg	41	44	44	n.a.
Netherlands	46	45	48	46
New Zealand	33	34	39	n.a.
Norway	47	48	48	45
Portugal	29	32	31	n.a.
Spain	24	29	33	34
Sweden	49	51	57	57
Switzerland	31	32	32	32
Turkey	22	20	24	24
United Kingdom	35	38	38	36
United States	30	29	30	n.a.
Unweighted average				
OECD Total	35	37	39	
OECD Europe	37	39	40	
EEC	36	39	41	

[a]Estimates
n.a. = not available
Source: "Revenue Statistics of OECD Member Countries 1965–1989" (OECD 1990) plus estimates for Iceland. Cited in OECD, *Taxation and International Capital Flows*, June 1990, p. 137.

TABLE 2
Share of Total Tax Revenues in 1989

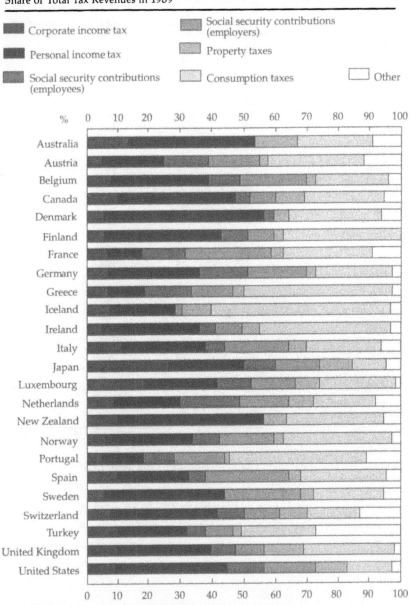

Source: Revenue Statistics of OECD Member countries, 1991.
Cited in OECD, Taxing Profits in a Global Economy 1991, p. 86.

TABLE 3
Balance of Payments: Current Account (1) (per cent of GDP)[a]

	1982	1983	1984	1985	1986	1987	1988
Per cent of GDP							
Canada	0.8	0.8	0.6	−0.6	−2.3	−2.1	−2.3
United States	−0.2	−1.3	−2.6	−3.0	−3.4	−3.5	−2.6
Japan	0.7	1.7	2.8	3.6	4.3	3.6	2.7
G–7	–	−0.2	−0.7	−0.8	−0.3	−0.5	−0.4
Other industrial	−2.3	−1.1	−0.6	−0.7	−0.3	−0.4	−0.4
Billions of $ U.S.							
Canada	2.3	2.5	2.1	−2.3	−8.2	−8.7	−11.3
United States	−7.0	−44.3	−99.0	−122.3	−145.4	−160.2	−126.2
Japan	6.9	20.8	35.0	49.2	85.8	87.0	79.6
G–7	−2.8	−12.7	−52.9	−59.5	−24.2	−48.9	−45.6
Other industrial	−23.2	−8.7	−0.9	−3.0	−2.9	−5.8	−8.3

[a]minus sign = deficits
Source: IMF: *World Economic Outlook* May 1991, May 1990

TABLE 4
World Economy: Real Output and Trade Growth (per cent change)

	1967–76 (per cent annual growth)	1980–91 (per cent annual change)
Output (real GDP)		
World	4.5	2.6
Industrial countries	3.7	2.5
LDCs	6.0	2.5
Canada	4.8	2.3
Trade volumes		
World	7.7	4.0
Industrial countries	7.8	4.4
LDCs	6.8	3.2
Canada	7.4	5.0

Source: IMF *World Economic Outlook* May 1992, April 1985

TABLE 5
Canadian Interest Rates 1970–90 (per cent average annual)

Year	(1) Canadian interest rate (3-month treasury bills)	(2) Differential above U.S. interest rate	(3) Inflation 4th quarter	(4) Real interest rate (1) minus (3)
1970–79	7.2	0.5	8.0	−0.8
1980–90	11.0	2.4	5.2	5.8
1985–90	10.1	3.0	4.1	6.0
1988–90	11.5	3.8	3.9	7.6

Source: Statistics Canada, *Canada's Balance of International Payments*. Historical Statistics 1991.

Bibliography

Barkin, D. 1991. "About Face." *NACLA, Report on the Americas*. North American Congress on Latin America, Vol. XXIV, No. 6, 30–36

Battle, K. 1992. "Limits of Social Policy." In *Finding Common Ground*, ed. J. Chrétien, 145–68. Hull: Voyageur Publishing

Bean, D.J.S. et al. 1991. *Taxation of International Portfolio Investment*. Ottawa: Institute for Research on Public Policy. Centre for Trade Policy and the Law

Betcherman, G. 1992. "The Declining Middle." In *Getting on Track: Social Democratic Strategies for Ontario*, ed. D. Drache, 124–35. Canadian Centre for Policy Alternatives, McGill-Queen's Press

Bienefeld, M. 1990. *Financial Deregulation and Its Implications for Canadian Political Economy*. Ottawa: Carleton University. Mimeo

Cameron, D., ed. 1988. *The Free Trade Deal*. Toronto: Lorimer

Campbell, Bruce. 1992. *Canada Under Siege*. Ottawa: Canadian Centre for Policy Alternatives

Campbell, B., and M. Barlow. 1991. *Take Back the Nation*. Toronto: Key Porter Books

Canada. 1984. *Agenda for Change*. Ottawa: Supply and Services

Canadian Labour Market Productivity Centre. 1991. "The Role of Consensus Bucking in Economic Performance." *Labour Market and Productivity Review*, Nos. 1–2. Summer. Ottawa

– 1991. "The Challenge of Economic Restructuring: An Overview of the Issues." *Labour Market and Productivity Review*. Fall. Ottawa

Canadian Manufacturers' Association. 1991. *Year End Review and Economic Outlook*. December. Toronto

Chrétien, J., ed. 1992. *Finding Common Ground*. Hull: Voyageur Publishing

Coopers and Lybrand. 1991. *Reshaping Canada to Compete*. Toronto

Courtis, K. 1992. "Globalization: The Economic Impact." In *Finding Common Ground*, ed. J. Chrétien, 15–22. Hull: Voyageur Publishing

Couzin, R. 1992. *Tax Options for Competitiveness*. Toronto: Canadian Tax Foundation

Cox, D. 1991. "The Global Political Economy A Social Choice." In *The New Era of Global Competition*, ed. D. Drache and M. Gertler, 335–50. Kingston and Montreal: McGill-Queen's University Press

Crane, D. 1992. *The Next Canadian Century: Building a Competitive Economy*. Toronto: Stoddart

Dagg, A., and A. Yalnizyan. 1992. *National and International Links: The Case of the Garment Workers*. Toronto. Mimeo

Daly, H. 1992. "Free Trade, Sustainable Development and Growth Alert." *Eco-Perspective*, 1: 10–13

Daly, H., and R. Goodland. 1992. *An Ecological Assessment of Deregulation of International Commerce under GATT*. Mimeo. Washington: World Bank, Environmental Department

Davidson, R. 1994. "Intellectual Property." *Canada Under Free Trade*, ed. D. Cameron and N. Watkins, 214–23. Toronto: Lorimer

Drache, D. 1992. *Social Democratic Strategies for Ontario*. Kingston and Montreal: McGill-Queen's University Press

Drache, D., and M. Gertler, eds. 1991. *The New Era of Global Competition: State Policies and Market Power*. Kingston and Montreal: McGill-Queen's University Press

Dungan, Peter. 1994. "The Economic Environment for Tax Reform in Ontario." In *The Economic and Social Environment for Tax Reform*, ed. Allan M. Maslove. Fair Tax Commission, Research Studies. Toronto: University of Toronto Press

Economic Council of Canada. 1990. *Good Jobs, Bad Jobs: Employment in the Service Economy*. Ottawa: Supply and Services Canada

Ecumenical Coalition for Economic Justice. 1991. *Ethical Reflections on North American Free Trade*. Toronto

Fieleke, N.S. 1988. *The International Economy under Stress*. New York, NY: Balinger Publishing

Fortin, P. 1991. "The Phillips Curve Macro Economic Policy and the Welfare of Canadians." *Canadian Journal of Economics*, XXIV, No. 4, November, 774–803

Friedman, B.M. 1990. *Implications of Increasing Corporate Indebtedness for Monetary Policy*. Occasion Papers 29. New York, NY: Group of Thirty

Galbraith, J.K. 1992. *The Culture of Contentment*. New York, NY: Houghton Mifflin Co.

Gillespie, I.W. 1991. *Tax, Borrow and Spend: Financing Federal Spending in Canada 1967–1990.* Ottawa: Carleton University Press

Gindin, S. 1992. "Putting the Con Back in the Economy." *This Magazine,* XXV: 17–21

Gold, M., and D. Leyton-Brown, eds. 1988. *Tradeoffs on Free Trade.* Toronto: Carswell

Gordon, M.J. 1984. *The Taxation of Canadian Subsidiaries of Foreign Corporations.* Occasional Paper No. 3. Toronto: Canadian Institute for Economic Policy

Grinspun, R., and M. Cameron. 1993. *The Political Economy of North American Free Trade.* McGill-Queen's Press, Canadian Centre for Policy Alternatives: Kingston

International Monetary Fund. 1985. *World Economic Outlook.* Washington. April

– 1992a. *World Economic Outlook,* Washington. May

– 1992b. *IMF Survey.* Washington. July 20

Investment Canada. 1991a. *A Multilateral Investment Accord: Issues, Models and Options.* June

– 1991b. *International Investment and Competitiveness.* Working Paper No. 9. October

Julius, D. 1990. *Global Companies and Public Policy: The Growing Challenge of Foreign Direct Investment.* London: Royal Institute of International Affairs

– 1991. *Foreign Direct Investment: The Neglected Twin of Trade,* Group of Thirty. New York

Junne, G. 1987. "Automation in the North: Consequences for Developing Countries Exports." In *A Changing International Division of Labour,* ed. J. Caporaso, 71–90. Boulder, CO: Lynne Reinner

Kenney-Wallace, G. 1992. "Innovation, Research and Development in Contemporary Canada: Competitiveness Options for a Caring Society." In *Finding Common Ground,* ed. J. Chrétien, 111–27. Hull: Voyageur Publishing

Laliberté, L. 1991. "Foreign Investment in the Canadian Bond Market, 1978–1990." *Canadian Economic Observer,* 3.19–3.34. Statistics Canada, June.

Laxer, J. 1991. *Inventing Europe: The Rise of a New World Power.* Toronto: Lester Publishing

Laxer, R. 1991. "Countries for Sale: Foreign Ownership in a Global Economy." CBC Radio, *Ideas,* 9 October 1991

Marchak, P. 1991. *The Integrated Circus: The New Right and the Restructuring of Global Markets.* Kingston and Montreal: McGill-Queen's University Press

Marshall, R. 1991. "Unions and Competitiveness." A paper presented at the United Steelworkers Conference, Empowering Workers in a Global Economy. October. Toronto

McQuaig, L. 1991. *The Quick and the Dead: Brian Mulroney, Big Business and the Seduction of Canada*. Toronto: Viking

Mead, W.R. 1992. *Harpers Magazine*, September 1992

Mersereau, B. 1992. "Characteristics of Importing Firms, 1978–86." *Canadian Economic Observer*, 4.1–4.15. Statistics Canada, August

Mimoto, H., and P. Cross. 1991. "The Growth of the Federal Debt." *Canadian Economic Observer*, 3.1–3.18. Statistics Canada, June

Mishel, L., and D. Frankel. 1991. *The State of Working America – 1990–91*. Washington, Economic Policy Institute and M.E. Sharpe Inc.

Myles, J. 1991. "Post-industrialism and the Service Economy." In *The New Era of Global Competition: State Policies and Market Power*, ed. D. Drache and M. Gertler, 350–66. Kingston and Montreal: McGill-Queen's University Press

Mytelka, L.K. 1987. "Knowledge Intensive Production and the Changing Internationalization Strategies of Multinational Firms." In *A Changing International Division of Labour*, ed. J. Caporaso, 43–70. Boulder, CO: Lynne Reinner

National Advisory Board on Science and Technology. 1991a. *Statement on Competitiveness*, Ottawa. March

– 1991b. *Innovation and National Prosperity, the Need for Canada to Change Course*, Ottawa. April.

Ontario, Attorney General. 1988. *A Legal Analysis of the Canada–U.S. Free Trade Agreement*. Mimeo. Toronto

Ontario. Ministry of Treasury and Economics. 1991. *Budget Paper E, Ontario in the 1990s: Promoting Equitable Structural Change*. Toronto: Queen's Printer

Organization for Economic Co-operation and Development, Fiscal Affairs Secretariat. 1990. "Recent Tax Reform in OECD Countries and Prospects for the 1990s." In *Taxation and International Capital Flows*, OECD, June. Paris

– 1991a. *Taxing Profits in a Global Economy: Domestic and International Issues*. Paris

– 1991b. *Economic Indicators*. Paris

Paquet, G. 1991. "The Canadian Malaise and Its External Impact." In *Canada Among Nations 1990–91: After the Cold War*, ed. F. Hamson and C. Maule, 25–40. Ottawa: Carleton University Press

Porter, M. 1991. *Canada at the Crossroads: The Reality of a New Competitive Environment*. Ottawa: Supply and Services Canada

Reich, R. 1991. *The Work of Nations – Preparing Ourselves for 21st Century Capitalism*. New York, NY: Alfred Knopf

Shaiken, H. 1990. *Mexico in the Global Economy*. San Diego: UCLA Press

Shaiken, H., and S. Herzenberg. 1987. *Automation and Global Production*. San Diego: UCLA Press

Statistics Canada. 1991. *The Labour Force Survey*. December. Cat. No. 71-001. Ottawa
- 1992a. *Canada's Balance of International Payments*, First Quarter. Cat. No. 67-001. Ottawa
- 1992b. *The Labour Force Survey*. August. Cat. No. 71-001. Ottawa
Strange, S. 1988. *States and Markets*. London: Basil Blackwell
Thurow, L. 1992. *Head to Head – The Coming Economic Battle among Japan, Europe and America*. New York, NY: Morrow
United Nations. Centre on Transnational Corporations. 1988. *CTC Reporter*, No. 26. Autumn
- 1989. UNCTAD Statistical Pocket Book. United Nations Conference on Trade and Development. New York, NY
- Centre on Transnational Corporations. 1991. *World Investment Report*. New York, NY
- United Nations Development Program. 1992. *Human Development Report*
Wilkins, J. 1990. "The Impact of the United States Tax Reform on Inward and Outward Capital Flows." In *Taxation and International Capital Flows*. June. Paris: OECD
Wilkinson, B.W. 1991. "Regional Trading Blocs: Fortress Europe vs Fortress North America." In *The New Era of Global Competition*, ed. D. Drache and M. Gertler. Kingston and Montreal: McGill-Queen's University Press
- 1993. "Trade Liberalization, the Market Ideology and Morality: Have We a Sustainable System?" In *The Political Economy of North American Free Trade*, ed. R. Grinspun and M. Cameron, 27–43. Kingston and Montreal: McGill-Queen's University Press
Williams, G. 1983. *Not for Export – Toward a Political Economy of Canada's Arrested Industrialization*. Toronto: McClelland and Stewart

3 The Economic Environment for Tax Reform in Ontario

PETER DUNGAN

Introduction

The work of the Fair Tax Commission has taken place against the backdrop of a rapidly shifting fiscal situation in Ontario and Canada. This paper is one of several prepared for the commission on the economic and fiscal environment in which Ontario tax reform will unfold over the next 15 years. My approach is to develop a numerical portrait of what the Canadian and Ontario economies could look like over the next 15 years under a reasonable set of trends and assumptions. Included in the portrait are the key economic indicators such as the gross domestic product (GDP), inflation, unemployment and interest rates, together with the fiscal details of the different levels of government adding up to the bottom line of deficits and debts. The basic portrait is supplemented by two variants that embody some of the more severe downside risks facing our economic future. Together, these economic images should give us a better idea of the pressures and challenges facing the tax system in Ontario in the years ahead.

How is my portrait of the future of the economy painted? I use the long-established method of developing an economic projection based on computer simulation models of the Canadian and Ontario economies.[1] In the present case I use the macroeconometric models FOCUS and FOCUS–Ontario, developed and maintained at the Institute for Policy Analysis, University of Toronto.[2] The models contain both "identities" that express the way economic and fiscal accounts and other economic data add up, together with "behavioural" equations that express my best estimates of the way segments of the economy (such as investment in machinery and equipment or consumption of automobiles) have performed and interacted with the rest of the economy in the past. I then combine the models with many numerical assumptions about the future economic environment outside Canada, about technological developments and population growth, and about future fiscal and monetary policies. Finally, I have used my own judgement when there is a need to reconcile the assumptions with each other, or with the model, or where I believe the future may break sharply with the lessons of the past embodied in the model.

What are the advantages of this approach? In two words, they are "quantification" and "consistency," with a coinciding advantage of allowing systematic "what if?" sensitivity analysis to be conducted. By quantification I mean the ability to resolve a problem not only into "good or bad" or "plus and minus," but into, roughly, "*how* good or bad." It is a valuable exercise to identify all the various factors that in future might affect government deficits, but the issues of whether deficits will grow or decline in the future, or whether the ratio of debt to GDP will rise or fall, ultimately require that numbers be put forward. While current deficits may appear large at either the national or provincial levels, it must be recalled that they are still relatively small percentages of revenues and of expenditures, and still small percentages of total economic output. Deficits are also subject to a variety of factors pushing them up (such as debt accumulation or revenue shortfalls) and down (such as lower interest rates and revenue growth in a period of economic recovery). No matter how rough it might be, a numerical ("quantitative") approach is required to sort out the relative importance of these various factors and determine whether the paths of these fiscal indicators lead to danger or eventual safety.

The second, and related, advantage of the model-based approach is "consistency"; the various factors affecting the economy are considered together and interact with each other. In a thought exercise it is possible to pile economic "bad news" into a truly terrifying heap – low growth, high unemployment, high real interest rates, uncompetitive wage growth – but the models quickly remind us that, while possible, it is often difficult for all of these negative factors to exist together for an extended period. Low growth, for example, will tend to lower real interest rates, and high unemployment will bring down real wages and restore competitiveness. Or

– to take an example that presented itself in the development of one of the alternatives – lower productivity growth must eventually lead to lower, real-wage gains in the private sector, and then lower real wages for the government payroll if the public sector emulates the private, which in turn mitigates the deficit impacts of the lower-growth assumption.

A third advantage of the models-based approach, once a "base-case" projection has been developed, is the ability to perform "what if?" sensitivity tests by varying the assumptions in the base case. In this way, one can check quite systematically how important the particular technological growth assumption is, or how sensitive the projected debt/GDP path might be to a sudden new recession in the later 1990s.

What then are the disadvantages of the model-based approach to studying the future of the economy? The disadvantages are almost the mirror images of the approach's strengths. The model-based approach relies on what is quantifiable and, to some extent, on the historical properties of the economy. This approach can be a poor guide when factors in the future are difficult to quantify or are out of historical experience. Two ready examples are the possible major effects due to global warming over the medium term, and some of the factors often associated with the "globalization" of the economy. These factors are part of a complete picture of the future of the Ontario and Canadian economies too, and the quantification exercises undertaken here should not lead us to forget them. That is why this paper includes "think" pieces that consider the unquantifiable, and ponder possible breaks with historical experience.

Outline

The paper proceeds in four sections. In the second section I outline in more general terms those issues that I have found most important in determining the fiscal futures of Canada and Ontario, and that are quantifiable in this framework. The third section presents the base projection for the Canadian economy together with the assumptions behind it and the fiscal implications for the federal government and the provinces combined. The fourth section presents the base projection for Ontario and for the Ontario provincial government (together with the federal, local, and hospital sectors in Ontario). The fifth section considers two major alternative projections for both Canada and Ontario. Each alternative explores a set of downside risks to the base projection of the third and fourth sections. In the first alternative I examine the implications of factors that could lead to an overall lower growth path for Canada and Ontario, while the second alternative considers the implications of a major recession and economic disturbance in the later 1990s from which the economies slowly recover. Finally, the sixth section presents some tentative conclusions.

Factors Affecting the Long-Term Economic Outlook for Canada and Ontario

This section is an annotated catalogue of the various factors that will affect the evolution of the Ontario economy over the next 10 to 15 years. I pay special attention to those factors that will affect the fiscal situation of the provincial government – most importantly, its tax revenues. The factors fall into eight somewhat overlapping categories:

- the fundamentals of potential growth;
- the closing of the output gap;
- the international environment;
- the Canadian constitutional framework;
- federal fiscal policy;
- monetary policy;
- Ontario provincial fiscal policy; and
- "environmental" issues and factors.

Before proceeding through this list, it is worth looking ahead briefly to the results of the base-case projection. To many, the base case will seem a very optimistic view of the future: economic growth in Canada and in Ontario is above 4 per cent for much of the rest of the decade and around 2.5 to 3 per cent for the period 2001 to 2008. Inflation, while rising gradually from the low 1992–93 levels, remains comfortably below 4 per cent for the entire period. Real interest rates are relatively high by long historical standards (although generally lower than in the 1980s) but nominal rates are low. Good growth and low nominal interest rates, combined with the taxation levels of 1993 and plausible spending paths, virtually eliminate the federal deficit problem by the late 1990s. The Ontario provincial deficit problem is somewhat more difficult to overcome, but requires neither drastic spending cuts nor massive tax increases to eliminate the deficit by about the year 2000.

Given the relatively optimistic picture emerging from the base case, this overview will concentrate on the key features leading to such a result. The discussion of alternatives under each category will focus on the downside risks – that is, what could go wrong, rather than what could go still better.

The Fundamentals of Potential Growth

In any longer-term economic projection, the dominant side of the analysis tends to be on the "supply side" – that is, on those factors that affect the economy's fundamental ability to produce output. There is less emphasis on the more volatile factors affecting demand (exports, consumption, or inventories) that move actual output around in the short run.

It is standard to divide the sources of this long-term, potential growth into three major elements – the contributions of labour, of physical capital, and of total factor productivity (TFP). The first two elements are straightforward: these are the workers and their factories, shops, and machines that are used in production. TFP accounts for everything else, and is most important for technological change and innovation, allowing a given amount of labour and physical capital to increase production. Note that TFP will also be affected by how labour and capital are measured (or mismeasured). For example, if labour is measured by persons (as in my model), changes in average hours worked or in labour quality will show up in TFP. Or if capital is prematurely scrapped under industrial restructuring, our usual capital stock measures will be too high (and TFP too low).

Labour

Projecting the labour component of potential growth requires projections for the working-age population, for trends in labour-force participation, and for the "full-employment" unemployment rate. None of these elements is terribly contentious – at least compared with some of the other factors in the sections below.

Population growth divides into natural increase (births and deaths) and net immigration. The former is very stable and basic projections developed by Statistics Canada are adequate. The latter is more volatile. My work assumes immigration averaging about 250,000 per year, with over 50 per cent coming to Ontario. Emigration from Canada averages between 60,000 and 70,000 per year. There is also some modest net in-migration to Ontario from interprovincial population flows.

Judgement is required on when and at what level the rising participation rates for women will level off and on the participation of women (and men) in the 55-and-older categories.

Estimates for the full-employment unemployment rate in the next two decades must take into account some conflicting pressures. On one hand, the recent tightening of unemployment insurance and a smaller share of younger workers in the labour force argue for a lower full-employment rate. On the other hand, an increased pace of structural change through the 1990s, and the aftermath of the 1990–92 recession argues for a higher full-employment rate. A higher rate may leave the present unemployed "scarred" with lower employability for the rest of their working lives (the "hysteresis" hypothesis).

As noted above, the labour component of potential growth is not one of the more contentious factors in the projection. Moreover, the effect of alternatives on the fiscal and tax situation may be ambiguous: a lower population, for example, means a lower tax base but also less demand for government services. I see greater risks to the future in the other components of aggregate supply.

Capital

The physical capital component of potential growth in the projection follows directly from the real investment generated in developing either the base case or the alternatives. Its contribution is high in the base case, especially in the 1990s, because investment growth is an important part of the projected recovery from the 1990–92 recession. One of the alternatives examined slows the pace of recovery by assuming less investment. This alternative automatically generates a smaller capital stock and therefore a lower potential growth path.

Finally, in constructing the base-case projection I recognize that some investment is made to restructure the Canadian economy for the Canada–U.S. FTA or for megaproject investments like Hibernia with delayed pay-offs. This portion of investment is not permitted to enter the capital stock for the purposes of estimating potential growth.

Total Factor Productivity

TFP is the most contentious component of potential growth. While even the measurement of past TFP growth is difficult, conventional wisdom is that it contributed 1 to 2 per cent to growth rates in the 1950s, 1960s, and early 1970s. Since the mid-1970s its contribution has fallen dramatically. Recent work by the Department of Finance suggests that TFP growth in the 1980s may have been virtually zero. The debate rages on as to why TFP fell off so much. Some blame the oil shocks of 1973 and 1980 that made a lot of physical capital built under low, real energy prices prematurely obsolete. The capital remained on the books but was not contributing to output and so measured TFP fell. Other analysts point to low research and development (R & D) expenditures, a failure of Canadian entrepreneurs and labour to embrace innovation and change, or to worsening educational levels. Obviously, pinpointing the cause matters for the projection since some of these causes will remain (perhaps low educational achievement?) and others, such as high real energy prices, have gone away.

My base-case projection takes the middle ground, assuming modest TFP gains for the next two decades (about 0.75 per cent per year), but much less than the levels before 1973. I assume an additional 3–4 per cent of GDP growth spread over the 1990s as a result of restructuring under the Canada–U.S. FTA, following the estimates of Richard Harris. I also think some more modest TFP gains will result from the elimination of the federal Manufacturers' Sales Tax, but I make no explicit addition to TFP growth.

One of my alternatives examines the impact of lower TFP growth (as part of a lower overall growth path). Lower TFP growth could emerge because the productivity gains from the FTA have been misestimated. Or the oil-shock explanation for the 1970s and 1980s may be incorrect and more fundamental problems of economic management or technological innovation are to blame and are likely to continue through the 1990s. TFP growth could also be negatively affected by a number of the factors listed in the categories below (for example, increased interprovincial trade barriers under new constitutional arrangements or outright separation). Naturally, lower TFP growth also has potentially severe implications for the tax and fiscal situation, since it will lower the tax base with no compensating decrease in pressures on government spending.

Closing the Output Gap

The recession of 1990–92 has left the Canadian and Ontario economies with a large gap between what they are currently producing and what they could produce at their full potential. (Among other things, this gap is evidenced by a national unemployment rate around 11 per cent – well above any reasonable measure of full employment.) The record of all past recessions or depressions is that eventually this "output gap" will be closed. The actual output of the economy, for a time, grows faster than its potential until the economy is again producing at or near its full potential level. Thus, for example, for a number of years after the 1981–82 recession, economic growth was above the underlying potential rate of around 3 per cent. Most of the output gap was closed by 1989.

Thus, an important factor underlying any projection for the next 15 years is the question of how quickly and in what ways the current output gap will be closed. In my national base case the closing of the gap requires 8 to 10 years, or somewhat longer than the 1980s recovery. Closing the gap would mean a number of years in which growth well exceeds a rough 3 per cent potential target. The dynamics of closing the gap, and the rate at which the gap is closed, are therefore important factors affecting the projection.

The essential idea behind why an output gap *must* close is that unemployed productive resources will force reductions in prices – whether actual commodity prices, wages, exchange rates, or real interest rates. Eventually it will pay to put the productive resources back to work. Combined with this is the idea that many demands can be postponed only temporarily. Demands for housing, automobiles, and other durables, and for real investment goods can easily be postponed for several quarters when prices or interest rates are high or the economic future uncertain. But eventually new housing is needed, the old autos and durables wear out, and new physical investment becomes increasingly profitable, at which point the pent-up demands are let loose. Note that these forces are not directly related to government actions. Fiscal and monetary policy can speed up or slow down the recovery, but the fundamental pressures come from the economy itself seeking to restore equilibrium. Or, so the mainline paradigm in macroeconomic analysis goes. But the speed at which the gap is closed can be highly variable and depends very much on the policy (and international) environments.

While the base-case projection embodies a closing of the gap in just under a decade, it is wise to consider an alternative in which the process is more prolonged. I have generated, therefore, an alternative in which another recessionary episode interrupts the economy's return to equilibrium. The interruption could stem from a number of factors discussed below. Nonetheless, the size of the current output gap is so large that I maintain that some closing of the gap over the next 10 to 15 years should be part of any reasonable economic base case or alternative. To maintain the current gap for any significant span would have only one historical antecedent in this century – the Great Depression.

The International Environment

Obviously, to a small, open economy, the international economic environment is critical. The evolution of the world economy and changes in Canada's relationships with its partners will affect Canadian potential growth, the closing of the output gap, and the fiscal implications of the projection.

The base-case or most-likely international projection is, in my view, also a relatively optimistic one. Closest to home, the U.S. economy recovers from its milder recession over the next several years and attains a potential growth rate of about 2.5 per cent. Growth is also projected to be strong in Asia and the Pacific. The economies of Eastern Europe restructure and begin to grow again as the 1990s progress, rather than remaining "basket cases" for an extended period. However, Asian and East European growth can be viewed as both good and bad: bad, in that these economies will compete strongly with Canadian goods, whether in manufactures (Asia and the former Soviet satellites) or in raw materials (Russia itself); and good, in that their growth contributes to a stronger world economy with greater sales and investment opportunities for all participants. My preliminary projection takes the positive effect as the predominant. But the more gradual closing of the output gap in my base case (compared with the 1980s) also incorporates a more prolonged period of structural adjustment in response to the continued emergence of the Asian and East European economies.

Another aspect of the international environment is changes in international trading relationships. The base projection assumes a continuation of the U.S.–Canada FTA and a gradual phase-in of the North American Free Trade Agreement (NAFTA), and in such a way that there is no major disruption to the U.S. economy. The FTA is already assumed to add to TFP growth through the 1990s, and the required restructuring adds to real investment and somewhat prolongs the return to full employment. The addition of Mexico to the trading arrangements adds slightly to all of these effects. I also assume that no major trade war breaks out between the emerging trade blocks – Europe, Japan and North America – and that modest trade liberalization continues throughout the world.

A final feature of the base case on the international side is the presence through the projection period of relatively high, real interest rates. More precisely, projected rates are high by long historical reference, but not in comparison to credit crunches before the 1990–92 recession or the 1981–82 recession. The story here is of a higher world demand for capital relative to world supply. The Asian and East European economies offer potentially very high returns to investment while the United States – through its government budget deficits – is also still absorbing world savings. Japan, with an ageing population and its own internal restructuring to do, ceases to be as predominant a source of world saving as in the past.

Given that many of these assumptions appear relatively optimistic, it is important to consider the downside risks on the international side.

The first risk would be of a shakier medium-term prognosis for the U.S. economy. A number of factors could prolong the recovery of the United States from its recession and lower its overall TFP growth path. These factors include fiscal muddling that leaves the structural federal deficit largely untouched and fails to provide for rebuilding of infrastructure and education. A major banking crisis following on the heels of the savings and loan problem could also worsen the U.S. situation. While a lower growth path for the United States does not condemn Canada to a lower growth path (as long as the fundamentals of our own potential growth are unaffected), it would certainly prolong our period of adjustment. Canada would be forced to restructure its economy to interact more with the rest of the world and less with the United States.

A second risk is for less optimistic outcomes in international trading arrangements. The biggest risk of all is that the United States – or more likely Canada – abrogates the FTA and trade barriers are re-erected between the United States and Canada. This would lead to significant TFP loss and adjustments that could push the economy well away from potential for a time. A trade war between North America and one or more of the other world trading areas would lower TFP growth in North America and prolong recovery to potential.

A third risk is that the TFP gains from the FTA may not be as large as has been widely estimated. This would mean a scenario with lower potential growth. A related risk is that the costs of restructuring the Canadian economy to take advantage of the FTA, of NAFTA, and of new competitors in Asia and Eastern Europe, will be higher than estimated in the base case. In this case the economy would need more investment (or less of the investment in the base case would add to potential) and there would be a more prolonged recovery to potential.

Another risk, or rather uncertainty, is the world inflation path. The base case assumes no major inflation surprises (like the oil-price shocks of the 1970s) over the next 15 years. It also assumes that most nations, including the United States, are content to keep inflation in the 2–5 per cent range. The alternative is that the rest of the world takes up the struggle for zero inflation with the same zeal shown in the past few years in Canada, guided by a re-rejuvenated Bundesbank and a more doctrinaire U.S. Federal Reserve. This alternative would make pursuit of lower inflation in Canada easier. But it might also obligate us to undergo, with the rest of the world, some additional slow-down and temporary increase of the output gap in the mid- to late 1990s.

A final risk is the possibility of higher world interest rates – which is incorporated as part of the "interrupted recovery" alternative. The story told above about why rates are high by historical standards in the base case is modified by some analysts to obtain even higher rates. They see still further world opportunities for capital to earn high returns and still fewer sources of savings.

The Canadian Constitutional Framework

The base-case projection effectively assumes little change in the current constitutional framework as it affects the economy. I assume that Quebec remains in the confederation. I also assume that there is little further reduction in interprovincial barriers to trade such as might have occurred under the original "economic union" proposals leading up to the Charlottetown Accord.

The principal alternative, of course, is that the confederation splits into Quebec and the Rest of Canada (ROC). There are then two further possibilities. The first is that the split is relatively amicable, with a common currency and customs union and with each partner still covered by the FTA. The second is that the breakup is nasty, with no common currency, disputes about the federal debt, and the erection of serious trade barriers between Quebec and the ROC.

An amicable breakup, if it occurred quickly and with little fuss, would probably have little impact on the projection for Ontario. A period of uncertainty surrounding the breakup would add to the factors causing an interrupted recovery. And real interest rates would likely have to rise to protect the dollar and to attract foreign capital into a regime of, at least temporarily, greater risk. Still, there would be little long-term effect. However, serious obstruction of trade would clearly lower TFP growth for a significant time – much as the FTA is estimated to be increasing TFP growth for the 1990s. Prolonged uncertainty would also lead to a reduction of trend growth on something like a 10-year horizon. I therefore treat the possibility of a contentious breakup as one of the factors leading to lower trend growth.

Federal Fiscal Policy

Obviously, federal fiscal policy is an important factor affecting the projection for Canada and Ontario. The primary impact is on the speed and nature of the closing of the output gap and not so much on underlying TFP or potential growth. However, even the latter can be affected by the overall stance of policy. For example, the base case projection shows a significant reduction in the demand for borrowing by the federal government through the later 1990s. This means that more national savings are available for private investment, which in turn increases the capital stock and adds to potential growth.

Fiscal policy in the base projection has the following features. First, no new taxes are added, but current taxes are maintained for most of the decade. Second, after the late 1990s some federal personal taxes are reduced. Third, federal current and capital spending continues to be restrained, growing in real terms but at less than potential GDP. Fourth, federal transfers to persons drop as a share of GDP as the output gap is closed. Finally, there are no major new spending initiatives.

In the model, these assumptions, combined with the dynamics of debt servicing, yield the result that the federal deficit falls away quickly through the 1990s and the debt/GDP ratio also peaks and begins a significant decline.

Now, left without changes in spending or taxation, the dynamics of deficit reduction would carry on to build up bigger and bigger federal surpluses. We view this as unlikely and must decide how federal fiscal policy will change gears. At the same time, my base-case projection work indicates that the provincial-local-hospital levels of government will have significant spending needs. My tentative solution is to assume that the federal government makes major increases in its transfers to the provincial governments while it also cuts personal taxes somewhat.

Two major alternatives to these federal fiscal assumptions can be suggested. The first, and most likely, is that the federal government will adopt an alternative solution to its incipient budget surplus "problem" in the late 1990s. Instead of increasing transfers to the provinces, the federal government might simply cut taxes more sharply (taking the political credit), and let provinces raise their taxes to fund their spending (and pay the political cost). The second alternative is for the federal government to increase its own spending in education, health, and social services – but the provinces might strongly resist further federal direct participation in these areas.

None of these alternatives matters much for underlying potential growth or the closing of the output gap unless the scenario leads to higher overall government spending that in turn reduces real investment. If it is simply a question of which level of government does the spending or taxation, the implications are important for fiscal analysis, but not for underlying growth. A secondary implication of more relevance for Ontario is that federal control of taxation, together with increased transfers, would likely mean more equalization among the provinces rather than the alternative of surrendering tax room and letting the provinces raise the taxes instead. Quebec, while it would likely benefit from greater equalization, would probably prefer more direct taxation control for its own political reasons.

Monetary Policy

There are two important features or assumptions about monetary policy and its effects in the base case. The first is that the early 1990s output gap will not be sufficient of itself to attain zero inflation, or even 2 per cent inflation, in the medium to long term. My present base case follows the U.S. projection in having the rate of inflation gradually increase through the year 2000 and beyond, but not above the 3–4 per cent range. Contributing to this result are indirect tax increases, the looming need for major price adjustments by utilities, the rebuilding of profit rates, and an element of catch-up by labour as the output gap closes. The failure to sustain 2 per cent inflation from the current recession is not entirely an assumption, but is also a finding of the modelling work itself.

The second monetary-policy assumption is that the federal government will not permit the Bank of Canada to undertake another round of monetary restriction to push the inflation rate permanently below 2 per cent. The political and economic costs of the 1990–92 round of inflation reduction will be too fresh in mind, I assume, to make another round a palatable choice. The choice would only become a serious option if some new and convincing evidence of the gains from zero inflation were brought forth or if the rest of the world also began to pursue zero inflation.

Either of these assumptions or features could be wrong. First, it is possible that the 1990–92 recession has been sufficient to lock in 2 per cent as the base inflation rate for the medium term. A scenario embodying this alternative would have the same underlying growth as the base but lower inflation rates and lower nominal interest rates – with obvious fiscal implications. To take the Bank of Canada's case one step further, we might want also to increase TFP growth through the medium term and reduce real interest rates. Each of these effects is supposed to result from a lower sustained inflation rate.

The second alternative to consider is, if 2 per cent inflation is not being achieved by 1995 or if a true zero rate is desired past 1995, that a second round of monetary restriction will then begin. This round of restriction would delay the closing of the current output gap – indeed it could open it up again somewhat – and would temporarily raise real interest rates, both results with fiscal implications. Just such a second round of monetary restriction is part of the rationale behind the interrupted recovery alternative.

Provincial Fiscal Policy

The current recession has left the provincial governments – and the Ontario government in particular – with a deficit problem akin to that facing the federal government in the wake of the 1981–82 recession. My base case assumes that all provincial governments will move swiftly over the next few years to get their deficits under control. They will restrain current and capital spending well below potential GDP growth, embark on no new major transfers initiatives, and will not scruple to raise taxes – primarily personal taxes and "green" or carbon taxes such as taxes on motive fuels. As a result, the provincial debt-to-GDP ratios should peak somewhere near the end of the 1990s, and the run-up in debts and deficits should be smaller than was the federal experience of the 1980s. This result is helped significantly by much lower nominal interest rates than in the previous decade. As mentioned, I also assume some increase in indirect taxes as these instruments are used to restrain carbon-based fuel usage and for other environmental goals. While this program might be directed federally, I assume that the actual indirect tax revenues will be allowed to go to the provincial treasuries.

The most likely alternatives to be considered in this area are a slower pace of adjustment back to fiscal equilibrium and different tax and spending mixes. These alternatives could also affect the speed at which the output gap was closed. A slower return to fiscal equilibrium would result from a greater reluctance to raise taxes or restrain spending. A different tax and spending mix would have implications for inflation (for example, if indirect taxes were changed significantly) and for the potential growth path (if there were a significant impact on real investment).

Environmental Issues

There are two major ways in which environmental matters can affect the projection for the Canadian and Ontario economies and the context of tax reform. The first way is that the environment does change in such a way as to affect economic growth or its mix. Over a horizon of the next 15 years this eventuality seems unlikely. Global warming at the present rate will have little effect and other environmental degradation – whether of land, water, or air – is advancing slowly, or in some cases already reversing. This not to say that some parts of the world (for example, desert or near-desert regions) might not undergo more traumatic environmental changes in the next 15 years, but these will have little effect on overall world growth, especially in the industrial countries. There is also the outside chance that world climate and environment may be subject to "catastrophic" (in the mathematical sense of the word) change once critical values are reached. However, too little is known about the likelihood of such shifts, or their nature, to allow us to model them.

The second way environmental matters can affect the economy is through the efforts undertaken to control or reverse environmental change in the long run. Thus, global warming itself may have little effect on Ontario in the next 15 years, but efforts taken over the next 15 years to control global warming in the more distant future could have potentially large effects.

The base projection assumes a continuation of gradual efforts to preserve and improve the environment. The relative prices of carbon-based fuels are assumed to be increased through indirect taxation (with the funds largely going to the provinces) and regulations are gradually tightened and improved year by year. The net result is a gentle push on inflation and some conservatism in my estimates of TFP growth. The latter is required because current economic measurements do not take adequate account of environmental improvements. For example, if a capital expenditure leaves output unchanged but lets cleaner air go up factory smokestacks, our current statistical measures show a lower TFP. The new capital has not added to economic output in the way that earlier real investment has. (Incidentally, efforts are underway to revise or add to the national accounts to include measures of environmental deterioration or improvement.)

A major alternative to be considered is that a much more concerted "green plan" policy will be instituted as the 1990s progress. This could result in major tax and spending shifts, possible pressures on inflation and real interest rates, increased investment, and possibly lower TFP growth (again using the standard economic growth measures). Sub-alternatives emerge when we ask whether Canada works alone in such an effort or is part of a larger movement on the part of the world economy. A go-it-alone green push could involve major industrial shifts as penalized sectors move abroad. This would delay closing of the output gap – or open a new gap temporarily – and would require proportionally more capital for restructuring, thereby lowering the potential growth path for a time. In my opinion, careful and concerted green policies need not have these kinds of disruptive effects; however, they may result in unnecessary disruptions if they are hastily or badly planned. And if green policies lower measured trend growth for a time, this may well be a cost worth paying; but it will be important to understand the fiscal implications. The possibility of an inflationary or disruptive environmental policy push will be one of the factors underlying the interrupted recovery alternative, while long-term environmental adjustment that lowers measured TFP growth can be viewed as a factor in the lower trend growth alternative.

The Canadian Economy through 2008

This section presents a projection of the Canadian economy through 2008, with special attention paid to fiscal issues at federal and lower government levels. The projection is my best estimate of how the Canadian economy will perform over the next 15 years. It is intended to stand alone as background to discussion of Ontario tax and fiscal issues, and also to serve as a base for my projection of the Ontario economy in the fourth section below.

The projection is developed from three principal sets of ingredients. First, there are a host of assumptions that must be made about the future economic environment outside Canada, about economic policies pursued by the different levels of government, and about underlying technology and population growth. The most important assumptions will be discussed further in the subsection "Assumptions Underlying the National Projection." The fifth section explores the sensitivity of the projection to two alternative sets of assumptions – one leading to lower trend growth and the other to a significant interruption of the economy's underlying return to balance.

Second, there is the computer simulation model of the Canadian economy (FOCUS) that is used to translate the assumptions into a numerical picture of the economy in detail (including output, employment, external trade, and deficits). The model contains both accounting "identities" that express the way the national accounts and other Canadian data add up, and "behavioural" equations that embody my best estimate of the way segments of the economy (such as investment or consumption) have performed or behaved in the past.

The third ingredient is the author's own judgement, which is used to coordinate and make consistent the previous two components. For example, initial assumptions about policy, when run through the model, may give a result that appears to be politically unsustainable in my judgement, causing me to change my assumptions. Or a particular model equation may be judged to be an unreliable guide at some point in the future and be overridden with judgemental assumptions instead. The economy remains sufficiently mysterious that the development of an economic projection is as much art as it is science.

There are two additional features of this projection – and any similar exercise – that should be noted. First, the specific numbers generated by the computer model must be considered only the middle of a range of possibilities that becomes more diffuse the further into the future we proceed. Despite the apparent precision of the numerical results, they are rough estimates only.

Second, beyond the immediate future and recovery from the current recessionary episode, the projection can only indicate trends for the future. Reality will no doubt include future business cycles. The projection can only represent an average through the ups and downs that will inevitably occur. I do assume that the result of future cycles is likely to be to keep the economy on average below its "full employment" or potential level, and this feature is built into my projected longer-term trends. The fifth section explores the sensitivity of the projection to the possibility of a more severe cyclical downturn in the mid-1990s.

Assumptions Underlying the National Projection

This section outlines and discusses the principal assumptions entering the national projection. These include assumptions about the economic prospects of Canada's major trading partners, and about Canadian fiscal, monetary, and exchange-rate policy. Table 1 summarizes many of the numerical assumptions incorporated in the projection.

The Foreign Environment

The U.S. projection used in this study is a mixture of elements from recent projections by Project LINK and by Data Resources Inc. – together with some additional judgement calls of my own. (For details see Table 1.)

In the near term, the U.S. recovery is projected to be less robust than normal, with real GDP growth of 2.1 per cent in 1992, and 2.5 per cent in 1993, up to 3.2 per cent in 1994, and dropping below 3 per cent after 1995. The U.S. projection assumes that U.S. inflation will remain below 4 per cent for the next decade. Potential growth in the United States is estimated to be about 2.5 per cent at the start of the 1990s and to decline gradually to just 2 per cent after the turn of the century.

Real short-term interest rates in the United States were very low in early 1993 but are projected to rise as the U.S. recovery becomes stronger. Real longer-term rates are projected to settle at about 5 per cent through the 1990s and beyond. These real rates – and especially the real long-term rate – will, of course, be those that will dominate the Canadian interest-rate projection. By broad historical averages the real, long-term, real rate is rather high, but this reflects the consensus that world savings will be relatively short compared with world demands for capital in at least the two decades to come.

Population and Labour-Force Participation

The population and household projections incorporated into the national projection (see Table 1) are based on those of Statistics Canada.[3] The projections have been updated for current population data and increases in immigration to a range of about 250,000 per year.

Gradual ageing of the source population for the labour force will likely have implications for the evolution of the full-employment unemployment rate; however, for the projection a flat figure of between 6.5 per cent and 7 per cent has been assumed as a rough benchmark. Note that no special upward adjustment has been made to the equilibrium rate to reflect above-normal industrial restructuring or regional imbalances which, it might be argued, would tend to make the labour market tighter than it appears both at present and through much of the first decade of the projection.

I have made several adjustments to the model's participation rate equations to reflect the easing or termination of some long-term trends. The rise in participation of the 15–24 age group is made to level off by the late 1990s to reflect increased returns on investment in education to this group and a greater availability of education as the number of young people declines relative to the size of the education sector. Most importantly, the long secular rise in the participation rate of females ages 25 to 54 is assumed to begin flattening. This participation rate keeps rising through 2008 but more and more slowly as it nears its maximum value. Finally, other adjustments accelerate the reduction in participation rates for older males (55 and over) to reflect both enhanced early retirement related to technological adjustments and a gradual rise in the average

TABLE 1
Canada Base Projection, September 1993: Principal Assumptions (% unless otherwise indicated)

	1991	1992	1993	1994	1995	1996	1997	1998	1999	2000
United States economy										
U.S. real GDP growth	−1.2	2.1	2.5	3.2	3.0	2.2	2.5	2.7	2.4	2.3
U.S. inflation (GDP deflator)	4.0	2.6	2.6	2.4	2.2	2.4	2.5	2.7	3.0	3.0
U.S. 90-day T-bill rate	5.4	3.5	3.0	3.3	3.6	3.5	3.6	4.4	4.9	4.9
U.S. industrial bond rate	9.2	8.5	7.6	7.3	7.6	7.6	7.6	8.0	8.4	8.4
Population, participation, and labour force										
Total population (millions)	26987	27388	27795	28188	28574	28951	29319	29680	30025	30359
(growth rate)	(1.46)	(1.49)	(1.48)	(1.42)	(1.37)	(1.32)	(1.27)	(1.23)	(1.16)	(1.11)
Labour-force source population ('000)	20746	21058	21388	21726	22046	22370	22674	22977	23275	23574
(growth rate)	(1.55)	(1.50)	(1.57)	(1.58)	(1.47)	(1.47)	(1.36)	(1.34)	(1.29)	(1.29)
Participation rate	66.3	65.5	65.4	65.9	66.5	66.8	67.2	67.4	67.6	67.8
Labour-force ('000)	13756	13796	13982	14318	14652	14952	15227	15490	15733	15978
(growth rate)	(0.55)	(0.29)	(1.35)	(2.40)	(2.34)	(2.05)	(1.84)	(1.73)	(1.57)	(1.56)
Policy										
Growth in real current and capital expenditure by government	2.4	0.7	1.2	0.8	1.6	1.8	1.9	2.0	2.0	2.0
Total government expenditures (excluding inter-government transfers) as % of GDP	50.5	51.4	51.2	49.6	48.6	47.6	46.8	46.2	45.7	45.0
Total government revenues (excluding inter-government transfers) as % of GDP	42.8	43.3	42.5	42.5	42.7	42.9	43.2	43.5	43.7	43.5

	2001	2002	2003	2004	2005	2006	2007	2008
United States economy								
U.S. real GDP growth	2.1	2.3	2.5	2.1	1.9	2.0	2.0	2.0
U.S. inflation (GDP deflator)	3.1	3.2	3.2	3.4	3.4	3.5	3.5	3.5
U.S. 90-day T-bill rate	4.9	4.9	4.9	4.8	4.8	4.8	4.7	4.7
U.S. industrial bond rate	8.5	8.5	8.5	8.5	8.5	8.5	8.5	8.4
Population, participation, and labour force								
Total population (millions)	30679	30992	31296	31589	31871	32144	32406	32658
(growth rate)	(1.05)	(1.02)	(0.98)	(0.94)	(0.89)	(0.86)	(0.82)	(0.78)
Labour-force source population ('000)	23869	24162	24451	24737	25021	25294	25560	25816
(growth rate)	(1.25)	(1.23)	(1.20)	(1.17)	(1.15)	(1.09)	(1.05)	(1.00)
Participation rate	67.9	67.9	67.9	67.7	67.5	67.3	67.1	66.9
Labour-force ('000)	16207	16403	16594	16745	16890	17026	17149	17269
(growth rate)	(1.43)	(1.21)	(1.16)	(0.91)	(0.87)	(0.81)	(0.72)	(0.70)
Policy								
Growth in real current and capital expenditure by government	2.1	2.2	2.2	2.3	2.2	2.6	2.4	2.2
Total government expenditures (excluding inter-government transfers) as % of GDP	44.4	43.9	43.4	43.0	42.6	42.4	42.2	42.0
Total government revenues (excluding inter-government transfers) as % of GDP	43.1	43.0	42.6	42.2	41.9	41.7	41.5	41.3

Source for all tables in this chapter: FOCUS Model, Institute for Policy Analysis age of this group. A rise in the participation rate of females 55 and over reflects the passage into this group of females who have entered the labour force over the past three decades.

Fiscal Policy

Setting fiscal policy in the model requires assumptions on certain spending categories and on a wide array of tax rates.

On a national income accounts basis, government expenditure can be roughly divided into current and capital spending, transfers and subsidies to persons and firms, transfers to other governments, and interest on the public debt. For current and capital spending I assumed real growth would be only 1.2 per cent in 1993, less than 1 per cent in 1994, and rising slowly thereafter to 2 per cent per year in 1998 and beyond. Naturally, these rates of growth are well below projected recovery growth rates for GDP (and below historical growth rates for these categories), so they ensure that the share of government current and capital spending to GDP falls. Current and capital spending growth is assumed to be lower at the federal than at the non-federal levels – the federal government will be cutting defence spending and rationalizing elsewhere, but the provincial, local, and hospital levels will have to provide both infrastructure and public services to a still-growing population.

Transfers to persons are largely determined by equations in the model. I assume in most cases that these spending categories will show their historical response to changes in unemployment, inflation, and population growth. I do not assume any new transfer programs, but I do assume that there will be a one-time ratcheting up of provincial (and local) transfers to persons as a result of the 1990–92 recession (and similar to what occurred after the 1981–82 recession). If, in fact, on this round the provinces are more successful in winding back their welfare and other transfers as the economy recovers, then the assumed increase in provincial transfers could leave room for a modest child-care initiative at the provincial level.

Interest on the debt is handled entirely within the model based on past debt stocks and interest rates. I have made no adjustments to these relationships.

Finally, I assume that transfers from the federal government to the provinces will grow somewhat less than nominal GDP until past the mid-1990s. Thereafter, however, much preliminary projection work convinced me that the federal government will have its deficit problem well in hand while the provinces (and local governments and hospitals) will still have strong expenditure requirements and pressing revenue needs. In this situation the pressure for the federal government either to increase transfers or to surrender tax room will, I judge, be virtually irresistible. I have decided that it is transfers that will be increased (partly with an eye to equalization and to maintaining the confederation) and so, after 1997, net federal transfers grow annually by 2–3 per cent in real terms. Meanwhile, provincial governments will also be increasing their transfers to the local and hospital levels to keep up with expenditure growth there.

On the revenue side there are the three main areas of corporate, personal, and indirect taxes to consider. (See the summary of tax rates in Table 2.)

I judge that there will be very little attempt to raise average corporate tax rates in the next decade and a half. It is now widely recognized that corporate rates must be kept internationally competitive, and the corporate tax system, with a lag of several years, will be showing good revenue growth at existing rates as corporate profits rebound from the cellar of the recent recession.

For personal income taxes I assume that the 3 per cent indexing floor will remain in place until into the next decade, yielding a slow but steady increase in personal income taxes at current rates. I assume that there will be further small reductions in the federal surtax rate later in the 1990s and after 2000. There have been major increases in personal income-tax rates in Ontario and elsewhere in 1993. These are assumed to be sustained through the remainder of the 1990s. Eventual success on the deficit permits the provinces to lower their tax rates in the next decade, with rates eventually falling well below even 1991 levels. (Alternatively, of course, federal transfers may not grow as fast and federal taxes could be further reduced.)

Starting in 1997, I assume that the unemployment insurance contribution rate drops by 0.1 per cent per year with a steady recovery in the unemployment rate and in the federal deficit. At the same time, the Canada and Quebec pension plan contribution rate, which is already scheduled to increase at a rate of 0.1 per cent per year, is moved up to an increase of 0.2 per cent per year. This additional rate increase is necessary to generate growing surpluses against the need to pay pensions to retiring baby boomers after 2010. The increasing CPP/QPP bite goes a long way towards offsetting the impacts of federal and provincial personal tax reductions on disposable income.

TABLE 2
Canada Base Projection, September 1993: Principal Tax Rates and Related Fiscal Indicators

	1991	1992	1993	1994	1995	1996	1997	1998	1999	2000
Federal "high" corporate tax rate	0.362	0.360	0.353	0.346	0.346	0.346	0.346	0.346	0.346	0.346
Provincial corporate tax rate	0.141	0.145	0.148	0.148	0.148	0.148	0.148	0.148	0.148	0.148
Indexing rate	1.833	2.831	0.000	0.000	0.000	0.000	0.000	0.000	0.000	0.000
Indexing "floor" rate	3.000	3.000	3.000	3.000	3.000	3.000	3.000	3.000	3.000	3.000
Basic federal PIT rate	0.198	0.198	0.198	0.198	0.198	0.198	0.198	0.198	0.198	0.198
Federal surtax rate (including high income)	0.058	0.053	0.038	0.038	0.038	0.038	0.038	0.038	0.028	0.028
Provincial PIT rate (% of basic federal) (including Quebec)	0.690	0.710	0.739	0.750	0.750	0.750	0.750	0.750	0.750	0.706
UI contribution rate (employee)	0.025	0.030	0.030	0.030	0.030	0.030	0.029	0.028	0.027	0.026
CPP contribution rate (employee)	0.023	0.024	0.025	0.026	0.027	0.028	0.030	0.032	0.034	0.036
"Other" provincial direct tax rate (as proportion of personal income)	0.005	0.006	0.006	0.006	0.006	0.006	0.006	0.006	0.006	0.006
GST rate	0.070	0.070	0.070	0.070	0.070	0.070	0.070	0.070	0.070	0.070
Average tariff rate (on non-auto imports)	0.034	0.036	0.026	0.022	0.020	0.018	0.017	0.016	0.015	0.014
Federal gasoline excise rate[a]	0.033	0.036	0.036	0.037	0.037	0.037	0.037	0.037	0.037	0.037
Federal alcohol/tobacco excise rate[a]	0.041	0.038	0.037	0.038	0.038	0.038	0.038	0.038	0.038	0.038
Average provincial sales tax rate (as proportion of approximate tax base)	0.090	0.089	0.088	0.090	0.090	0.090	0.090	0.090	0.090	0.090
Provincial gasoline tax rate[a]	0.045	0.050	0.050	0.052	0.055	0.060	0.065	0.070	0.075	0.080
Provincial liquor board profit tax rate[a]	0.022	0.021	0.021	0.021	0.021	0.021	0.021	0.021	0.021	0.021
Provincial other indirect tax rate[b]	0.015	0.016	0.016	0.016	0.016	0.016	0.016	0.016	0.016	0.016

	2001	2002	2003	2004	2005	2006	2007	2008
Federal "high" corporate tax rate	0.346	0.346	0.346	0.346	0.346	0.346	0.346	0.346
Provincial corporate tax rate	0.148	0.148	0.148	0.148	0.148	0.148	0.148	0.148
Indexing rate	0.000	0.000	2.651	2.738	2.938	3.038	3.163	3.238
Indexing "floor" rate	3.000	3.000	0.000	0.000	0.000	0.000	0.000	0.000
Basic federal PIT rate	0.198	0.198	0.198	0.198	0.198	0.198	0.198	0.198
Federal surtax rate (including high income)	0.018	0.018	0.006	-0.015	-0.032	-0.047	-0.068	-0.090
Provincial PIT rate (% of basic federal) (including Quebec)	0.673	0.650	0.629	0.613	0.600	0.594	0.589	0.583
UI contribution rate (employee)	0.025	0.024	0.023	0.022	0.021	0.020	0.020	0.020
CPP contribution rate (employee)	0.038	0.040	0.042	0.044	0.047	0.049	0.052	0.054
"Other" provincial direct tax rate (as proportion of personal income)	0.006	0.006	0.006	0.006	0.006	0.006	0.006	0.006
GST rate	0.070	0.070	0.070	0.070	0.070	0.070	0.070	0.070
Average tariff rate (on non–auto imports)	0.013	0.012	0.011	0.010	0.009	0.009	0.008	0.008
Federal gasoline excise rate[a]	0.037	0.037	0.037	0.037	0.037	0.037	0.037	0.037
Federal alcohol/tobacco excise rate[a]	0.038	0.038	0.038	0.038	0.038	0.038	0.038	0.038
Average provincial sales tax rate (as proportion of approximate tax base)	0.090	0.090	0.090	0.090	0.090	0.090	0.090	0.090
Provincial gasoline tax rate[a]	0.080	0.078	0.076	0.074	0.072	0.070	0.068	0.066
Provincial liquor board profit tax rate[a]	0.021	0.021	0.021	0.021	0.021	0.021	0.021	0.021
Provincial other indirect tax rate[b]	0.016	0.016	0.016	0.016	0.016	0.016	0.016	0.016

[a] tax as a rate on total consumer non-durable spending
[b] tax as a rate on nominal GDP

On the indirect tax side, the GST rate stays at 7 per cent throughout the projection. If the GST were to be replaced I assume that a similar amount of indirect federal tax revenues would be raised – although other options such as personal tax increases certainly exist. On the provincial side I assume that only minor additions will be made to general sales taxes (largely through additions to the tax base). But I assume that gasoline taxes will be gradually increased to almost double their current values. The temptation to do something about global warming combined with a need for cash should make these taxes a major target. At the local level, property and other indirect taxes are assumed to increase, but by less than GDP growth.

Monetary and Exchange-Rate Policy

In the near term (1994–95), monetary policy remains sufficiently tight to meet the targets announced for inflation in 1991 (within the bands of error). Primarily because of the huge output gap that opened with the recession, but also because of the productivity gains assumed to stem from adjustment to free trade, Canadian inflation is projected to remain well below that of the United States over the next decade while real growth remains strong. The inflation rate in Canada remains below 3 per cent through the 1990s, and the inflation differential between Canada and the United States is not expected to close until after the projection horizon of 2008.

One result of this overall orientation of monetary policy is that real interest rates continue to decline in the years 1993 to 1995 from the heights of 1989–90. But the scope for further real rate reductions is then quite modest for the rest of the 1990s – mostly because of the world demand for capital in Asia, Eastern Europe, and the Middle East.

Projections for exchange rates are notorious for error. My projection features an average exchange rate of about 76 cents U.S. for 1993. Naturally the rate can be expected to vary around this value. After 1993–94, the lower Canadian rate of inflation (compared with the United States) allows for a gradual appreciation of the Canada–U.S. exchange rate, which reaches almost 86 cents U.S. by 2008.

Obviously, the long-run projection assumes that the objective of zero inflation will be abandoned in the mid-1990s (in part because the U.S. projection used assumes it will never be adopted there), but that the objective of maintaining low inflation will be kept, with only a gradual creeping up towards the rate of our major trading partner being allowed. I view the long-run projection for the un-employment rate at 7 per cent as somewhat above the long-term equilibrium rate, reflecting some constant element of slack in the system to resist probable asymmetric upward shocks to the inflation rate. The possibility that the Bank of Canada will initiate a further round of monetary tightness in the later 1990s to achieve something closer to zero inflation is investigated as part of the interrupted recovery alternative in the section dealing with alternatives.

Free Trade and Other Assumptions

The projection assumes the full implementation of the Canada–U.S. Free Trade Agreement (FTA), and later in the 1990s the addition of the North American Free Trade Agreement (NAFTA). In the model, tariffs are reduced over ten years, direct investment inflows are augmented and private investment is increased to reflect the investment required for restructuring and rationalization.[4] Additional adjustments are required to obtain a higher rate of total factor productivity (TFP) growth as a result of the agreements. Due to the recession and the period of dollar overvaluation, some of the more positive impacts of the FTA have been delayed into the mid-1990s. Overall TFP gains from the FTA as built into the projection are approximately 3–4 per cent of GDP. Some additional investment and productivity stimulus is assumed to come from the removal of the inefficient Manufacturers' Sales Tax (MST).

Finally, the projection assumes that the Hibernia Oil project, although delayed, will proceed through the mid-1990s (further increasing the share of investment and demand for capital) and that one or more other major energy-related investments will commence sometime toward the end of the decade (for example, further oil sands exploitation or Beaufort Sea development).

The National Projection: An Overview

The basics of the national projection are summarized in Table 3 and Figure 1. The years 1993 and 1994 are of course dominated by the struggle to put the recession of 1990–92 firmly behind us. By the end of 1993, with a projected growth of 2.5 per cent, I estimate that, relative to 1989, an output gap of over 10 per cent will have opened. In 1994 recovery at last begins in earnest, with growth of 4.2 per cent. The unemployment rate averages 11.3 per cent in 1992 and 1993 and begins to fall gradually starting in 1994, with labour productivity growth in the range of 2 per cent. The GDP price deflator, as a result of a large gap relative to our economic potential, grows at only about 1 per cent in 1993 and 1994 – the lowest rates in recent memory. This rate is expected to move gradually upward over the next decade.

The medium term (1994–99) is dominated by recovery from the 1990–92 recession together with adjustments to free trade, and to the elimination of the MST and other structural changes. The underlying growth in potential is strong (averaging above 3 per cent) and the potential output gap is being closed, together giving an average GDP growth rate well above 4 per cent through the period. Because an output gap persists throughout, and because there are productivity improvements associated with the structural adjustments, there is little increase in inflation over the period; much of the inflation is simply imported from the U.S. projection, although some wage catch-up is allowed for as the unemployment rate falls. Labour productivity growth is also vigorous, as is normal in a recovery, although compounded by the efficiency gains of the structural adjustments.

Given the large output gap still present in the 1992–94 period, it might be argued that the inflation rate should continue to fall over this period, instead of rising slightly as in the projection. My analysis indicates that some of the inflation reduction achieved through the end of 1991 has actually been borrowed from the future – first through the recession's being induced by an overvalued dollar, and, second, through the extent to which the recession has reduced corporate profits, which have been driven to a postwar low relative to GDP. While in 1993 and 1994 (and beyond) real wages will be rising much less than productivity (as the unemployment gap would suggest), the downward impact on inflation is offset by the after-effects of the exchange-rate depreciation of 1992, by indirect green tax hikes, and especially by increased profit margins required to rebuild the profit share of national income.

Finally, the long-term trend projection (after 2000) shows growth rates largely at potential.[6] Real growth declines gradually after the year 2000 along with potential growth, primarily due to declining population growth rates.

My projection for the 1990s especially may appear optimistic to

FIGURE 1
Canada: Main Indicators

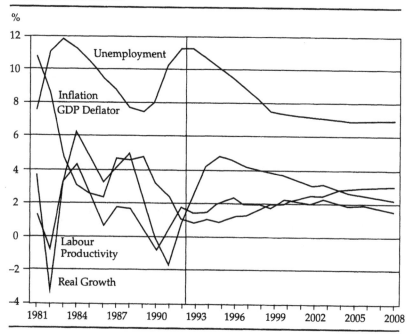

Source for all figures in this chapter: FOCUS Model, Institute for Policy Analysis

those who focus on the economic malaise of 1992 and 1993. It is important to recall that economic pessimism was similarly widespread on the threshold of the recovery from the 1981–82 recession and that the strength of that recovery was almost uniformly underpredicted (including by me). Yet, as Figure 2 shows, the current output gap versus potential is as large or larger than the gap that developed in the entire recessionary episode from 1979 through 1982, and the rate at which I project the gap to close is slower than what occurred in the 1980s recovery.

Sources of Aggregate Demand

Next I look more closely at the sources of final demand that largely determine the path of GDP through the projection in the short and medium term. Figure 3 shows the evolution of expenditure shares of GDP while details on expenditure and income shares of GDP are given in Table 4.

TABLE 3
Canada Base Projection, September 1993: Summary of Projection

	1991	1992	1993	1994	1995	1996	1997	1998	1999	2000
Real gross domestic product (% change)	-1.7	0.7	2.5	4.2	4.8	4.7	4.3	4.1	3.9	3.8
Expenditure on personal consumption	-2.0	1.1	1.3	2.2	3.7	3.3	3.2	3.3	3.2	3.5
Expenditure by governments	2.4	0.7	1.2	0.8	1.6	1.8	1.9	2.0	2.0	2.0
Investment expenditure	-3.0	-2.1	1.0	8.8	8.2	8.5	7.1	7.5	7.0	5.7
Residential construction	-12.3	6.3	-4.1	10.4	7.0	5.5	4.5	4.0	4.0	3.5
Non-residential construction	-2.5	-15.1	-6.5	5.0	5.1	5.8	4.8	5.2	6.0	4.8
Machinery and equipment	3.9	0.8	8.7	9.7	10.3	11.5	9.6	10.4	8.9	7.2
Exports	0.8	7.9	8.3	8.9	7.0	6.8	6.2	5.5	5.0	4.8
Imports	2.7	4.9	6.5	6.1	5.2	5.2	4.9	5.4	4.8	4.8
Implicit deflator for GDP (% change)	2.5	1.1	0.9	1.0	0.9	1.2	1.3	1.6	2.0	2.1
Inflation rate (CPI)	5.6	1.5	1.9	1.5	1.1	1.3	1.5	1.8	2.2	2.3
Unemployment rate	10.3	11.3	11.3	10.8	10.1	9.6	8.9	8.3	7.6	7.4
Employment (% change)	-1.8	-0.8	1.3	3.0	3.1	2.6	2.6	2.4	2.3	1.8
Participation rate	66.3	65.5	65.4	65.9	66.5	66.8	67.2	67.4	67.6	67.8
Finance Company 90-day paper rate	8.9	6.6	5.1	4.6	4.7	4.5	4.6	5.3	5.8	5.8
Finance Company 90-day paper rate (real)	6.4	5.4	4.2	3.6	3.8	3.3	3.3	3.7	3.8	3.7
Industrial bond rate	10.8	9.9	8.9	8.1	8.1	7.8	7.6	7.8	8.3	8.2
Industrial bond rate (real)	8.3	8.8	8.1	7.0	7.2	6.6	6.3	6.2	6.2	6.1
Annual wage per employee – private (% change)	2.5	2.4	1.7	1.8	2.4	3.1	3.0	3.6	4.0	4.6
Real annual wage per employee – private (% change)	-3.0	0.9	-0.1	0.3	1.3	1.8	1.5	1.7	1.8	2.3

Labour productivity – private (% change)	0.5	1.8	1.5	1.5	2.0	2.4	1.9	2.0	1.8	2.2
Real capital stock (% change)	4.0	3.4	2.6	2.9	3.3	3.9	4.4	4.8	5.1	5.3
Exchange rate (U.S.$/Cdn$)	0.873	0.827	0.777	0.768	0.778	0.788	0.797	0.805	0.813	0.820
Terms of trade (% change)	-1.1	-0.8	0.1	-0.1	0.0	0.0	0.0	0.0	0.0	0.0
Balance on current account ($ bill)	-29.0	-27.7	-26.0	-21.9	-18.5	-14.8	-11.4	-9.8	-7.9	-6.3
Cumulative current account as % of GDP	21.6	25.5	28.3	30.0	30.9	31.1	30.8	30.2	29.4	28.4
Balance on long-term capital ($ bill)	18.4	10.3	31.6	14.3	17.4	16.5	15.4	14.1	12.7	11.7
Total government balance (National accounts basis) ($ bill)	-42.4	-45.8	-51.2	-42.1	-35.1	-26.3	-18.6	-11.3	-4.6	-0.3
Balance as % of GDP	-6.3	-6.6	-7.2	-5.6	-4.4	-3.1	-2.1	-1.2	-0.5	0.0
Debt as % of GDP	47.0	52.5	57.8	61.0	62.4	62.5	61.6	59.7	57.1	54.0
Federal balance (National accounts basis) ($ bill)	-30.7	-26.4	-29.9	-24.7	-21.5	-16.5	-12.5	-9.4	-7.4	-4.3
Federal balance as % of GDP	-4.5	-3.8	-4.2	-3.3	-2.7	-2.0	-1.4	-1.0	-0.7	-0.4
Federal debt as % of GDP	45.1	48.2	50.7	51.8	51.8	51.1	50.0	48.4	46.5	44.4
Provincial balance (National accounts basis) ($ bill)	-14.6	-20.7	-21.5	-17.6	-13.8	-10.1	-7.1	-3.6	0.5	1.0
Personal savings rate (%)	10.1	10.6	11.0	10.5	10.3	10.2	10.1	10.0	10.0	10.0
Real personal disposable income (% change)	-2.7	0.8	1.2	1.4	3.4	3.0	3.0	3.2	3.2	3.4
Nominal after-tax corporate profits (% change)	-45.1	-10.9	55.6	50.7	25.3	17.2	11.5	9.2	7.8	6.5
Estimated potential growth	3.0	3.0	3.0	3.1	3.2	3.2	3.3	3.3	3.3	3.3
Cumulative potential GDP gap	-7.8	-10.1	-10.6	-9.5	-7.8	-6.3	-5.3	-4.5	-3.9	-3.4

TABLE 3 (continued)
Canada Base Projection, September 1993: Summary of Projection

	2001	2002	2003	2004	2005	2006	2007	2008
Real gross domestic product (% change)	3.5	3.2	3.2	2.9	2.7	2.6	2.4	2.2
Expenditure on personal consumption	3.4	2.9	3.2	3.1	2.8	2.6	2.5	2.4
Expenditure by governments	2.1	2.2	2.2	2.3	2.2	2.6	2.4	2.2
Investment expenditure	4.4	4.6	3.2	2.9	2.5	2.0	1.9	1.6
Residential construction	3.0	2.5	2.3	1.9	1.8	1.8	1.7	1.6
Non-residential construction	3.6	3.9	2.6	2.4	1.9	1.5	1.4	1.2
Machinery and equipment	5.4	5.8	3.9	3.5	2.9	2.2	2.1	1.7
Exports	4.3	3.7	3.7	3.3	3.2	2.8	2.7	2.5
Imports	4.0	3.7	3.2	3.2	3.0	2.5	2.4	2.4
Implicit deflator for GDP (% change)	2.3	2.5	2.6	2.8	2.9	3.0	3.0	3.1
Inflation rate (CPI)	2.5	2.7	2.7	3.0	3.1	3.2	3.2	3.3
Unemployment rate	7.3	7.2	7.2	7.1	7.0	7.0	7.0	7.0
Employment (% change)	1.5	1.3	1.2	1.0	1.0	0.8	0.7	0.7
Participation rate	67.9	67.9	67.9	67.7	67.5	67.3	67.1	66.9
Finance Company 90-day paper rate	5.8	5.9	5.9	5.8	5.8	5.9	5.8	5.8
Finance Company 90-day paper rate (real)	3.5	3.4	3.3	3.0	2.9	2.9	2.8	2.7
Industrial bond rate	8.3	8.4	8.4	8.5	8.5	8.6	8.6	8.6
Industrial bond rate (real)	6.0	5.9	5.8	5.7	5.7	5.6	5.5	5.5
Annual wage per employee – private (% change)	5.0	5.2	5.3	5.3	5.1	5.2	5.2	5.1
Real annual wage per employee – private (% change)	2.4	2.4	2.5	2.2	2.0	2.0	1.9	1.7

Labour productivity – private (% change)	2.2	2.1	2.3	2.1	1.9	1.9	1.9	1.7
Real capital stock (% change)	5.3	5.1	5.0	4.6	4.3	4.0	3.7	3.4
Exchange rate (U.S.$/Cdn$)	0.827	0.832	0.838	0.842	0.847	0.851	0.855	0.858
Terms of trade (% change)	0.0	0.0	0.0	0.0	0.0	0.0	0.0	0.0
Balance on current account ($ bill)	-3.8	-2.2	1.6	4.7	8.8	13.8	18.7	23.6
Cumulative current account as % of GDP	27.2	26.0	24.6	22.9	21.2	19.2	17.2	15.0
Balance on long-term capital ($ bill)	11.5	9.3	6.5	5.1	2.0	-0.6	-3.0	-5.1
Total government balance (National accounts basis) ($ bill)	2.6	6.3	8.4	9.0	10.0	10.8	11.8	12.7
Balance as % of GDP	0.2	0.5	0.7	0.7	0.7	0.7	0.8	0.8
Debt as % of GDP	50.9	47.7	44.4	41.3	38.4	35.6	33.0	30.6
Federal balance (National accounts basis) ($ bill)	-2.1	0.9	2.3	2.4	2.4	2.4	2.5	2.5
Federal balance as % of GDP	-0.2	0.1	0.2	0.2	0.2	0.2	0.2	0.2
Federal debt as % of GDP	42.2	39.9	37.5	35.3	33.2	31.3	29.5	27.8
Provincial balance (National accounts basis) ($ bill)	1.0	1.0	1.0	1.0	1.1	1.0	1.0	1.0
Personal savings rate (%)	10.0	10.0	10.0	10.0	10.0	10.0	10.0	10.0
Real personal disposable income (% change)	3.2	2.8	3.1	2.9	2.7	2.5	2.4	2.2
Nominal after-tax corporate profits (% change)	6.1	4.5	6.8	8.0	7.9	8.5	7.7	6.9
Estimated potential growth	3.2	3.0	3.1	2.8	2.7	2.5	2.4	2.3
Cumulative potential GDP gap	-3.1	-2.9	-2.8	-2.6	-2.5	-2.5	-2.4	-2.4

FIGURE 2
Potential Output Gaps

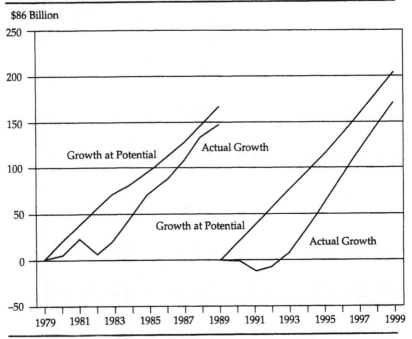

The overall pattern of the components of GDP is relatively simple. Through the 1990s it is primarily large increases in net exports and in non-residential investment spending – the latter fuelled by free trade, tax reform, and major projects – that propel growth in aggregate demand. Investment as a share of GDP reaches heights not achieved – let alone sustained – since at least the early 1960s. In 1994 and 1995 there is also a significant contribution by a recovery in residential housing. The share of consumption falls away in turn while those of imports and exports continue their long historical rise – in the present case pushed along by free trade. As the Canadian dollar has ceased to be overvalued, the share of real exports once again begins to surpass that of real imports. After the turn of the century the investment boom levels off and consumption out of the new potential created becomes a more important component of GDP growth. Net exports now make an increasingly more positive contribution to growth as Canada pays the higher capital-service charges left over from the overvaluation pe-

FIGURE 3
Expenditure Shares of GDP

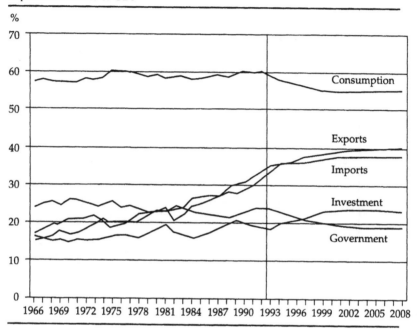

riod and the investment boom and as less and less foreign capital either for government deficits or for private-sector development is required. The expenditure share of government also stops falling at the projection horizon, with reduced expenditure constraints and increased social requirements. Growth in consumption is well below that of GDP through the late 1990s, after being the engine of growth for the economy in 1985–1988. Each of these years saw a major reduction in the personal saving rate but no further significant declines are projected. Instead, during much of the 1990s the share of consumption decreases owing to a fall in the share of real disposable income. Real disposable incomes fall because the output gap resulting from the recession depresses real wage growth, and because of increased taxes – including increases in personal income taxation (due to incomplete indexation and to increases in provincial income tax rates), increased gas taxes, and the steady rise in pension-plan premiums.

After the 1990s, however, growth in personal income is boosted

TABLE 4
Canada Base Projection, September 1993
GDP: Expenditure and Income Shares (share)

	1991	1992	1993	1994	1995	1996	1997	1998	1999	2000
Expenditure shares										
Consumption	0.597	0.599	0.592	0.581	0.575	0.567	0.561	0.557	0.553	0.552
Residential construction	0.055	0.059	0.055	0.058	0.059	0.060	0.060	0.060	0.060	0.060
Non-residential construction	0.054	0.046	0.042	0.042	0.042	0.043	0.043	0.043	0.044	0.045
Machinery and equipment	0.085	0.085	0.090	0.095	0.100	0.106	0.112	0.118	0.124	0.128
Government	0.239	0.239	0.236	0.228	0.221	0.215	0.210	0.206	0.202	0.198
Exports	0.299	0.320	0.338	0.353	0.361	0.368	0.375	0.380	0.384	0.388
Imports	0.324	0.338	0.351	0.357	0.358	0.360	0.362	0.367	0.370	0.373
Income shares										
Wages and salaries	0.564	0.570	0.566	0.558	0.554	0.551	0.549	0.548	0.548	0.548
Interest and miscellaneous investment	0.084	0.082	0.076	0.075	0.074	0.073	0.072	0.072	0.071	0.071
Corporate profits	0.049	0.046	0.055	0.066	0.073	0.079	0.083	0.085	0.086	0.086
Inventory valuation adjustment	0.004	−0.005	−0.004	−0.003	−0.003	−0.003	−0.003	−0.003	−0.003	−0.002
Non-farm unincorporated	0.054	0.054	0.054	0.054	0.054	0.054	0.054	0.054	0.054	0.054
Farm unincorporated	0.005	0.005	0.006	0.006	0.006	0.006	0.006	0.006	0.005	0.005
Indirect taxes	0.140	0.143	0.142	0.142	0.140	0.139	0.138	0.137	0.137	0.137
Subsidies	−0.020	−0.020	−0.017	−0.017	−0.017	−0.016	−0.016	−0.015	−0.015	−0.015
Capital consumption allowance	0.118	0.120	0.119	0.117	0.116	0.116	0.116	0.116	0.116	0.117
Statistical discrepancy	0.004	0.004	0.003	0.003	0.002	0.001	0.001	0.000	0.000	0.000
Personal income	0.897	0.903	0.892	0.879	0.874	0.867	0.862	0.861	0.860	0.857
Personal disposable income	0.689	0.693	0.690	0.675	0.667	0.658	0.651	0.646	0.643	0.642

Wages and salaries	0.564	0.570	0.566	0.558	0.554	0.551	0.549	0.548	0.548	0.548
Farm income	0.004	0.006	0.006	0.006	0.006	0.006	0.006	0.006	0.005	0.005
Unincorporated income	0.054	0.054	0.054	0.054	0.054	0.054	0.054	0.054	0.054	0.054
Interest income	0.127	0.115	0.106	0.102	0.104	0.103	0.103	0.104	0.106	0.105
Transfers from government	0.145	0.155	0.158	0.156	0.153	0.150	0.148	0.147	0.145	0.143
Other income	0.004	0.003	0.003	0.003	0.003	0.003	0.003	0.003	0.002	0.002
Direct taxes	0.208	0.210	0.202	0.204	0.207	0.209	0.211	0.215	0.217	0.215

TABLE 4 (*continued*)
Canada Base Projection, September 1993
GDP: Expenditure and Income Shares (share)

	2001	2002	2003	2004	2005	2006	2007	2008
Expenditure Shares								
Consumption	0.552	0.550	0.550	0.551	0.551	0.552	0.552	0.553
Residential construction	0.059	0.059	0.058	0.058	0.057	0.057	0.056	0.056
Non-residential construction	0.045	0.045	0.045	0.044	0.044	0.044	0.043	0.043
Machinery and equipment	0.131	0.134	0.135	0.136	0.136	0.135	0.135	0.134
Government	0.196	0.194	0.192	0.191	0.190	0.190	0.190	0.190
Exports	0.391	0.393	0.395	0.396	0.398	0.399	0.400	0.401
Imports	0.375	0.377	0.377	0.378	0.379	0.378	0.379	0.379
Income shares								
Wages and salaries	0.548	0.550	0.551	0.551	0.551	0.551	0.552	0.553
Interest and miscellaneous investment	0.070	0.069	0.068	0.067	0.066	0.065	0.064	0.063
Corporate profits	0.086	0.085	0.085	0.086	0.087	0.088	0.088	0.089
Inventory valuation adjustment	−0.002	−0.002	−0.002	−0.002	−0.002	−0.002	−0.002	−0.002
Non-farm unincorporated	0.054	0.054	0.054	0.054	0.054	0.054	0.054	0.054
Farm unincorporated	0.005	0.005	0.005	0.005	0.005	0.004	0.004	0.004
Indirect taxes	0.136	0.136	0.135	0.135	0.135	0.135	0.134	0.134
Subsidies	−0.014	−0.014	−0.014	−0.013	−0.013	−0.012	−0.012	−0.012
Capital consumption allowance	0.117	0.118	0.118	0.118	0.118	0.118	0.118	0.117
Statistical discrepancy	0.000	0.000	0.000	0.000	0.000	0.000	0.000	0.000
Personal income	0.855	0.853	0.851	0.849	0.848	0.847	0.848	0.848
Personal disposable income	0.642	0.641	0.641	0.642	0.643	0.644	0.645	0.646

Wages and salaries	0.548	0.550	0.551	0.551	0.551	0.551	0.552	0.553
Farm income	0.005	0.005	0.005	0.005	0.005	0.004	0.004	0.004
Unincorporated income	0.054	0.054	0.054	0.054	0.054	0.054	0.054	0.054
Interest income	0.102	0.100	0.098	0.096	0.095	0.094	0.093	0.092
Transfers from government	0.143	0.142	0.142	0.142	0.142	0.142	0.143	0.143
Other income	0.002	0.002	0.002	0.002	0.002	0.002	0.002	0.002
Direct taxes	0.213	0.213	0.210	0.207	0.205	0.204	0.203	0.202

FIGURE 4
Federal Expenditure Items (as % of GDP)

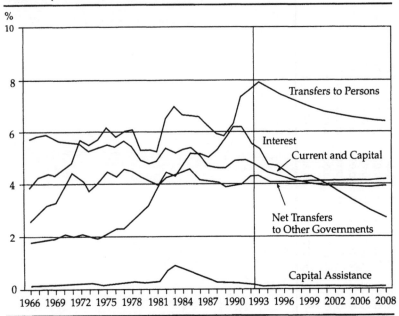

by increased productivity and real wage gains, and consumption growth gradually comes to equal the growth of GDP. The result of this growth pattern is a fall in the GDP share of consumption in the 1990s, bottoming out after the turn of the century at a historically low level.

The Government Sector: Deficits and Debt

I now turn to a more detailed examination of the projection for the government sector at the national level, beginning with the federal government.

The Federal Government

Figures 4 through 7 and Table 5 show detailed expenditure, revenue, deficit, and debt projections for the federal government. As noted in the discussion of fiscal assumptions above, federal

FIGURE 5
Federal Revenue Items (as % of GDP)

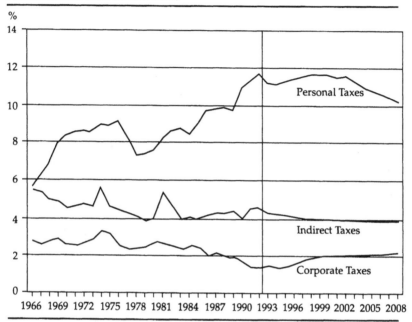

spending on real current and capital goods is held well below GDP growth until near the end of the projection. Naturally, this causes the ratio of such spending to GDP to fall, but as can be seen in Figure 4, the decline in this spending category's share of GDP is not greater than that seen on average in past decades. Transfers to persons (including and especially UI payments) fall from their recession peak just as they did after the 1981–82 recession; indeed, it might be argued that the rate of decline should be even steeper.[7] Transfers to provinces have already fallen as a share of GDP from their mid-1980s peak; I assume the share holds steady until after the mid-1990s, when funding pressures at lower levels of government combined with increasing fiscal good health at the federal level should lead to irresistible arguments for increasing transfers. Finally, interest on the federal debt declines steadily as a share of GDP, as the debt comes to be more and more financed at lower interest rates, and as the ratio of debt to GDP begins to fall.

Figure 5 shows the major federal revenue categories as shares

FIGURE 6
Federal Deficit (as % of GDP)

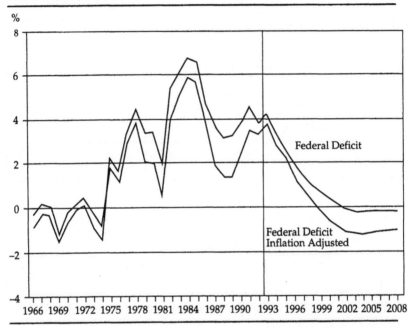

of GDP. The personal-tax share continues to climb through the mid-1990s, peaking in 1996, then remaining relatively steady for a decade – in part because gradual reductions in the surtax rate offset the upward push of less-than-full indexation, and also because personal income itself is weak relative to GDP over the period. Elimination of the deficit problem permits several reductions in the Personal Income Tax (PIT) share thereafter. Federal indirect taxes fall slightly as a share of GDP through the projection largely because the indirect-tax base share falls. This is because growth in the projection is led by investment and exports, neither of which is subject to federal indirect taxes since the elimination of the MST. Finally, the share of corporate tax revenue is projected to return to the levels seen in the late 1980s.

The projection for the federal deficit is shown in Figure 6. The federal deficit relative to GDP continues its downward movement in 1994 after a small surge in 1993. It is presumed that a small surplus becomes the target after the turn of the century. When

FIGURE 7
Federal Debt (as % of GDP)

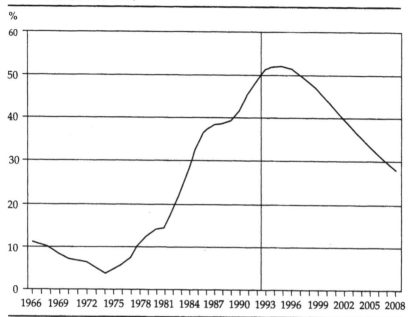

inflation adjustment is taken into account the federal deficit is actually "eliminated" by the mid-1990s.

Figure 7 shows past and projected ratios of the federal debt to GDP, where the debt is defined as the accumulation of national income accounts (NIA) deficits. The federal debt/GDP ratio does finally peak in 1995. This measure then diminishes significantly under the assumed settings for expenditure and taxation. At the projection horizon of 2008 it is back to a level comparable to that of the early 1980s.

The Provincial Government Sector

Figures 8 through 11 and Table 6 show detailed expenditure, revenue, deficit, and debt projections for the provincial governments in aggregate. The fiscal fate of the provinces is intimately connected with that of the municipalities and the hospital sector, and therefore current and capital spending at the local and hospital level is com-

TABLE 5
Canada Base Projection, September 1993: Federal Government Revenues and Expenditures (millions of dollars)[a]

	1991	1992	1993	1994	1995	1996	1997	1998	1999	2000
Revenues										
Indirect taxes	30605	31452	30855	31927	33247	34576	36126	37919	39913	42108
	(15.29)	(2.77)	(−1.90)	(3.47)	(4.14)	(4.00)	(4.48)	(4.96)	(5.26)	(5.50)
Direct taxes: corporate and government business enterprises	9889	9749	10548	10261	11384	13524	15699	17733	19560	21286
	(−15.13)	(−1.42)	(8.19)	(−2.72)	(10.95)	(18.80)	(16.08)	(12.96)	(10.30)	(8.82)
Direct taxes and transfers from persons	76379	80403	79626	83547	89648	95898	101875	108878	115857	122691
	(4.17)	(5.27)	(−0.97)	(4.92)	(7.30)	(6.97)	(6.23)	(6.87)	(6.41)	(5.90)
Direct taxes on non-residents	1506	1568	1562	1679	1788	1905	2028	2160	2301	2450
Investment income	12675	12844	12680	13187	13715	14263	14834	15427	16044	16686
Net transfers from (+), to (−) other governments	−27506	−29436	−30837	−31000	−32550	−34340	−36401	−38585	−40900	−43354
	(3.09)	(7.02)	(4.76)	(0.53)	(5.00)	(5.50)	(6.00)	(6.00)	(6.00)	(6.00)
Expenditures										
Current expenditures on goods and services	30966	31183	30850	30931	31753	32796	34078	35592	37326	39119
	(1.53)	(0.70)	(−1.07)	(0.26)	(2.66)	(3.28)	(3.91)	(4.44)	(4.87)	(4.80)
Gross capital formation	2172	2379	2436	2495	2577	2664	2741	2832	2937	3045
	(−4.40)	(9.53)	(2.40)	(2.43)	(3.27)	(3.39)	(2.89)	(3.31)	(3.74)	(3.67)
Transfers to persons	49816	52778	56267	58070	59981	62129	64442	66843	69472	72203
	(17.67)	(5.95)	(6.61)	(3.20)	(3.29)	(3.58)	(3.72)	(3.73)	(3.93)	(3.93)
Subsidies	7003	5617	5027	5250	5408	5570	5737	5966	6205	6453
	(45.68)	(−19.79)	(−10.51)	(4.45)	(3.00)	(3.00)	(3.00)	(4.00)	(4.00)	(4.00)
Capital assistance	1418	1152	887	905	923	941	960	979	1009	1039
Transfers to non-residents	2589	2587	2345	2495	2577	2653	2734	2820	2916	3024

Interest on the public debt	41885 (0.82)	38944 (−7.02)	38278 (−1.71)	36012 (−5.92)	37457 (4.01)	37643 (0.50)	38168 (1.39)	40214 (5.36)	42779 (6.38)	43864 (2.53)
Capital consumption allowances	1564	1657	1724	1829	1943	2061	2183	2307	2436	2570
Surplus (+) or deficit (−)	−30737 (−5325)	−26403 (4334)	−29933 (−3530)	−24728 (5205)	−21500 (3227)	−16507 (4993)	−12516 (3991)	−9407 (3110)	−7433 (1974)	−4310 (3123)

[a]% changes (or levels changes) in parentheses

TABLE 5 (continued)
Canada Base Projection, September 1993: Federal Government Revenues and Expenditures (millions of dollars)[a]

	2001	2002	2003	2004	2005	2006	2007	2008
Revenues								
Indirect taxes	44410	46779	49356	52094	54890	58111	61173	64706
	(5.47)	(5.33)	(5.51)	(5.55)	(5.37)	(5.87)	(5.27)	(5.78)
Direct taxes: corporate and government								
business enterprises	22869	24350	25987	27630	29393	31356	33340	35331
	(7.44)	(6.48)	(6.72)	(6.32)	(6.38)	(6.68)	(6.33)	(5.97)
Direct taxes and transfers from persons	128840	136370	142098	146791	151758	157165	163043	168675
	(5.01)	(5.84)	(4.20)	(3.30)	(3.38)	(3.56)	(3.74)	(3.45)
Direct taxes on non-residents	2609	2779	2960	3152	3357	3575	3807	4055
Investment income	17270	17874	18500	19147	19817	20511	21229	21972
Net transfers from (+) to (−) other	−45955	−48712	−51635	−54733	−58017	−61498	−65188	−69099
governments	(6.00)	(6.00)	(6.00)	(6.00)	(6.00)	(6.00)	(6.00)	(6.00)
Expenditures								
Current expenditures on goods and services	41066	43266	45597	48138	50814	53852	57012	60247
	(4.98)	(5.36)	(5.39)	(5.57)	(5.56)	(5.98)	(5.87)	(5.67)
Gross capital formation	3162	3296	3432	3578	3728	3932	4142	4355
	(3.84)	(4.22)	(4.15)	(4.23)	(4.22)	(5.45)	(5.34)	(5.15)
Transfers to persons	75568	79093	82784	86813	91040	95472	100121	104997
	(4.66)	(4.66)	(4.67)	(4.87)	(4.87)	(4.87)	(4.87)	(4.87)
Subsidies	6711	6913	7120	7334	7554	7780	8014	8134
	(4.00)	(3.00)	(3.00)	(3.00)	(3.00)	(3.00)	(3.00)	(1.50)
Capital assistance	1070	1102	1135	1169	1204	1241	1278	1316
Transfers to non-residents	3138	3261	3393	3531	3681	3839	4006	4182

Interest on the public debt	44085	44449	44483	44315	44116	44140	44007	43729
	(0.50)	(0.83)	(0.08)	(−0.38)	(−0.45)	(0.06)	(−0.30)	(−0.63)
Capital consumption allowances	2708	2851	2999	3154	3314	3482	3658	3843
Surplus (+) or deficit (−)	−2051	910	2321	2358	2376	2446	2483	2522
	(2260)	(2961)	(1411)	(37)	(17)	(70)	(38)	(39)

[a]% changes (or levels changes) in parentheses

FIGURE 8
Provincial Expenditure Items (as % of GDP)

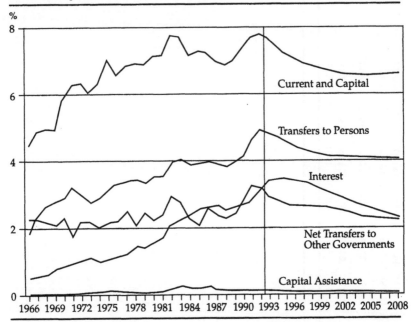

pared with provincial and federal current and capital spending in Figure 12, while Figure 13 shows local government taxes (largely property taxes) in relation to federal and provincial income taxes (and CPP/QPP contributions).

On the provincial expenditure side, current and capital spending by provinces rose by over 3 per cent of GDP from the mid-1960s through 1980. Thereafter this form of spending kept pace with GDP until GDP began to fall in the 1990–92 recession. Since current and capital spending has fallen relatively little, its GDP share again rose and is back to the heights of the 1981–82 recession. I assume significant medium-term current and capital spending restraint; this, coupled with the recovery of real GDP growth, will gradually push the share of provincial current and capital spending to GDP back to its pre-recession levels. Note, however, that even this assumption on average allows for some real per capita current-spending growth.

Provincial transfers to persons decline only slowly from their recession peak; again, I am assuming some permanent ratcheting up in this category such as occurred after the 1981–82 recession. Trans-

FIGURE 9
Provincial Revenue Items (as % of GDP)

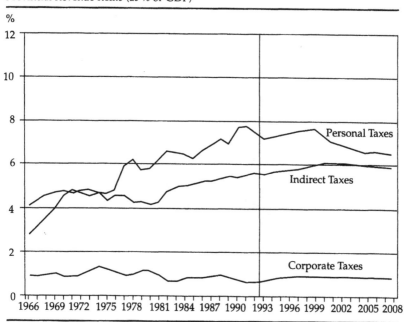

fers to local governments and hospitals decline as a share of GDP as GDP recovers and as real expenditure restraints take effect. As can be seen from Figure 12, local government current spending is assumed to be restrained in line with provincial spending, reducing its share of GDP as the recovery proceeds. On the other hand, I have assumed that hospital spending will be more difficult to restrain and that there will be no major reduction from current levels of hospital spending to GDP.

Finally, interest on the debt rises as a share of GDP well into the 1990s, reflecting the continued accumulation of provincial debt. However, the run-up in debt payments is not as severe as it was for the federal government in the 1980s, because the deficits are brought under control earlier and nominal interest rates are not nearly as high.

Provincial revenues (Figure 9) show some recovery of the PIT base lost in the 1990–92 recession, while indirect taxes are increased through gasoline or other green taxes. Corporate taxes remain a

FIGURE 10
Total Provincial Deficits (as % of GDP)

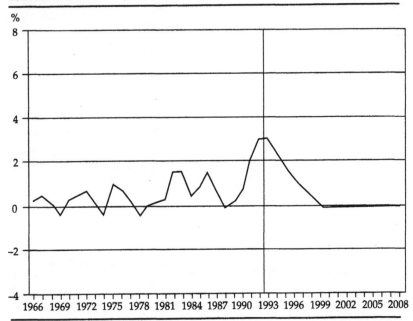

very small part of provincial government revenues but do recover in relation to GDP at the same time that corporate profits do.

Finally, local taxes must figure in the provincial calculations, as the provinces are ultimately responsible for local governments' fiscal health. As can be seen in Figure 13, I have assumed that the recent recession has pushed local taxes as a share of GDP as high or higher than can be sustained and that over the recovery period local taxes will rise much more slowly than GDP, pushing their GDP share back to prerecession levels and below.

These revenues estimates and assumptions, combined with economic recovery, yield the deficit path of Figure 10. As can be seen, when measured in relation to GDP, the provincial deficit problem in the 1990-92 recession is about twice as bad as that which emerged in the 1981-82 recession. With some major ups and downs, that earlier deficit situation was eliminated in about six years – only to be struck by the recent recession. The recovery period for the current episode lasts through the year 2000, and, thereafter, pro-

FIGURE 11
Provincial Debt (Estimated) (as % of GDP)

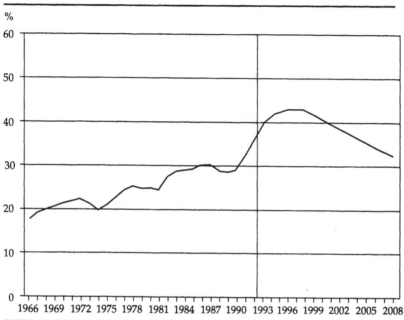

vincial deficits are assumed to be kept roughly at zero. The resulting debt/GDP ratio for the provinces is shown in Figure 11: the National Income Accounts (NIA) debt/GDP ratio rises another 15 per cent to 20 per cent from current levels before finally levelling off in the later 1990s and declining slowly thereafter.

The Government Sector Combined

I conclude this section by examining the deficit and debt situation of the consolidated government sector, which includes the Canada and Quebec pension plans as well as the three levels of government and hospitals. I have assumed that the municipal and hospital sectors will continue to run small NIA surpluses into the future, as they have through much of the past. In the model the provincial governments, through their transfers to these levels of government, are ultimately responsible for attaining this fiscal objective. But, as noted above, I have also assumed real expenditure restraint at both

TABLE 6
Canada Base Projection, September 1993: Provincial Government Revenues and Expenditures (millions of dollars)[a]

	1991	1992	1993	1994	1995	1996	1997	1998	1999	2000
Revenues										
Indirect taxes	37655	39031	40008	42679	45468	48664	51987	55705	59820	64211
	(2.20)	(3.65)	(2.50)	(6.68)	(6.53)	(7.03)	(6.83)	(7.15)	(7.39)	(7.34)
Direct taxes: corporate and government business enterprises	4459	4467	5110	6083	6868	7648	8320	8919	9466	9999
	(−14.12)	(0.18)	(14.39)	(19.04)	(12.91)	(11.36)	(8.79)	(7.20)	(6.13)	(5.64)
Direct taxes and transfers from persons	52667	52080	51657	55021	58920	63158	67083	71696	76882	78146
	(2.13)	(−1.17)	(−0.81)	(6.51)	(7.09)	(7.19)	(6.22)	(6.88)	(7.23)	(1.65)
Investment income	18141	18711	19513	20338	21202	22107	23054	24344	25709	26942
	(−0.09)	(3.14)	(4.29)	(4.23)	(4.25)	(4.27)	(4.29)	(5.59)	(5.61)	(4.79)
Net transfers from (+), to (−) other governments	−21800	−21852	−20875	−21120	−21451	−22360	−23469	−24751	−26098	−27327
	(16.23)	(0.24)	(−4.47)	(1.17)	(1.57)	(4.23)	(4.96)	(5.47)	(5.44)	(4.71)
Expenditures										
Current expenditures on goods and services	46961	48846	49823	50579	52027	53894	56167	58719	61580	64475
	(6.16)	(4.01)	(2.00)	(1.52)	(2.86)	(3.59)	(4.22)	(4.54)	(4.87)	(4.70)
Gross capital formation	5040	4648	4863	4986	5144	5318	5483	5670	5888	6110
	(1.41)	(−7.78)	(4.63)	(2.53)	(3.17)	(3.39)	(3.09)	(3.41)	(3.84)	(3.27)
Transfers to persons	31119	33770	34356	35204	36260	37348	38468	40103	41807	43584
	(12.09)	(8.52)	(1.74)	(2.47)	(3.00)	(3.00)	(3.00)	(4.25)	(4.25)	(4.25)
Subsidies	5623	6908	6431	6652	6852	7057	7269	7487	7711	7943
	(5.66)	(22.85)	(−6.90)	(3.43)	(3.00)	(3.00)	(3.00)	(3.00)	(3.00)	(3.00)
Capital assistance	834	698	697	711	725	739	754	769	792	816
Interest on the public debt	19366	21560	24106	25921	27359	28587	29632	30562	31331	31988
	(7.37)	(11.33)	(11.81)	(7.53)	(5.55)	(4.49)	(3.66)	(3.14)	(2.51)	(2.10)

Capital consumption allowances	3180	3316	3393	3452	3520	3595	3677	3766	3863	3970
Surplus (+) or deficit (−)	−14611	−20677	−21471	−17599	−13840	−10132	−7120	−3631	533	1025
	(−9604)	(−6066)	(−794)	(3872)	(3759)	(3708)	(3012)	(3489)	(4165)	(492)

a% changes (or levels changes) in parentheses

TABLE 6 (continued)
Canada Base Projection, September 1993: Provincial Government Revenues and Expenditures (millions of dollars)[a]

	2001	2002	2003	2004	2005	2006	2007	2008
Revenues								
Indirect taxes	68035 (5.95)	71733 (5.44)	75657 (5.47)	79796 (5.47)	83973 (5.23)	88280 (5.13)	92749 (5.06)	97345 (4.96)
Direct taxes: corporate and government business enterprises	10531 (5.31)	10994 (4.40)	11582 (5.35)	12238 (5.67)	12901 (5.42)	13607 (5.47)	14269 (4.86)	14878 (4.26)
Direct taxes and transfers from persons	80309 (2.77)	83353 (3.79)	86220 (3.44)	89611 (3.93)	93284 (4.10)	97971 (5.02)	102939 (5.07)	107991 (4.91)
Investment income	27912 (3.60)	28918 (3.60)	29960 (3.60)	31040 (3.60)	32159 (3.60)	33318 (3.60)	34519 (3.61)	35764 (3.61)
Net transfers from (+), to (−) other governments	−28090 (2.79)	−28931 (3.00)	−29648 (2.48)	−30692 (3.52)	−31834 (3.72)	−33431 (5.02)	−35055 (4.86)	−36548 (4.26)
Expenditures								
Current expenditures on goods and services	67750 (5.08)	71450 (5.46)	75372 (5.49)	79650 (5.68)	83997 (5.46)	89018 (5.98)	94242 (5.87)	99589 (5.67)
Gross capital formation	6351 (3.95)	6625 (4.32)	6914 (4.35)	7234 (4.64)	7569 (4.63)	7982 (5.45)	8409 (5.34)	8842 (5.15)
Transfers to persons	45981 (5.50)	48510 (5.50)	51178 (5.50)	53993 (5.50)	56963 (5.50)	60096 (5.50)	63401 (5.50)	66888 (5.50)
Subsidies	8141 (2.50)	8345 (2.50)	8554 (2.50)	8767 (2.50)	8987 (2.50)	9211 (2.50)	9441 (2.50)	9678 (2.50)
Capital assistance	840	866	892	918	946	974	1003	1034
Interest on the public debt	32703 (2.23)	33466 (2.33)	34184 (2.14)	34887 (2.06)	35633 (2.14)	36319 (1.93)	36982 (1.82)	37682 (1.89)

Capital consumption allowances	4085	4212	4349	4499	4662	4841	5038	5252
Surplus (+) or deficit (−)	1015	1016	1028	1042	1052	986	980	968
	(−10)	(1)	(12)	(14)	(10)	(−66)	(−6)	(−12)

a% changes (or levels changes) in parentheses

FIGURE 12
Current and Capital Spending by Level of Government (as % of GDP)

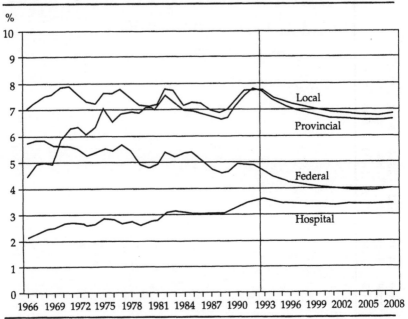

these levels of government, so that provincial transfers, as a share of GDP, can gradually return to late-1980s levels by the projection horizon (see Figure 8).

As noted under my fiscal assumptions, the Canada and Quebec pension plans will require an increase in their contribution rates beginning soon if they are to continue to build up their surpluses to meet the pension requirements of retiring baby boomers (after 2010). Figure 13 shows federal and provincial personal taxes together with the pension plan contributions. As can be seen, while it is possible for the federal and provincial governments to give tax room after the year 2000, the share of pension plan contributions in GDP can and must keep rising.[8]

Finally, Figure 14 plots both federal and total government debt /GDP ratios. Each debt is calculated on an accumulated National Incomes Account deficit basis. Because the local, hospital, and pension plan levels of government have typically run surpluses (often quite large ones in the case of the pension plans) the accumulated NIA debt of the non-federal government levels has been much

FIGURE 13
Government Revenue Items (as % of GDP)

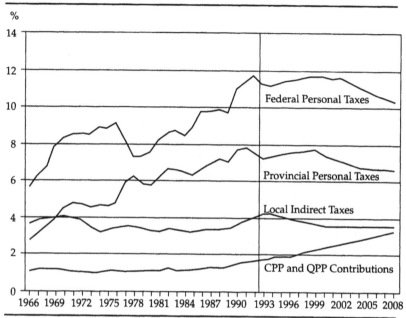

smaller than the NIA federal debt. Indeed, as can be seen during the early 1980s, the non-federal levels of government were in an overall net asset position (the sum of total government NIA debts was less than the federal). This position has unravelled in the face of recent provincial deficits and the disappearance of the pension plan surpluses. As can be seen in Figure 14, total government NIA debt is projected to peak at about 60 per cent of GDP in 1995 or 1996. On a public accounts basis, my rough estimate is that the debt/GDP ratio will peak at just under 95 per cent.[9]

The Ontario Economy through 2008

This section presents a projection of the Ontario economy through 2008 – again with special attention paid to fiscal issues. The projection is developed from the same three sets of ingredients as the national projection: a variety of assumptions about demographics; underlying productivity growth and fiscal policies; a macroeconometric model (the FOCUS–Ontario model) to translate the assump-

FIGURE 14
Government Debt (as % of GDP)

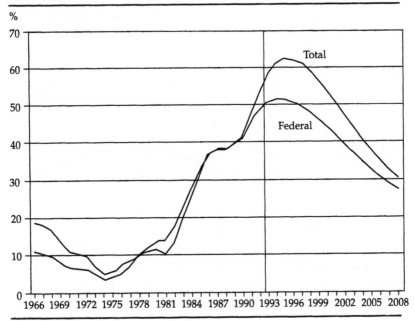

tions into a consistent and detailed numerical picture of the Ontario economy; and the author's own judgement to coordinate the two. The same cautions also apply, including the need to treat the projections not as precise forecasts, but rather as estimates indicating trends, especially in the later years.

A further caution is required regarding data sources: The provincial data, and especially the provincial fiscal data, are on the whole less precise and less timely than their national equivalents. The FOCUS–Ontario model is based on quarterly figures for provincial income and expenditure that are developed jointly by Statistics Canada and the Ontario Ministry of Finance. Over time, these data have been subject to considerable revision. The present projection was developed in September 1993 based on income and expenditure data through 1993:1. Moreover, these provincial accounts do not include detail on government expenditures, revenues, and surpluses/ deficits – unlike the quarterly national income accounts. The fiscal detail in the FOCUS–Ontario model comes from the annual provincial accounts developed by Statistics Canada, but these data are only available with a significant lag. In the present case, the last available data are for 1991, and therefore all the 1992 fiscal detail presented below and used as a starting point for the projection are estimates, rather than published data. I have coordinated my estimates as much as possible to the 1992 income and expenditure data available, and to the quarterly budgetary reports issued by the Ontario Ministry of Finance. Nonetheless, the reader must be aware that the 1992 fiscal detail from which the projection proceeds are themselves very soft. In my opinion, this is not a serious concern for medium- and long-term analysis; potential errors in the starting point will not much affect the medium- and long-term trends and lessons of the projection.

Assumptions Underlying the Ontario Projection

Naturally, many of the assumptions underlying the national projection are also critical to the projection for Ontario. These include assumptions about foreign economies, federal fiscal policy, monetary, and exchange-rate policy. Assumptions specific to Ontario include those for demographics, for fiscal policy below the federal level, and for supply and productivity conditions within the province.

Population

As for Canada as a whole, the population projection for Ontario (see Table 8) is based on work by Statistics Canada. The projection has also been updated for current population data and for recent increases in immigration. My assumption is that roughly half of all new immigrants will settle in Ontario, and that there will be a modest amount of net interprovincial inmigration over the next 15 years. Despite this, Ontario population growth gradually slows as does the overall Canadian growth rate. From a population of just over 10 million in 1992, Ontario is projected to have just over 12 million inhabitants by 2008.

Provincial Fiscal Policy

In the Ontario model, just as in the national model, setting fiscal policy requires assumptions on a range of spending categories by level of government and on an array of tax rates.

Current and capital spending at all levels of government is assumed to grow only slightly in real per capita terms for the rest of the 1990s, and only slightly faster after that. Compared with the country as a whole, I assume that federal current and capital spending will grow in Ontario at the national rate, while provincial spending growth will be slightly (less than 0.5 per cent per year) below average provincial current spending growth due to greater deficit pressures and the already somewhat higher level of public services. Real spending at the municipal and hospital levels is assumed to grow at the national average through the year 2000 (which means at a slightly lower per capita rate than the rest of the country, since Ontario's population growth is projected to be higher). After the year 2000, provincial, local, and hospital current spending are assumed to grow at something above the national average, in line with Ontario's higher population growth rate.

In the area of transfers to persons my assumptions again follow those made at the national level. Ontario gets its share of federal transfers based on population and unemployment levels. At the provincial level, a significant ratcheting up of transfers to persons in the wake of the 1990–92 recession is assumed. If I have been overly cautious in estimating how much transfers can be cut down as the economy recovers, then the assumed increase in transfers could perhaps allow for a modest child-care initiative.

As in the national model, interest on the provincial debt is handled entirely in the model based on accumulated debt stocks and the interest rates determined in the national model.

Finally, transfers from the province to the local and hospital levels are set in the model as whatever is required to keep these two levels of government in a very modest surplus condition (as has historically been the case in the provincial accounts data). Expenditure restraint at each of these two levels of government permits transfers as a share of provincial GDP to fall back to prerecession levels by the end of the decade.

On the revenue side I first assume no significant change in corporate taxation for reasons of competitiveness – just as at the federal level and in the national projection. (See the summary of Ontario tax rates in Table 7.)

For personal income taxes I assume that there will be no major increases beyond the large hike in rates introduced in 1993. I do assume some small additions to the tax base (closing of loopholes) and to high-income surtaxes in 1994, and that these PIT rates are then sustained until the deficit problem is solved. I further assume that under improved auditing and enforcement, together with economic recovery, there will be some recovery of the PIT tax base that has apparently been lost or gone underground in the 1991–93 period. Once the deficit has been eliminated, I let the provincial PIT rate gradually decline so as to keep the modest budget surplus then attained from rising further.

For indirect taxes I assume no increase in the provincial sales tax rate. But as in the national projection I assume a gradual increase in gasoline taxes (which represents a range of possible carbon or green taxes). The current level of gasoline taxes (relative to consumer spending) is assumed to approximately double by the end of the decade – although, again, the tax increase may be diffused through a much broader range of fuels or pollutants.

Finally, at the local level, as in the national projection, property and other indirect taxes are assumed to increase by less than the growth of GDP, reducing their importance in relative terms.

Productivity

The growth in the Ontario economy from the supply side is made up of growth in its labour force and capital stock and growth in TFP. As noted above, population and labour-force growth in Ontario are assumed to be above the national average, tending to give Ontario a higher potential growth rate. Capital stock growth is determined within the model. But TFP growth must be assumed. For most years I assume that Ontario's TFP growth is the same as Canada's, but I have added an extra 0.25 per cent per year for the period from 1997 to 2000 to represent extra gains expected under the FTA, given that Ontario is more exposed to, and has more to gain from, the industrial restructuring and efficiency gains that the FTA is estimated to generate.

The Ontario Projection: An Overview

The Ontario projection is summarized in Table 8 and Figure 15. As for the national projection, the Ontario outlook appears optimistic; real growth averages well above 4 per cent through the year 2000, and the unemployment rate falls from just under 11 per cent to just under 7 per cent in the same span. With the country as a whole, Ontario enjoys a historically low inflation rate and a reasonably high rate of labour productivity.

The twin themes behind the growth projection are again potential

TABLE 7
Ontario Base Projection, September 1993: Principal Tax Rates and Related Fiscal Indicators

	1991	1992	1993	1994	1995	1996	1997	1998	1999	2000
Effective rate of corporate tax	0.412	0.410	0.403	0.396	0.396	0.396	0.396	0.396	0.396	0.396
Provincial corporate tax rate	0.150	0.150	0.150	0.150	0.150	0.150	0.150	0.150	0.150	0.150
Provincial PIT rate (% of basic federal rate)	0.530	0.549	0.587	0.592	0.600	0.600	0.600	0.600	0.600	0.600
"Other" provincial direct tax rate (on YP)*	0.010	0.012	0.011	0.011	0.011	0.011	0.012	0.012	0.012	0.012
Provincial sales tax rate	0.080	0.080	0.080	0.080	0.080	0.080	0.080	0.080	0.080	0.080
Gasoline tax rate (on CNDV)**	0.046	0.051	0.054	0.055	0.059	0.065	0.071	0.077	0.083	0.090
Other provincial indirect tax rate (on GDPV)	0.010	0.011	0.010	0.010	0.010	0.010	0.010	0.010	0.010	0.010

	2001	2002	2003	2004	2005	2006	2007	2008
Effective rate of corporate tax	0.396	0.396	0.396	0.396	0.396	0.396	0.396	0.396
Provincial corporate tax rate	0.150	0.150	0.150	0.150	0.150	0.150	0.150	0.150
Provincial PIT rate (% of basic federal rate)	0.600	0.600	0.587	0.578	0.570	0.569	0.568	0.565
"Other" provincial direct tax rate (on YP)*	0.012	0.012	0.012	0.012	0.012	0.012	0.012	0.012
Provincial sales tax rate	0.080	0.080	0.080	0.080	0.080	0.080	0.080	0.080
Gasoline tax rate (on CNDV)**	0.092	0.091	0.091	0.090	0.090	0.089	0.089	0.089
Other provincial indirect tax rate (on GDPV)	0.010	0.010	0.010	0.009	0.009	0.009	0.008	0.008

*tax as a rate on total personal income
**tax as a rate on non-durables consumption
***tax as a rate on nominal GDP

FIGURE 15
Ontario: Main Indicators

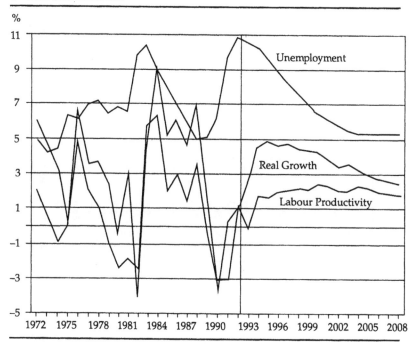

growth and recovery from the current output gap – except that in Ontario's case each item is larger.

First, the underlying potential growth of the Ontario economy is projected to be in the range of 3.3 to 3.6 per cent over the 1990s, in excess of the national potential growth rate by several tenths of a percentage point. This stronger potential growth is based on a somewhat higher population growth rate (largely the result of higher immigration) and on higher relative TFP gains to Ontario from the FTA.

Second, Ontario has a larger output gap to spring back from than the rest of the country. As can be seen in Figure 16, I estimate the Ontario output gap relative to potential in 1993 to be over 14 per cent of GDP. The process of closing the gap continues well beyond the year 2000, with over 5 per cent of the gap assumed never to be closed. This last assumption allows for the possibility that Ontario was well above potential in 1989 – in my opinion a very cautious estimate. In addition, allowing well over a decade for

TABLE 8
Ontario Base Projection, September 1993: Summary of Projection

	1991	1992	1993	1994	1995	1996	1997	1998	1999	2000
Real provincial product (% change)	-3.0	0.9	2.5	4.6	4.9	4.7	4.7	4.5	4.4	4.3
Real GDP, Canada (% change)	-1.7	0.7	2.6	4.2	4.8	4.7	4.3	4.1	3.9	3.8
Ontario/Canada (%)	39.2	39.3	39.3	39.4	39.4	39.4	39.6	39.8	40.0	40.2
Consumption	-2.2	0.9	1.1	2.2	3.1	2.9	3.1	3.5	3.5	3.3
Government	3.6	1.1	1.6	1.1	1.5	1.7	1.8	1.9	1.9	1.9
Private investment	-3.4	-0.4	0.1	9.4	9.3	9.6	8.2	8.5	7.8	6.6
Residential construction	-15.1	7.2	-5.3	10.9	7.7	6.5	5.4	4.8	4.3	3.9
Non-residential construction	-7.9	-19.4	-14.1	3.3	5.3	6.0	5.1	5.2	5.9	4.9
Machinery and equipment	7.2	4.0	8.1	10.3	11.2	12.0	10.2	10.8	9.7	8.1
Exports	-3.5	8.0	10.6	9.3	6.9	6.0	6.1	4.7	4.6	4.8
Imports	2.0	6.3	9.1	7.7	5.5	5.1	4.9	4.4	4.4	4.1
Nominal gross provincial product (% change)	-0.7	1.4	2.9	5.6	5.6	5.7	5.9	6.0	6.3	6.2
Deflator, Ontario gross provincial expenditure (% change)	2.4	0.5	0.4	0.9	0.7	1.0	1.1	1.4	1.8	1.9
Unemployment rate (%)	9.6	10.8	10.6	10.2	9.5	8.9	8.3	7.7	7.0	6.5
Employment (% change)	-3.4	-1.2	2.4	3.2	3.5	3.0	2.9	2.6	2.5	2.1
Employment ('000)	4769	4714	4826	4980	5156	5312	5468	5609	5749	5873
Labour force (% change)	0.1	0.2	2.1	2.8	2.7	2.3	2.3	1.9	1.7	1.6
Participation rate	68.3	67.3	67.4	68.1	68.8	69.3	69.9	70.2	70.5	70.7
Population (% change)	1.7	1.8	1.9	1.7	1.4	1.4	1.3	1.2	1.2	1.2
Population ('000)	9909	10091	10285	10464	10615	10764	10900	11034	11165	11296
Source population (% change)	1.7	1.7	1.9	1.7	1.6	1.6	1.5	1.4	1.4	1.3

CPI Ontario, inflation rate	4.7	1.0	1.7	1.5	1.1	1.4	1.5	1.8	2.2	2.3
Annual wage per employee, private (% change)	4.2	1.7	1.5	1.9	1.8	2.4	2.9	3.6	4.0	4.4
Real annual wage per employee, private (% change)	-0.4	0.6	-0.2	0.4	0.7	1.0	1.4	1.8	1.7	2.1
Labour productivity (% change)	0.4	2.1	0.1	1.3	1.3	1.6	1.7	1.9	1.8	2.1
Consolidated government balance ($ bill)	-10.4	-11.9	-13.5	-9.5	-6.1	-2.6	1.2	4.3	7.0	10.7
Federal balance in Ontario (NA basis) ($ bill)	-5.4	-3.5	-3.7	-1.0	0.5	2.4	4.5	6.0	6.8	8.5
Provincial government balance (NA basis) ($ bill)	-8.4	-11.7	-12.9	-11.3	-9.1	-7.5	-6.0	-4.6	-3.0	-1.2
Provincial balance as % of GDP	-3.1	-4.3	-4.6	-3.8	-2.9	-2.2	-1.7	-1.2	-0.8	-0.3
Ratio: Provincial debt (accumulated NA deflator)/GDP (%)	10.6	14.3	18.4	21.4	23.4	24.5	25.0	25.0	24.4	23.5
Provincial government balance (public accounts) ($ bill)	-9.0	-11.7	-11.8	-10.3	-8.1	-6.5	-5.0	-3.6	-2.0	-0.2
Provincial balance (public accounts) as % of GDP	-3.3	-4.3	-4.2	-3.5	-2.6	-1.9	-1.4	-1.0	-0.5	-0.1
Ratio: Provincial debt (public accounts)/GDP (%)	17.2	21.2	24.8	27.0	28.1	28.5	28.4	27.7	26.6	25.1
Personal savings rate (%)	12.7	13.5	14.3	13.9	13.7	13.6	13.5	13.4	13.4	13.4
Real personal disposable income (% change)	-1.5	1.1	1.2	1.5	2.8	2.7	2.9	3.3	3.5	3.1
Nominal after-tax corporate profits (% change)	-34.5	-1.4	10.7	47.4	25.6	14.8	10.0	6.9	6.5	4.0
Estimated potential growth	3.0	3.0	3.0	3.3	3.4	3.3	3.6	3.6	3.6	3.6
Cumulative potential GDP gap (from 1989)	-12.0	-14.1	-14.6	-13.3	-11.8	-10.5	-9.3	-8.4	-7.6	-6.9

TABLE 8 *(continued)*
Ontario Base Projection, September 1993: Summary of Projection

	2001	2002	2003	2004	2005	2006	2007	2008
Real provincial product (% change)	3.9	3.5	3.6	3.3	3.1	2.8	2.6	2.5
Real GDP, Canada (% change)	3.5	3.2	3.2	2.9	2.7	2.6	2.4	2.2
Ontario/Canada (%)	40.3	40.4	40.6	40.7	40.9	40.9	41.0	41.2
Consumption	3.3	3.0	3.6	3.3	3.0	2.6	2.5	2.5
Government	2.1	2.2	2.3	2.3	2.2	2.6	2.5	2.3
Private investment	5.3	5.3	3.9	3.5	3.0	2.4	2.2	1.9
Residential construction	3.6	3.4	2.8	2.6	2.4	2.2	2.1	2.0
Non-residential construction	3.7	4.2	2.8	2.5	2.2	1.8	1.6	1.5
Machinery and equipment	6.3	6.3	4.5	4.0	3.4	2.6	2.3	1.9
Exports	4.5	3.8	3.7	3.3	3.0	3.1	3.0	3.1
Imports	4.1	3.7	3.5	3.1	2.7	2.7	2.7	2.8
Nominal gross provincial product (% change)	6.1	6.0	6.1	6.1	5.9	5.8	5.7	5.6
Deflator, Ontario gross provincial expenditure (% change)	2.1	2.4	2.5	2.7	2.8	2.9	3.0	3.0
Unemployment rate (%)	6.2	5.9	5.5	5.4	5.4	5.4	5.4	5.4
Employment (% change)	1.8	1.6	1.7	1.2	1.0	0.9	0.8	0.8
Employment ('000)	5980	6076	6180	6252	6312	6369	6421	6473
Labour force (% change)	1.5	1.3	1.3	1.1	1.0	0.9	0.8	0.8
Participation rate	70.8	70.8	70.7	70.6	70.4	70.2	69.9	69.7
Population (% change)	1.1	1.1	1.1	1.1	1.0	1.0	0.9	0.9
Population ('000)	11424	11555	11686	11818	11936	12050	12160	12267
Source population (% change)	1.3	1.3	1.3	1.3	1.2	1.2	1.1	1.1

CPI Ontario, inflation rate	2.5	2.7	2.7	3.0	3.0	3.2	3.2	3.3
Annual wage per employee, private (% change)	4.8	5.0	4.8	5.1	5.1	5.0	4.9	4.8
Real annual wage per employee, private (% change)	2.3	2.3	2.0	2.0	1.9	1.7	1.6	1.5
Labour productivity (% change)	2.1	1.9	1.8	2.1	2.1	1.9	1.8	1.7
Consolidated government balance ($ bill)	13.7	16.8	18.5	19.6	20.8	22.0	23.3	24.6
Federal balance in Ontario (NA basis) ($ bill)	9.8	11.7	13.0	13.8	14.5	15.4	16.2	17.1
Provincial government balance (NA basis) ($ bill)	0.0	0.9	1.0	1.0	0.9	0.9	0.9	1.0
Provincial balance as % of GDP	0.0	0.2	0.2	0.2	0.2	0.2	0.1	0.1
Ratio: Provincial debt (accumulated NA deflator)/GDP (%)	22.2	20.8	19.4	18.1	16.9	15.8	14.8	13.9
Provincial government balance (public accounts) ($ bill)	1.0	1.9	2.0	1.9	1.9	1.9	1.9	2.0
Provincial balance (public accounts) as % of GDP	0.2	0.4	0.4	0.4	0.3	0.3	0.3	0.3
Ratio: Provincial debt (public accounts)/GDP (%)	23.4	21.7	20.0	18.5	17.2	15.9	14.7	13.6
Personal savings rate (%)	13.4	13.4	13.4	13.4	13.4	13.4	13.4	13.4
Real personal disposable income (% change)	3.1	2.8	3.3	3.1	2.8	2.4	2.3	2.3
Nominal after-tax corporate profits (% change)	12.4	7.5	7.7	6.1	5.6	5.4	5.1	5.1
Estimated potential growth	3.4	3.2	3.4	3.1	2.9	2.8	2.6	2.5
Cumulative potential GDP gap (from 1989)	-6.4	-6.1	-5.9	-5.7	-5.6	-5.6	-5.5	-5.5

FIGURE 16
Potential Output Gaps

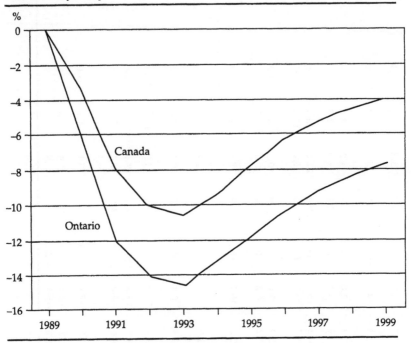

the output gap to be closed permits plenty of time for significant structural adjustments.

Past and projected real growth and unemployment for Ontario and Canada are compared in Figure 17. Note both the extent to which Ontario growth outpaced Canada's in the mid-1980s and then the relative shortfall in the last recession. As can be seen, the projection shows relatively higher growth for Ontario in the 1990s and beyond that is well within historical ranges. Note too how the Ontario unemployment rate has closed on the national rate in the current recession. I project that the Ontario rate will once again begin to fall well below the national rate – but only after the middle of the decade. Thereafter, the Ontario unemployment rate returns to a position substantially below the average national unemployment rate, although the gap never gets as large as it was in the late 1980s.

FIGURE 17
Canada and Ontario - Growth and Unemployment

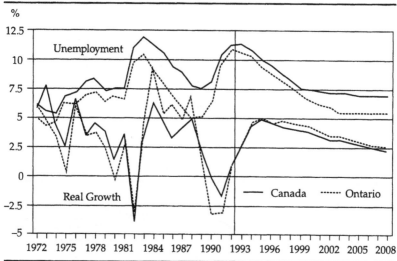

Sources of Aggregate Demand

Figure 18 and Table 9 present a closer look at the sources of
final demand that help determine the path of GDP through the
medium term. Not surprisingly, the story is little changed from the
national, but it bears repetition. The chief engines of growth in
the short and medium term are investment and net exports (where
the latter is made up of both export growth and substitution away
from imports and to domestic production). In the Ontario data, exports and imports include exports to and imports from the rest of
Canada as well as to and from foreign countries, so their share
of GDP is much larger than the share of exports and imports for
Canada. As net exports and investment lead growth and increase
their share of Ontario GDP, there is a corresponding decline in
the shares of consumption and government current and capital
spending - both of which still grow, but at less than the rate of
growth of GDP.

As for Canada as a whole, strength in net exports is based on
increased competitiveness from low wage inflation, good labour productivity growth, and the depreciations of the Canadian dollar
through 1993 (from a position I judge to have been badly over-

FIGURE 18
Expenditure Shares of GDP

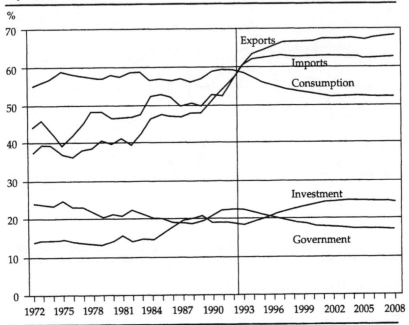

valued). There also remain significant advantages to be exploited from the FTA. The strength in investment is based on relatively good after-tax returns to investment, despite high real borrowing costs, a strong recovery in corporate cash flow, the existence of major investment and restructuring opportunities from the FTA, and the elimination of the MST, together with pent-up demand from the past several years of very high real rates, economic uncertainty, and very poor corporate cash flow.

Figure 18 should serve to remind also that, for Ontario even more than for Canada, while the growth picture is optimistic, the prospects for real incomes and consumption are less so. The growth of the next 15 years is highly concentrated in both reducing our dependence on foreign savings (the rise in net exports) and in accumulating and renewing our capital stock (the rise in investment). This leaves proportionally less for us to consume – whether outright as private consumers or via our governments – although there is still room for modest growth in each in per capita terms.

The Government Sector in Ontario

The government sector in Ontario is, in essence, the bottom line of this study, and I move now to examine it in some detail.

The Federal Government

The expenditures and revenues of the federal government in Ontario are shown in Tables 10 and 11. Historically, Statistics Canada develops these data by allocating federal expenditures and revenues across the provinces (and externally). While in some cases the allocation is straightforward (the payout of civil service salaries or UI benefits, for example), in other cases it is quite difficult and some rather arbitrary judgements may be needed (for example, in the case of public-debt payments to a pension plan held by workers across the country, or corporate taxes paid by a corporation active in many provinces). Because of these allocation problems, too much weight cannot be put, for example, on measures of the federal deficit (in fact, usually a surplus) in Ontario.

Briefly, I have simply extended the national story for the federal government through to the province. Federal spending grows in Ontario at the national rate, UI is paid out based on the Ontario unemployment rate, and federal taxes are collected from their bases in the Ontario model multiplied by the federal tax rates. Based on the Statistics Canada allocations, the federal government ran a deficit of about $5 billion in Ontario in 1991, compared with a national deficit of over $20 billion and notwithstanding that Ontario's economy had fallen more than the national. It should be no surprise then that as Ontario rebounds faster than the national economy (it has further to come back and a higher potential growth) and as the national federal deficit falls, the federal government in Ontario moves into a significant surplus (over $8 billion) by the end of the decade, and that the surplus grows larger still into the next decade.

The Provincial Government Sector

I will consider the provincial government sector together with the local and hospital levels for which it is ultimately responsible. Tables 12 and 13 give detailed projections for provincial revenues and expenditures, both in levels and as a share of provincial GDP. Table

TABLE 9
Ontario Base Projection, September 1993: GDP: Expenditure and Income Shares (share)

	1991	1992	1993	1994	1995	1996	1997	1998	1999	2000
GDP expenditure shares										
Consumption	0.594	0.593	0.585	0.572	0.562	0.553	0.544	0.539	0.535	0.529
Residential construction	0.053	0.057	0.052	0.055	0.057	0.058	0.058	0.058	0.058	0.058
Non-residential construction	0.043	0.034	0.029	0.029	0.029	0.029	0.029	0.029	0.030	0.030
Machinery and equipment	0.096	0.099	0.104	0.110	0.116	0.125	0.131	0.139	0.146	0.151
Government	0.226	0.227	0.225	0.217	0.210	0.204	0.199	0.193	0.189	0.185
Exports	0.525	0.562	0.607	0.634	0.647	0.655	0.663	0.665	0.666	0.669
Imports	0.539	0.568	0.604	0.622	0.626	0.628	0.629	0.628	0.628	0.627
GDP income shares										
Wages and salaries	0.598	0.605	0.605	0.596	0.592	0.589	0.588	0.588	0.588	0.590
Interest and miscellaneous investment	0.042	0.041	0.042	0.042	0.040	0.039	0.037	0.035	0.034	0.034
Corporate profits	0.054	0.051	0.053	0.065	0.074	0.079	0.083	0.084	0.084	0.082
Inventory valuation adjustment	0.004	−0.006	−0.008	−0.007	−0.006	−0.006	−0.006	−0.006	−0.006	−0.005
Non-farm unincorporated	0.056	0.056	0.054	0.054	0.054	0.054	0.054	0.054	0.054	0.054
Farm unincorporated	0.003	0.003	0.003	0.003	0.003	0.003	0.003	0.003	0.003	0.003
Indirect taxes	0.146	0.148	0.149	0.148	0.147	0.147	0.146	0.146	0.146	0.146
Subsidies	−0.012	−0.011	−0.010	−0.010	−0.010	−0.009	−0.009	−0.009	−0.009	−0.008
Capital consumption allowances	0.110	0.113	0.111	0.108	0.106	0.104	0.104	0.104	0.104	0.105
Statistical discrepancy	−0.003	−0.002	−0.003	−0.003	−0.003	−0.002	−0.002	−0.002	−0.002	−0.002
Personal income	0.911	0.917	0.918	0.902	0.894	0.886	0.879	0.876	0.874	0.871
Personal disposable income	0.697	0.702	0.702	0.685	0.674	0.664	0.655	0.649	0.646	0.642

Wages and salaries	0.598	0.605	0.605	0.596	0.592	0.589	0.588	0.588	0.588	0.590
Farm income	0.003	0.003	0.003	0.003	0.003	0.003	0.003	0.003	0.003	0.003
Unincorporated income	0.056	0.056	0.054	0.054	0.054	0.054	0.054	0.054	0.054	0.054
Interest income	0.124	0.113	0.109	0.105	0.104	0.102	0.099	0.097	0.097	0.095
Transfers from government	0.127	0.139	0.145	0.142	0.139	0.137	0.134	0.132	0.130	0.128
Other income	0.004	0.002	0.000	0.001	0.001	0.001	0.001	0.001	0.001	0.001
Direct taxes	0.211	0.212	0.212	0.213	0.217	0.219	0.221	0.223	0.224	0.226

TABLE 9 (*continued*)
Ontario Base Projection, September 1993: GDP: Expenditure and Income Shares (share)

	2001	2002	2003	2004	2005	2006	2007	2008
GDP expenditure shares								
Consumption	0.527	0.524	0.524	0.524	0.524	0.523	0.522	0.522
Residential construction	0.058	0.058	0.058	0.057	0.057	0.056	0.056	0.056
Non-residential construction	0.030	0.030	0.030	0.030	0.029	0.029	0.029	0.028
Machinery and equipment	0.155	0.159	0.160	0.162	0.162	0.162	0.161	0.160
Government	0.181	0.179	0.177	0.175	0.174	0.173	0.173	0.173
Exports	0.673	0.675	0.676	0.676	0.676	0.678	0.680	0.684
Imports	0.628	0.630	0.629	0.628	0.626	0.625	0.626	0.627
GDP income shares								
Wages and salaries	0.593	0.596	0.599	0.600	0.601	0.602	0.603	0.604
Interest and miscellaneous investment	0.033	0.032	0.031	0.031	0.030	0.029	0.029	0.028
Corporate profits	0.085	0.085	0.085	0.085	0.085	0.085	0.085	0.085
Inventory valuation adjustment	-0.005	-0.005	-0.005	-0.005	-0.004	-0.004	-0.004	-0.004
Non-farm unincorporated	0.054	0.054	0.054	0.054	0.054	0.054	0.054	0.054
Farm unincorporated	0.003	0.003	0.003	0.003	0.003	0.003	0.003	0.003
Indirect taxes	0.145	0.145	0.144	0.143	0.141	0.141	0.140	0.139
Subsidies	-0.008	-0.008	-0.008	-0.008	-0.008	-0.007	-0.007	-0.007
Capital consumption allowances	0.100	0.098	0.097	0.097	0.097	0.098	0.098	0.098
Statistical discrepancy	-0.002	-0.002	-0.002	-0.001	-0.001	-0.001	-0.001	-0.001
Personal income	0.869	0.869	0.867	0.864	0.862	0.860	0.858	0.856
Personal disposable income	0.639	0.637	0.637	0.638	0.638	0.637	0.637	0.637

Wages and salaries	0.593	0.596	0.599	0.600	0.601	0.602	0.603	0.604
Farm income	0.003	0.003	0.003	0.003	0.003	0.003	0.003	0.003
Unincorporated income	0.054	0.054	0.054	0.054	0.054	0.054	0.054	0.054
Interest income	0.092	0.090	0.086	0.083	0.080	0.077	0.075	0.072
Transfers from government	0.126	0.125	0.124	0.124	0.123	0.123	0.123	0.123
Other income	0.001	0.001	0.001	0.001	0.001	0.001	0.001	0.001
Direct taxes	0.227	0.230	0.227	0.224	0.221	0.220	0.219	0.217

TABLE 10
Ontario Base Projection, September 1993: Federal Government Balance, Revenue, and Expenditure Shares of GDP (share)

	1991	1992	1993	1994	1995	1996	1997	1998	1999	2000
Federal surplus/deficit	−0.020	−0.013	−0.013	−0.003	0.002	0.007	0.013	0.016	0.017	0.020
Federal expenditure	0.233	0.231	0.229	0.216	0.211	0.206	0.200	0.196	0.193	0.190
Current goods & services expenditure	0.042	0.041	0.041	0.039	0.038	0.037	0.036	0.036	0.035	0.035
Capital expenditure	0.004	0.004	0.004	0.004	0.004	0.004	0.004	0.003	0.003	0.003
Transfers to persons	0.061	0.064	0.064	0.062	0.060	0.058	0.057	0.055	0.054	0.053
Transfers to provincial & local governments	0.024	0.029	0.029	0.028	0.028	0.027	0.027	0.027	0.027	0.027
Other expenditure	0.009	0.007	0.006	0.006	0.006	0.006	0.005	0.005	0.005	0.005
Interest on the debt	0.094	0.086	0.084	0.078	0.076	0.073	0.070	0.069	0.068	0.067
Federal revenue	0.211	0.216	0.213	0.211	0.210	0.211	0.210	0.210	0.208	0.207
Direct taxes, persons	0.124	0.128	0.130	0.130	0.131	0.132	0.132	0.132	0.131	0.132
Direct taxes, corporations	0.014	0.014	0.013	0.011	0.010	0.011	0.012	0.012	0.013	0.012
Indirect taxes	0.049	0.050	0.049	0.048	0.047	0.046	0.045	0.044	0.044	0.043
Other revenue (interest & non-residents)	0.024	0.024	0.022	0.021	0.021	0.021	0.021	0.021	0.020	0.020

	2001	2002	2003	2004	2005	2006	2007	2008
Federal surplus/deficit	0.022	0.025	0.026	0.026	0.026	0.026	0.025	0.025
Federal expenditure	0.185	0.182	0.178	0.174	0.171	0.168	0.165	0.162
Current goods & services expenditure	0.035	0.034	0.034	0.034	0.034	0.034	0.034	0.034
Capital expenditure	0.003	0.003	0.003	0.003	0.003	0.003	0.003	0.003
Transfers to persons	0.051	0.050	0.049	0.049	0.048	0.047	0.047	0.046
Transfers to provincial & local governments	0.027	0.027	0.027	0.027	0.027	0.027	0.027	0.027
Other expenditure	0.005	0.005	0.005	0.005	0.005	0.005	0.004	0.004
Interest on the debt	0.064	0.062	0.059	0.057	0.054	0.052	0.050	0.048

Federal revenue	0.205	0.204	0.201	0.197	0.194	0.191	0.188	0.186
Direct taxes, persons	0.131	0.131	0.129	0.126	0.123	0.120	0.118	0.116
Direct taxes, corporations	0.012	0.011	0.011	0.011	0.011	0.011	0.012	0.012
Indirect taxes	0.043	0.043	0.042	0.042	0.042	0.042	0.041	0.041
Other revenue (interest & non-residents)	0.020	0.019	0.019	0.018	0.018	0.018	0.017	0.017

TABLE 11
Ontario Base Projection, September 1993: Federal Revenues and Expenditures, Ontario (millions of dollars)[a]

	1991	1992	1993	1994	1995	1996	1997	1998	1999	2000
Revenues										
Total	57127	59354	60239	62859	66262	70167	74214	78538	82841	87602
	(−1.17)	(3.90)	(1.49)	(4.35)	(5.41)	(5.89)	(5.77)	(5.83)	(5.48)	(5.75)
Indirect taxes	13151	13834	13757	14290	14766	15254	15896	16638	17479	18322
	(−2.17)	(5.19)	(−0.56)	(3.87)	(3.33)	(3.31)	(4.21)	(4.67)	(5.05)	(4.83)
Direct taxes, corporate and government business enterprise	3873	3792	3733	3327	3278	3674	4196	4637	4993	5265
	(−19.19)	(−2.08)	(−1.57)	(−10.88)	(−1.46)	(12.06)	(14.23)	(10.50)	(7.67)	(5.46)
Direct taxes and transfers from persons	33645	35162	36641	38867	41442	44103	46648	49463	52242	55561
	(2.59)	(4.51)	(4.21)	(6.08)	(6.62)	(6.42)	(5.77)	(6.04)	(5.62)	(6.35)
Direct taxes on non-residents	738	769	719	771	949	1076	1172	1247	1312	1366
Investment income	5704	5780	5373	5588	5812	6044	6286	6538	6799	7071
	(−0.96)	(1.33)	(−7.03)	(4.00)	(4.00)	(4.00)	(4.00)	(4.00)	(4.00)	(4.00)
Other current transfers from persons	16	16	16	16	16	16	16	16	16	16
Expenditures										
Total	63168	63462	64621	64543	66540	68543	70601	73391	76936	80115
	(6.96)	(0.46)	(1.83)	(−0.12)	(3.09)	(3.01)	(3.00)	(3.95)	(4.83)	(4.13)
Current expenditures on goods and services	11296	11375	11574	11688	11998	12392	12875	13447	14102	14781
	(0.82)	(0.70)	(1.75)	(0.99)	(2.65)	(3.28)	(3.90)	(4.44)	(4.87)	(4.81)
Gross capital formation	963	1056	1119	1151	1189	1229	1264	1306	1355	1405
	(4.11)	(9.62)	(5.98)	(2.89)	(3.26)	(3.38)	(2.88)	(3.31)	(3.74)	(3.68)
Transfers to persons	16506	17487	18181	18445	18920	19440	20021	20645	21374	22178
	(21.79)	(5.95)	(3.96)	(1.45)	(2.58)	(2.75)	(2.99)	(3.12)	(3.53)	(3.76)
Subsidies	2061	1653	1491	1515	1560	1607	1656	1722	1791	1862
	(37.22)	(−19.79)	(−9.80)	(1.61)	(3.00)	(3.00)	(3.00)	(4.00)	(4.00)	(4.00)

Interest on the public debt	25375 (−0.50)	23593 (−7.02)	23790 (0.84)	23228 (−2.36)	23945 (3.09)	24474 (2.21)	24841 (1.50)	25754 (3.67)	27189 (5.57)	28120 (3.42)
Capital assistance	411	334	243	247	254	262	269	277	286	294
Transfers to provinces	6207 (10.41)	7590 (22.27)	7789 (2.63)	7831 (0.53)	8222 (5.00)	8674 (5.50)	9195 (6.00)	9746 (6.00)	10331 (6.00)	10951 (6.00)
Transfers to municipalities	349	373	433	439	452	465	479	494	508	524
Capital consumption allowances	592	628	667	707	752	797	844	892	942	994
Surplus (+) or deficit (−)	−5449 (−4749)	−3480 (1969)	−3715 (−235)	−977 (2738)	473 (1450)	2422 (1948)	4458 (2036)	6040 (1582)	6847 (807)	8481 (1634)

a% changes (or levels changes) in parentheses

TABLE 11 (continued)
Ontario Base Projection, September 1993: Federal Revenues and Expenditures, Ontario (millions of dollars)[a]

	2001	2002	2003	2004	2005	2006	2007	2008
Revenues								
Total	91876 (4.88)	96919 (5.49)	101380 (4.60)	105561 (4.12)	109907 (4.12)	114632 (4.30)	119364 (4.13)	124324 (4.16)
Indirect taxes	19248 (5.05)	20201 (4.95)	21285 (5.37)	22417 (5.32)	23552 (5.06)	24902 (5.73)	26102 (4.82)	27588 (5.69)
Direct taxes, corporate and government business enterprise	5261 (−0.08)	5297 (0.68)	5515 (4.13)	5913 (7.20)	6351 (7.41)	6842 (7.73)	7369 (7.71)	7908 (7.31)
Direct taxes and transfers from persons	58573 (5.42)	62259 (6.29)	65055 (4.49)	67337 (3.51)	69738 (3.57)	72241 (3.59)	74855 (3.62)	77386 (3.38)
Direct taxes on non-residents	1459 (3.50)	1571 (3.50)	1668 (3.50)	1765 (3.50)	1852 (3.50)	1938 (3.50)	2025 (3.50)	2115 (3.50)
Investment income	7319 (3.50)	7575 (3.50)	7840 (3.50)	8114 (3.50)	8398 (3.50)	8692 (3.50)	8996 (3.50)	9311 (3.50)
Other current transfers from persons	16	16	16	16	16	16	16	16
Expenditures								
Total	83073 (3.69)	86328 (3.92)	89551 (3.73)	93012 (3.86)	96665 (3.93)	100619 (4.09)	104616 (3.97)	108746 (3.95)
Current expenditures on goods and services	15517 (4.98)	16348 (5.36)	17227 (5.37)	18187 (5.57)	19198 (5.56)	20350 (6.00)	21544 (5.87)	22766 (5.67)
Gross capital formation	1459 (3.85)	1520 (4.22)	1583 (4.13)	1650 (4.23)	1720 (4.22)	1814 (5.48)	1911 (5.34)	2009 (5.15)
Transfers to persons	23027 (3.83)	23940 (3.96)	24917 (4.08)	25998 (4.34)	27137 (4.38)	28332 (4.40)	29595 (4.46)	30915 (4.46)
Subsidies	1937 (4.00)	2014 (4.00)	2095 (4.00)	2179 (4.00)	2266 (4.00)	2356 (4.00)	2451 (4.00)	2549 (4.00)

Interest on the public febt	28683	29333	29793	30252	30742	31256	31644	32017
	(2.00)	(2.27)	(1.57)	(1.54)	(1.62)	(1.67)	(1.24)	(1.18)
Capital sssistance	303	312	322	331	341	351	362	373
Transfers to provinces	11608	12305	13043	13826	14655	15534	16466	17454
	(6.00)	(6.00)	(6.00)	(6.00)	(6.00)	(6.00)	(6.00)	(6.00)
Transfers to municipalities	539	556	572	589	607	625	644	663
Capital consumption allowances	1047	1103	1160	1220	1282	1347	1415	1486
Surplus (+) or deficit (−)	9850	11694	12989	13770	14523	15360	16162	17065
	(1369)	(1844)	(1296)	(781)	(753)	(837)	(802)	(902)

a% changes (or levels changes) in parentheses

14 details local and hospital revenues and expenditures as a share
of provincial GDP while Tables 15 and 16 give the local and hospital
accounts in levels form. My aim in providing all these numbers with
the report is to give readers the opportunity to make their own
detailed analysis of the Ontario fiscal projections and to double-
check my assumptions and conclusions.

On the expenditure side, it can be seen from Figure 19 that provincial current and capital spending had been holding at just over
5 per cent of provincial GDP for much of the 1980s after an upsurge
caused by the 1981–82 recession. The current recession has increased the share of current and capital spending to over 6 per cent
– largely because GDP has fallen and not from a significant rise
in this category of spending itself. My assumption is of very modest
per capita real growth in this spending category that serves gradually
to reduce its share of GDP back to mid-1980s levels by about the
end of the decade.

When speaking of current and capital spending, it should be noted
that local government spending of this type in Ontario is almost
2 per cent of GDP higher than provincial spending (see Figure 20).
As can be seen, the local governments have also seen their ratio
of spending to GDP rise massively during the recession after maintaining a relatively constant share in the 1980s. My assumptions
on local government spending restraint are slightly less severe than
for provincial spending and serve to reduce their ratio of spending
to GDP back to prerecession levels only well after 2000. Hospitals,
on the other hand, have seen their spending/GDP ratio rise rather
less than the other two levels of government in the recession. I
assume that there will be stronger upward spending pressure in
this level of government in the future, and that the recession level
of spending to GDP will be largely constant over the next decade
and beyond.

Returning to the other types of spending at the provincial level,
note the massive increase in transfers to persons in the most recent
recession (from under 3 per cent to well over 4 per cent of GDP).
The cause of this increase is both a decline in GDP itself and an
increase in the levels of transfers above its normal rate. Naturally,
much of this extra increase will also be recession induced. As at
the national level, I have been very cautious in assuming that this
spending category can be swiftly reduced as a share of GDP as
the economy recovers. For now I assume that a certain amount of
welfare dependency, together with the need to support a large

FIGURE 19
Provincial Expenditure Items (as % of GDP)

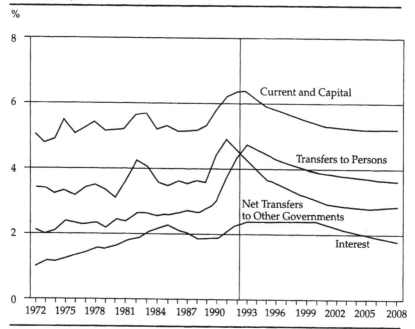

amount of economic (and social) restructuring, will keep the ratio of transfers to GDP at very high rates well into the recovery period and beyond.

Transfers to other governments are driven by their net revenue needs. As we have seen, we have been able to assume proportionally less spending restraint relative to GDP growth at the hospital level and so transfers to this level are projected to show significant growth. At the local level, on the other hand, more spending restraint is assumed possible; this, together with positive impacts on local tax revenues from a strong recovery, permits transfers to local governments to be held virtually flat for the 1993–95 period and to grow only modestly for several years thereafter. The net result is to reduce transfers to local governments and hospitals, as a share of GDP, back to their 1980s levels by the late 1990s, with further reductions thereafter.

Finally, provincial payments on the public debt, after diminishing slightly as a share of GDP in the later 1980s, are calculated to grow by under a percentage point of GDP through the late 1990s, at

FIGURE 20
Government Current and Capital Expenditure (as % of GDP)

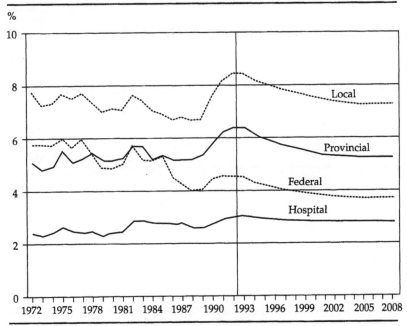

which point both debt-interest payments and the debt/GDP ratio both crest.

The revenue side of the provincial balance is shown in Figure 21. An important part of the deficit reduction that I project for Ontario rests on an increased personal-tax share of GDP – partly the automatic result of economic recovery, partly from the 1992 and 1993 increases in the provincial income-tax rate, and partly from a modest recouping of some of the PIT base lost in the 1991–93 years. As can be seen, the provincial income tax take is calculated to increase by about 1 per cent of provincial GDP through the 1990s; thereafter, with the provincial deficit largely eliminated, I have assumed that some reductions will be possible. Indirect taxes also are increased as a share of GDP; again, I have assumed that these are principally gasoline or other carbon or green taxes.

It should be noted from Figure 21 that local taxes take a bite of GDP comparable to all provincial indirect taxes (which include alcohol and tobacco taxes as well as the retail sales tax). The share of local taxes to GDP has increased significantly in the recession

FIGURE 21
Provincial Revenue Items (as % of GDP)

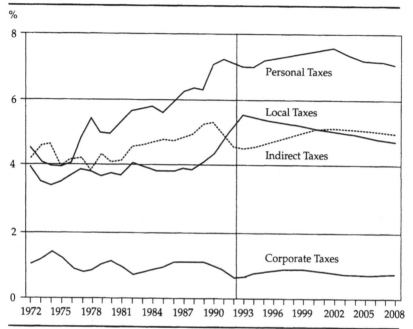

%

as dollar assessments have stayed up while GDP has fallen away. I have assumed that, under the dual pressures of spending needs and low transfers from the province, local governments will continue slowly to raise their tax revenues, but not their rates, in the 1990s, but at less than the strong GDP growth projected. The result will be a gradual fall in the ratio of local taxes to GDP, but not a full return to 1980s levels.

A final important note on incomes concerns federal transfers. Recall that I have assumed that success in fighting the federal deficit will lead to strong pressures to increase transfers to lower governments once more (or to release tax room). I have assumed that federal transfers to Ontario will increase at the same rate as to the provinces in total.

The result of my assumptions and calculations for Ontario's deficit and debt are shown in Figures 22 and 23. Ontario's deficit/GDP ratio (on a provincial accounts basis) had formerly peaked at just over 2 per cent in the mid-1970s and again in the 1981–82 recession. I project that the deficit/GDP ratio will peak at about

TABLE 12
Ontario Base Projection, September 1993: Provincial Government Balance, Revenue, and Expenditure Shares of GDP (share)

	1991	1992	1993	1994	1995	1996	1997	1998	1999	2000
Provincial surplus/deficit	-0.031	-0.043	-0.046	-0.038	-0.029	-0.022	-0.017	-0.012	-0.008	-0.003
Provincial expenditure	0.174	0.180	0.183	0.176	0.169	0.165	0.161	0.158	0.154	0.151
Current goods & services expenditure	0.057	0.058	0.058	0.056	0.054	0.053	0.052	0.051	0.050	0.049
Capital expenditure	0.005	0.006	0.006	0.006	0.005	0.005	0.005	0.005	0.005	0.005
Transfers to persons	0.037	0.043	0.047	0.046	0.045	0.043	0.042	0.041	0.040	0.039
Net transfers to/from governments	0.049	0.046	0.043	0.040	0.037	0.035	0.034	0.033	0.032	0.030
Other expenditure	0.004	0.004	0.004	0.004	0.004	0.004	0.004	0.004	0.004	0.004
Interest on the debt	0.021	0.023	0.024	0.024	0.024	0.024	0.024	0.024	0.024	0.024
Provincial revenue	0.140	0.135	0.133	0.135	0.137	0.139	0.141	0.142	0.144	0.145
Direct taxes & transfers, persons	0.073	0.072	0.070	0.070	0.072	0.073	0.073	0.074	0.074	0.075
Direct taxes, corporations	0.008	0.007	0.007	0.008	0.008	0.009	0.009	0.009	0.009	0.009
Indirect taxes	0.049	0.046	0.045	0.046	0.046	0.047	0.048	0.049	0.050	0.051
Interest and royalties	0.010	0.011	0.011	0.011	0.011	0.011	0.010	0.010	0.010	0.010

	2001	2002	2003	2004	2005	2006	2007	2008
Provincial surplus/deficit	0.000	0.002	0.002	0.002	0.002	0.002	0.001	0.001
Provincial expenditure	0.148	0.146	0.144	0.142	0.140	0.140	0.139	0.138
Current goods & services expenditure	0.049	0.048	0.048	0.048	0.048	0.048	0.048	0.048
Capital expenditure	0.005	0.005	0.005	0.004	0.004	0.004	0.004	0.004
Transfers to persons	0.039	0.038	0.038	0.037	0.037	0.037	0.037	0.036
Net transfers to/from governments	0.029	0.029	0.029	0.028	0.028	0.028	0.028	0.029
Other expenditure	0.003	0.003	0.003	0.003	0.003	0.003	0.003	0.003
Interest on the debt	0.023	0.022	0.021	0.021	0.020	0.019	0.019	0.018

Provincial revenue	0.145	0.145	0.143	0.141	0.140	0.139	0.138	0.137
Direct taxes & transfer, persons	0.076	0.076	0.075	0.073	0.072	0.072	0.072	0.071
Direct taxes, corporations	0.008	0.008	0.008	0.008	0.008	0.008	0.008	0.008
Indirect taxes	0.051	0.052	0.051	0.051	0.051	0.051	0.050	0.050
Interest and royalties	0.010	0.010	0.010	0.009	0.009	0.009	0.009	0.009

TABLE 13
Ontario Base Projection, September 1993: Provincial Revenues and Expenditures, Ontario (millions of dollars)[a]

	1991	1992	1993	1994	1995	1996	1997	1998	1999	2000
Revenues										
Total	44180 (−1.73)	44590 (0.93)	45552 (2.16)	48026 (5.43)	51555 (7.35)	55107 (6.89)	58940 (6.96)	63029 (6.94)	67581 (7.22)	72210 (6.85)
Indirect taxes	13381 (−7.80)	12570 (−6.07)	12775 (1.63)	13618 (6.60)	14585 (7.10)	15734 (7.88)	16963 (7.81)	18363 (8.25)	19935 (8.56)	21599 (8.35)
Direct taxes, corporate and government business enterprise	2230 (−18.88)	1791 (−19.69)	1912 (6.76)	2355 (23.19)	2634 (11.81)	2940 (11.63)	3180 (8.16)	3371 (6.02)	3559 (5.57)	3635 (2.15)
Direct taxes and transfers from persons	19005 (1.37)	19047 (0.22)	19279 (1.22)	20281 (5.20)	22002 (8.48)	23467 (6.66)	25122 (7.05)	26824 (6.77)	28774 (7.27)	30803 (7.05)
Investment income	2646 (−0.15)	2921 (10.41)	3120 (6.79)	3252 (4.23)	3390 (4.25)	3534 (4.27)	3686 (4.29)	3892 (5.59)	4110 (5.61)	4307 (4.79)
Other current transfers from persons	679	637	642	655	688	722	758	796	836	878
Transfers from federal government	6207 (10.41)	7590 (22.27)	7789 (2.63)	7831 (0.53)	8222 (5.00)	8674 (5.50)	9195 (6.00)	9746 (6.00)	10331 (6.00)	10951 (6.00)
Transfers from municipalities	32	34	35	35	35	36	36	36	37	37
Expenditures										
Total	53476 (10.89)	57216 (6.99)	59436 (3.88)	60331 (1.51)	61608 (2.12)	63600 (3.23)	65936 (3.67)	68709 (4.21)	71664 (4.30)	74559 (4.04)
Current expenditures on goods and services	15547 (6.45)	16023 (3.06)	16402 (2.37)	16653 (1.53)	17060 (2.44)	17601 (3.17)	18270 (3.80)	19023 (4.12)	19871 (4.46)	20724 (4.29)
Gross capital formation	1315 (4.61)	1512 (14.97)	1601 (5.87)	1643 (2.68)	1695 (3.16)	1753 (3.38)	1807 (3.08)	1868 (3.41)	1940 (3.84)	2013 (3.78)
Transfers to persons	10095 (22.47)	11871 (17.59)	13418 (13.03)	13706 (2.15)	14047 (2.49)	14397 (2.49)	14756 (2.49)	15307 (3.74)	15878 (3.74)	16471 (3.74)

Subsidies	770	932	977	994	1024	1055	1086	1119	1153	1187
	(−5.87)	(21.07)	(4.81)	(1.76)	(3.00)	(3.00)	(3.00)	(3.00)	(3.00)	(3.00)
Interest on the public debt	5803	6399	6828	7188	7540	7981	8530	9088	9583	9989
	(12.01)	(10.28)	(6.70)	(5.26)	(4.91)	(5.84)	(6.87)	(6.55)	(5.44)	(4.24)
Capital assistance	394	275	277	281	290	298	307	316	326	336
Transfers to municipalities	11147	11538	11243	10963	10746	10946	11195	11527	11916	12292
	(12.35)	(3.50)	(−2.55)	(−2.49)	(−1.98)	(1.87)	(2.27)	(2.97)	(3.38)	(3.15)
Transfers to hospitals	8405	8666	8692	8904	9207	9571	9989	10463	11000	11550
	(6.64)	(3.11)	(0.30)	(2.45)	(3.40)	(3.95)	(4.37)	(4.75)	(5.13)	(5.00)
Capital consumption allowances	872	917	945	962	980	1001	1024	1049	1076	1106
Surplus (+) or deficit (−)	−8424	−11709	−12939	−11343	−9072	−7492	−5972	−4631	−3006	−1243
	(−5972)	(−3285)	(−1231)	(1596)	(2271)	(1581)	(1520)	(1341)	(1625)	(1764)

a% changes (or levels changes) in parentheses

TABLE 13 (*continued*)
Ontario Base Projection, September 1993: Provincial Revenues and Expenditures, Ontario (millions of dollars)[a]

	2001	2002	2003	2004	2005	2006	2007	2008
Revenues								
Total	76733 (6.26)	81372 (6.05)	85256 (4.77)	89445 (4.91)	93834 (4.91)	98873 (5.37)	104113 (5.30)	109494 (5.17)
Indirect taxes	23053 (6.73)	24473 (6.16)	25942 (6.00)	27368 (5.50)	28815 (5.29)	30312 (5.19)	31891 (5.21)	33579 (5.29)
Direct taxes, corporate and government business enterprise	3694 (1.62)	3727 (0.88)	3849 (3.28)	4054 (5.34)	4271 (5.34)	4511 (5.62)	4764 (5.62)	5022 (5.42)
Direct taxes and transfers from persons	32955 (6.99)	35240 (6.93)	36578 (3.80)	38130 (4.24)	39793 (4.36)	41974 (5.48)	44198 (5.30)	46384 (4.95)
Investment income	4463 (3.60)	4623 (3.60)	4790 (3.60)	4963 (3.60)	5141 (3.60)	5327 (3.60)	5519 (3.61)	5718 (3.61)
Other current transfers from persons	922	968	1016	1067	1120	1176	1235	1297
Transfers from federal government	11608 (6.00)	12305 (6.00)	13043 (6.00)	13826 (6.00)	14655 (6.00)	15534 (6.00)	16466 (6.00)	17454 (6.00)
Transfers from municipalities	37	38	38	38	39	39	40	40
Expenditures								
Total	77885 (4.46)	81658 (4.84)	85503 (4.71)	89742 (4.96)	94188 (4.95)	99278 (5.40)	104571 (5.33)	110003 (5.19)
Current expenditures on goods and services	21756 (4.98)	22962 (5.55)	24239 (5.56)	25635 (5.76)	27055 (5.54)	28702 (6.09)	30410 (5.95)	32161 (5.76)
Gross capital formation	2094 (4.00)	2186 (4.41)	2283 (4.42)	2391 (4.72)	2503 (4.71)	2643 (5.56)	2786 (5.43)	2932 (5.23)

Transfers to persons	17292 (4.98)	18153 (4.98)	19057 (4.98)	20006 (4.98)	21003 (4.98)	22049 (4.98)	23147 (4.98)	24300 (4.98)
Subsidies	1223 (3.00)	1260 (3.00)	1297 (3.00)	1336 (3.00)	1376 (3.00)	1418 (3.00)	1460 (3.00)	1504 (3.00)
Interest on the public debt	10315 (3.27)	10585 (2.61)	10817 (2.19)	11063 (2.28)	11309 (2.22)	11554 (2.17)	11799 (2.12)	12043 (2.07)
Capital assistance	346	356	367	378	389	401	413	425
Transfers to municipalities	12719 (3.48)	13333 (4.83)	13918 (4.39)	14636 (5.16)	15440 (5.49)	16535 (7.09)	17685 (6.95)	18852 (6.60)
Transfers to hospitals	12146 (5.16)	12829 (5.62)	13530 (5.47)	14302 (5.71)	15121 (5.73)	15987 (5.73)	16883 (5.61)	17798 (5.42)
Capital consumption allowances	1138	1173	1211	1253	1299	1348	1403	1463
Surplus (+) or deficit (−)	−15 (1228)	887 (902)	964 (76)	957 (−7)	945 (−12)	944 (−1)	946 (2)	954 (8)

[a]% changes (or levels changes) in parentheses

TABLE 14
Ontario Base Projection, September 1993: Other Government Revenue and Expenditure Shares of GDP (share)

	1991	1992	1993	1994	1995	1996	1997	1998	1999	2000
Municipal										
Surplus/deficit	0.007	0.008	0.009	0.008	0.006	0.006	0.006	0.005	0.005	0.005
Current goods & services expenditure	0.070	0.073	0.073	0.071	0.070	0.068	0.067	0.067	0.066	0.065
Capital expenditure	0.011	0.011	0.011	0.011	0.011	0.011	0.011	0.011	0.011	0.010
Transfers to persons	0.007	0.008	0.008	0.008	0.008	0.008	0.008	0.008	0.008	0.008
Net transfers to/from governments	−0.042	−0.043	−0.041	−0.038	−0.035	−0.034	−0.033	−0.032	−0.031	−0.030
Interest on the debt	0.002	0.002	0.002	0.002	0.002	0.002	0.002	0.002	0.002	0.002
Indirect taxes	0.048	0.052	0.055	0.055	0.054	0.054	0.053	0.053	0.052	0.052
Interest and royalties	0.002	0.002	0.003	0.003	0.003	0.002	0.002	0.002	0.002	0.002
Hospitals										
Surplus/deficit	0.004	0.004	0.003	0.003	0.002	0.002	0.002	0.002	0.002	0.002
Current goods & services expenditure	0.028	0.028	0.028	0.028	0.027	0.027	0.027	0.027	0.027	0.027
Capital expenditure	0.002	0.002	0.002	0.002	0.002	0.002	0.002	0.002	0.002	0.002
Net transfers to/from governments	−0.031	−0.032	−0.031	−0.030	−0.029	−0.029	−0.028	−0.028	−0.028	−0.027
Pension plans										
Surplus/deficit	0.002	0.000	−0.001	−0.001	−0.001	−0.001	0.000	0.000	0.001	0.002
Payments to persons	0.022	0.024	0.026	0.026	0.027	0.027	0.028	0.028	0.028	0.029
Direct taxes, persons	0.016	0.017	0.018	0.019	0.019	0.020	0.021	0.022	0.023	0.024
Interest	0.008	0.008	0.008	0.007	0.007	0.007	0.007	0.007	0.006	0.006

TABLE 14 (continued)
Ontario Base Projection, September 1993: Other Government Revenue and Expenditure Shares of GDP (share)

	2001	2002	2003	2004	2005	2006	2007	2008
Municipal								
Surplus/deficit	0.004	0.004	0.004	0.004	0.004	0.003	0.003	0.003
Current goods & services expenditure	0.064	0.064	0.063	0.063	0.063	0.063	0.063	0.063
Capital expenditure	0.010	0.010	0.010	0.010	0.010	0.010	0.010	0.010
Transfers to persons	0.007	0.007	0.007	0.007	0.007	0.007	0.007	0.007
Net transfers to/from governments	−0.029	−0.029	−0.029	−0.028	−0.028	−0.029	−0.029	−0.029
Interest on the debt	0.002	0.002	0.002	0.002	0.002	0.001	0.001	0.001
Indirect taxes	0.051	0.051	0.050	0.050	0.049	0.049	0.048	0.048
Interest and royalties	0.002	0.002	0.002	0.002	0.002	0.002	0.002	0.002
Hospitals								
Surplus/deficit	0.002	0.002	0.001	0.001	0.001	0.001	0.001	0.001
Current goods & services expenditure	0.026	0.027	0.026	0.026	0.027	0.027	0.027	0.027
Capital expenditure	0.002	0.002	0.002	0.002	0.002	0.002	0.002	0.002
Net transfers to/from governments	−0.027	−0.027	−0.027	−0.027	−0.027	−0.027	−0.027	−0.027
Pension Plans								
Surplus/deficit	0.002	0.003	0.004	0.004	0.004	0.005	0.005	0.006
Payments to persons	0.029	0.029	0.030	0.030	0.031	0.032	0.033	0.033
Direct taxes, persons	0.026	0.027	0.028	0.029	0.030	0.031	0.032	0.034
Interest	0.006	0.006	0.006	0.006	0.006	0.006	0.006	0.006

TABLE 15
Ontario Base Projection, September 1993: Municipal Revenues and Expenditures, Ontario (millions of dollars)[a]

	1991	1992	1993	1994	1995	1996	1997	1998	1999	2000
Revenues										
Total	25392	27128	28198	28631	29202	30250	31420	32742	34224	35731
	(11.63)	(6.84)	(3.94)	(1.54)	(1.99)	(3.59)	(3.87)	(4.21)	(4.53)	(4.40)
Indirect taxes	12939	14220	15655	16331	17068	17863	18730	19664	20698	21768
	(8.71)	(9.90)	(10.09)	(4.32)	(4.51)	(4.66)	(4.85)	(4.98)	(5.26)	(5.17)
Investment income	661	680	733	763	793	825	858	892	928	965
	(4.26)	(2.90)	(7.81)	(4.00)	(4.00)	(4.00)	(4.00)	(4.00)	(4.00)	(4.00)
Other current transfers from persons	296	317	134	137	143	151	158	166	174	183
Transfers from federal government	349	373	433	439	452	465	479	494	508	524
	(−0.29)	(7.02)	(16.04)	(1.21)	(3.00)	(3.00)	(3.00)	(3.00)	(3.00)	(3.00)
Transfers from provincial government	11147	11538	11243	10963	10746	10946	11195	11527	11916	12292
	(12.35)	(3.50)	(−2.55)	(−2.49)	(−1.98)	(1.87)	(2.27)	(2.97)	(3.38)	(3.15)
Expenditures										
Total	25053	26452	27258	28159	29158	30338	31646	33111	34740	36401
	(7.98)	(5.58)	(3.04)	(3.31)	(3.55)	(4.05)	(4.31)	(4.63)	(4.92)	(4.78)
Current expenditures on goods and services	19015	20130	20662	21180	21913	22789	23772	24899	26164	27450
	(8.15)	(5.86)	(2.64)	(2.51)	(3.46)	(4.00)	(4.31)	(4.74)	(5.08)	(4.92)
Gross capital formation	3059	3081	3222	3325	3464	3638	3813	3994	4196	4402
	(−3.53)	(0.73)	(4.55)	(3.22)	(4.17)	(5.02)	(4.82)	(4.74)	(5.07)	(4.91)
Transfers to persons	1877	2099	2209	2468	2567	2670	2790	2916	3047	3184
	(35.13)	(11.85)	(5.23)	(11.73)	(4.00)	(4.00)	(4.50)	(4.50)	(4.50)	(4.50)
Subsidies	433	443	446	452	465	479	494	509	524	540
	(7.44)	(2.36)	(0.60)	(1.36)	(3.00)	(3.00)	(3.00)	(3.00)	(3.00)	(3.00)
Interest on the public debt	630	657	678	691	705	719	734	749	764	779
	(1.29)	(4.26)	(3.16)	(2.02)	(2.02)	(2.02)	(2.02)	(2.02)	(2.02)	(2.02)

Transfers to provinces	32	34	35	35	35	36	36	36	37	37
Transfers to hospitals	7	7	7	7	8	8	8	8	9	9
Capital consumption allowances	1508	1601	1706	1826	1955	2087	2224	2366	2513	2667
	(8.96)	(6.13)	(6.56)	(7.07)	(7.02)	(6.77)	(6.57)	(6.38)	(6.23)	(6.11)
Surplus (+) or deficit (−)	1847	2277	2647	2300	2000	2000	2000	2000	2000	2000
	(919)	(430)	(371)	(−347)	(−300)	(0)	(0)	(0)	(0)	(0)

a% changes (or levels changes) in parentheses

TABLE 15 (continued)
Ontario Base Projection, September 1993: Municipal Revenues and Expenditures, Ontario (millions of dollars)[a]

	2001	2002	2003	2004	2005	2006	2007	2008
Revenues								
Total	37320	39121	40986	43053	45220	47714	50296	52942
	(4.45)	(4.82)	(4.77)	(5.04)	(5.03)	(5.52)	(5.41)	(5.26)
Indirect taxes	22872	23998	25216	26499	27795	29124	30484	31887
	(5.07)	(4.92)	(5.08)	(5.09)	(4.89)	(4.78)	(4.67)	(4.60)
Investment income	999	1034	1070	1107	1146	1186	1228	1271
	(3.50)	(3.50)	(3.50)	(3.50)	(3.50)	(3.50)	(3.50)	(3.50)
Other current transfers from persons	192	202	212	222	234	245	258	270
Transfers from federal government	539	556	572	589	607	625	644	663
	(3.00)	(3.00)	(3.00)	(3.00)	(3.00)	(3.00)	(3.00)	(3.00)
Transfers from provincial government	12719	13333	13918	14636	15440	16535	17685	18852
	(3.48)	(4.83)	(4.39)	(5.16)	(5.49)	(7.09)	(6.95)	(6.60)
Expenditures								
Total	38151	40119	42158	44409	46771	49469	52265	55132
	(4.81)	(5.16)	(5.08)	(5.34)	(5.32)	(5.77)	(5.65)	(5.49)
Current expenditures on goods and services	28803	30341	31934	33708	35575	37740	39986	42288
	(4.93)	(5.34)	(5.25)	(5.55)	(5.54)	(6.09)	(5.95)	(5.76)
Gross capital formation	4623	4870	5125	5404	5692	6009	6335	6666
	(5.02)	(5.33)	(5.24)	(5.44)	(5.33)	(5.56)	(5.43)	(5.23)
Transfers to persons	3327	3477	3633	3797	3968	4146	4333	4528
	(4.50)	(4.50)	(4.50)	(4.50)	(4.50)	(4.50)	(4.50)	(4.50)
Subsidies	556	572	590	607	626	644	664	684
	(3.00)	(3.00)	(3.00)	(3.00)	(3.00)	(3.00)	(3.00)	(3.00)
Interest on the public debt	795	811	827	844	861	878	896	914
	(2.02)	(2.02)	(2.02)	(2.02)	(2.02)	(2.02)	(2.02)	(2.02)

Transfers to provinces	37	38	38	38	39	39	40	40
Transfers to hospitals	10	10	10	11	11	12	12	13
Capital consumption allowances	2826 (5.99)	2993 (5.90)	3168 (5.84)	3351 (5.78)	3543 (5.73)	3745 (5.69)	3957 (5.66)	4179 (5.62)
Surplus (+) or deficit (−)	2000 (0)	2000 (0)	2000 (0)	2000 (0)	2000 (0)	2000 (0)	2000 (0)	2000 (0)

a% changes (or levels changes) in parentheses

TABLE 16
Ontario Base Projection, September 1993: Public Hospital and Canada Pension Plan Revenues and Expenditures (millions of dollars)[a]

	1991	1992	1993	1994	1995	1996	1997	1998	1999	2000
Public hospital revenues and expenditures										
Revenues										
Total	8575	8847	8875	9092	9402	9773	10199	10682	11227	11787
	(6.67)	(3.17)	(0.32)	(2.44)	(3.41)	(3.95)	(4.36)	(4.73)	(5.11)	(4.98)
Transfers from persons	102	111	112	114	120	126	132	139	146	153
Investment income	61	62	65	66	67	69	70	71	73	74
Transfers from provincial government	8405	8666	8692	8904	9207	9571	9989	10463	11000	11550
	(6.64)	(3.11)	(0.30)	(2.45)	(3.40)	(3.95)	(4.37)	(4.75)	(5.13)	(5.00)
Transfers from municipal government	7	7	7	7	8	8	8	8	9	9
Expenditures										
Total	8002	8292	8580	8865	9229	9656	10141	10684	11293	11917
	(7.54)	(3.62)	(3.48)	(3.31)	(4.11)	(4.63)	(5.02)	(5.36)	(5.69)	(5.53)
Current expenditures on goods and services	7474	7760	8025	8294	8640	9047	9511	10031	10612	11211
	(8.35)	(3.83)	(3.41)	(3.36)	(4.17)	(4.71)	(5.13)	(5.46)	(5.80)	(5.64)
Gross capital formation	513	517	539	555	574	595	616	639	666	693
	(−3.02)	(0.73)	(4.39)	(2.94)	(3.36)	(3.69)	(3.49)	(3.82)	(4.15)	(3.99)
Interest on the public debt	15	15	17	16	15	15	14	14	14	14
Capital consumption allowances	416	442	473	523	577	633	692	752	815	881
Surplus (+) or deficit (−)	989	996	768	750	750	750	750	750	750	750

Canada Pension Plan revenues and expenditures

Revenues										
Total	6636 (3.70)	6896 (3.91)	7205 (4.49)	7738 (7.40)	8324 (7.57)	8921 (7.18)	9816 (10.03)	10782 (9.84)	11835 (9.77)	13013 (9.95)
Employer and employee contributions	4401 (4.64)	4717 (7.18)	5066 (7.39)	5580 (10.15)	6090 (9.14)	6609 (8.52)	7423 (12.32)	8305 (11.88)	9271 (11.64)	10320 (11.32)
Investment income	2235 (1.92)	2179 (−2.52)	2140 (−1.79)	2159 (0.89)	2234 (3.50)	2313 (3.50)	2394 (3.50)	2477 (3.50)	2564 (3.50)	2692 (5.00)
Expenditures										
Total	6636 (3.70)	6896 (3.91)	7205 (4.49)	7738 (7.40)	8324 (7.57)	8921 (7.18)	9816 (10.03)	10782 (9.84)	11835 (9.77)	13013 (9.95)
Current expenditures on goods and services	121	128	137	140	144	149	155	162	169	177
Transfers to persons	5921 (10.98)	6709 (13.31)	7313 (8.99)	7862 (7.51)	8428 (7.20)	9052 (7.40)	9730 (7.50)	10470 (7.60)	11255 (7.50)	12099 (7.50)
Surplus (+) or deficit (−)	594	58	−244	−263	−248	−280	−70	150	411	737

a % changes (or levels changes) in parentheses

TABLE 16 (continued)
Ontario Base Projection, September 1993: Public Hospital and Canada Pension Plan Revenues and Expenditures (millions of dollars)[a]

	2001	2002	2003	2004	2005	2006	2007	2008
Public hospital revenues and expenditures								
Revenues								
Total	12392	13085	13796	14579	15409	16287	17196	18124
	(5.14)	(5.59)	(5.44)	(5.68)	(5.69)	(5.70)	(5.58)	(5.40)
Transfers from persons	161	169	177	186	195	205	215	226
Investment income	76	77	79	80	82	84	85	87
Transfers from provincial government	12146	12829	13530	14302	15121	15987	16883	17798
	(5.16)	(5.62)	(5.47)	(5.71)	(5.73)	(5.73)	(5.61)	(5.42)
Transfers from municipal government	10	10	10	11	11	12	12	13
Expenditures								
Total	12591	13354	14140	15001	15912	16875	17874	18897
	(5.65)	(6.06)	(5.88)	(6.09)	(6.08)	(6.05)	(5.92)	(5.72)
Current expenditures on goods and services	11855	12586	13338	14161	15034	15949	16898	17871
	(5.75)	(6.17)	(5.97)	(6.17)	(6.16)	(6.09)	(5.95)	(5.76)
Gross capital formation	721	753	788	825	864	912	961	1011
	(4.10)	(4.51)	(4.52)	(4.72)	(4.71)	(5.56)	(5.43)	(5.23)
Interest on the public debt	14	14	15	15	15	15	15	15
Capital consumption allowances	949	1020	1094	1172	1253	1338	1428	1523
Surplus (+) or deficit (−)	750	750	750	750	750	750	750	750

Canada Pension Plan revenues and expenditures

Revenues								
Total	14272 (9.68)	15619 (9.44)	17082 (9.37)	18596 (8.86)	20385 (9.62)	22291 (9.35)	24329 (9.14)	26507 (8.95)
Employer and employee contributions	11445 (10.90)	12651 (10.53)	13965 (10.39)	15324 (9.73)	16949 (10.60)	18683 (10.23)	20541 (9.94)	22529 (9.68)
Investment income	2827 (5.00)	2968 (5.00)	3117 (5.00)	3272 (5.00)	3436 (5.00)	3608 (5.00)	3788 (5.00)	3978 (5.00)
Expenditures								
Total	14272 (9.68)	15619 (9.44)	17082 (9.37)	18596 (8.86)	20385 (9.62)	22291 (9.35)	24329 (9.14)	26507 (8.95)
Current expenditures on goods and services	185	193	202	212	222	236	250	264
Transfers to persons	13007 (7.50)	13982 (7.50)	15059 (7.70)	16264 (8.00)	17614 (8.30)	19076 (8.30)	20659 (8.30)	22373 (8.30)
Surplus (+) or deficit (−)	1081	1443	1821	2121	2549	2980	3421	3870

[a]% changes (or levels changes) in parentheses

5 per cent in the wake of the 1990–92 recession and will fall rather steeply thereafter, reaching zero just after the end of the decade. The fall in the deficit/GDP ratio is the combined result of the expenditure restraint and revenue increases discussed above, against a background of a healthy, if prolonged, recovery to economic equilibrium.

Nonetheless, the result of a long string of deficits, even if they are steadily falling as a share of GDP, is a stock of debt relative to GDP that keeps rising through much of the 1990s (see Figure 23).[10] The debt/GDP ratio crests near the end of the 1990s at about twice its current estimated value and then falls steadily thereafter as the debt itself remains roughly constant (there is a balanced provincial budget) and nominal GDP continues to grow.

Alternatives: Testing the Sensitivity of the Province's Fiscal Situation

The third and fourth sections above presented a projection for the Canadian and Ontario economies in which the fiscal situation for both federal and provincial governments was under control. Expenditure restraints and (in the case of the provincial government) some tax increases were projected, but they were far from drastic, in that expenditures per capita still rose somewhat in the 1990s and tax increases were no larger than those already introduced in recent years. As a result of real growth, expenditure restraint and these tax increases, both the federal and provincial debt/GDP ratios peak and then fall significantly. Fiscal improvements are such that after the turn of the century, reductions in personal income taxes and some acceleration in spending is possible.

To some, these fiscal results may appear very optimistic. It is therefore important to examine how sensitive they are to the possibility that economic growth and other economic conditions in the 1990s will be less conducive to debt/GDP stabilization and reduction. This section presents two such alternatives, each of which is significantly more pessimistic than the base case.

As I noted in the second section above and in the discussion of the base-case projections, there are two principal factors or sets of factors underlying the projected real-growth path. The first is the growth in the production potential of the economy itself, and the second is the speed at which the economy returns to an equilibrium near full employment from its present large output gap

FIGURE 22
Ontario Provincial Deficit (as % of provincial GDP)

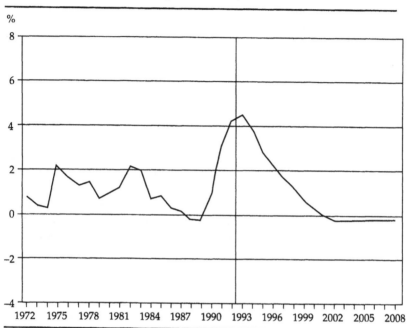

below potential. The growth of potential and the rate of recovery, in turn, are each affected by the eight special factors underlying long-term growth identified in the second section.

The first alternative projection, "Lower Trend Growth," looks at the possibility that the productive potential of the economy will grow significantly more slowly than in the base case. The second alternative, "Interrupted Recovery," considers the possibility of a sharp interruption in the recovery of the economy towards full employment.

Lower trend growth could have a number of causes. First, as explained in the second section, it is not yet fully understood why TFP growth fell so much during the late 1970s and the 1980s, as compared with the 1950s and 1960s. Factors prominent in some of the more popular explanations – such as high energy prices or a proportionally younger and more inexperienced workforce – would appear now to have gone away, and I have assumed a modest recovery in TFP growth rates on average over the 1990s and beyond.

But this assumption may be wrong, and basic TFP growth may continue to be low. Second, it is possible that the TFP gains from major structural adjustments such as the introduction of the Canada–U.S. Free Trade Agreement have been overestimated. A third possibility would be a break-up of Canada, which would lead to severe trade barriers between Quebec and the rest of Canada or even among the remaining provinces. These trade barriers would increase inefficiencies and lower TFP growth for a lengthy period. Finally, it is possible that major environmental regulations or environmental tax shifting will also reduce measured GDP growth as more capital and technology are shifted to increasing unmeasured environmental gains. While this may be socially desirable, the fact remains that taxes are collected on measured, or "dollar," incomes and lower measured trend growth will reduce tax revenues.

An interrupted recovery could also result from a number of different causes. First, the world economy may be hit by a new recession based on some kind of economic or political disruption. A constitutional crisis in Canada – even if successfully resolved in the long run – could lead to a rapid if temporary run-up in real interest rates and a short-term reduction in confidence with impacts on consumption and investment spending. Or the Bank of Canada and federal government may be more insistent than has been assumed on keeping inflation around 2 per cent or lowering it still more, and may induce another economic slow-down to drop the long-term inflation path still further.

In each of the alternatives I will examine the fiscal implications at both the federal and provincial level. In neither alternative are the fundamental assumptions made about fiscal policy changed. Real current and capital spending grow at the same rate as in the base case (even though in each scenario GDP is growing less), and tax and transfer rates also remain unchanged from the base case. In other words, the two alternatives can tell us what kind of fiscal trouble these more pessimistic views of the future will give the federal and Ontario governments, but not what they could do to get out of that trouble.

Alternative 1: Lower Trend Growth

In the lower trend growth alternative I assume that underlying TFP growth is 0.5 per cent per year instead of the 0.75 per cent in the base case. I further assume that there are no TFP gains from the

Canada–U.S. FTA; this removes another 0.25 per cent of growth per year from 1993 to 1996 and 2000 to 2001 and 0.5 per cent of growth per year from 1997 to 1999. As a result, by 2000, Canadian GDP is almost 5 per cent lower than in the base case, and by 2008 it is 7 per cent below base. (See Figure 24 for a comparison of the base-case and lower trend growth rates by year). For Ontario I assume an additional loss of 0.25 per cent of GDP for the 1997–2000 period, just as I assumed an extra TFP gain for Ontario under the FTA. Therefore, for Ontario by 2000 the loss of GDP is just under 6 per cent of base case and by 2008 it is 8 per cent of base GDP (See Figure 27.)

To simplify the alternative, I assume that the lower growth is forthcoming at the same inflation rate, the same interest rates, and the same exchange rate as the base case. I also assume the same employment growth as in the base case, and thus the same unemployment rate. Recall that in this alternative, the output gap is being closed at the same rate as in the base case; thus the unemployment rate falls from 1993 levels at the same rate. But productivity growth is assumed to be lower so that, as employment rises, less is added to GDP. With the same output gap as in the base case it is reasonable to assume the same pressures on inflation. And since the assumption is that the lower productivity growth is confined to Canada, there is no reason to change interest rates. Indeed, if lower productivity growth is also assumed in the rest of the world, returns to capital and lower real interest rates might be reduced.

With lower trend productivity, however, real wages and real incomes do grow more slowly than in the base – and this can have a major effect on revenues.

On the demand side, I assume that the reduced GDP is made up of proportional reductions in investment, exports, and imports, while real consumption is reduced so as to keep the personal savings rate the same as in the base case. Real government current and capital expenditure, as noted above, is not reduced.

Canada

The lower trend growth alternative for Canada is summarized in Tables 17 and 18 and in Figures 24, 25, and 26. Table 17 shows key indicators for the Canadian economy under the alternative, while Table 18 shows changes in the same indicators relative to the base case. The three figures plot base-case and alternative indicators together for comparison.

As the tables and figures show, the growth decline in this alternative is a severe one. Averaged over the 1993–2000 period (and uncompounded), the real growth rate is 3.4 per cent, down 0.6 from the 4 per cent in the base case. The average potential growth rate over the 1993–2000 span drops from 3.2 per cent in the base to 2.6 per cent, roughly level with the U.S. potential growth in the base case.

Primary attention is placed on the impact of this lower growth alternative on the Canadian fiscal situation. Recall that this is an alternative of lower growth but unchanged inflation, interest rates, unemployment, and real government spending. Therefore most revenues will be lower than in the base case, but most expenditures will be unchanged – including UI payments, transfers to persons, and interest on the debt. However, there is one factor working to reduce government expenditures that must be noted: because of lower productivity growth, the scenario shows lower real wage inflation in the private sector (and, therefore, lower nominal wage increases given that price inflation is unchanged from the base case). In the FOCUS model government sector nominal wages follow the private sector and fall by about 80 per cent of the decline in private-sector wages. This is an important mechanism in keeping the fiscal situation under control in the lower-growth alternative and demonstrates the importance of keeping public and private sector wages and salaries in line with each other.

Naturally, deficits and debt – and, even more, deficits and debt relative to GDP – ought to rise in this alternative, and indeed they do, as shown in the tables and in Figures 24 and 25 for the federal government. By 2000, the federal deficit is almost $8 billion worse in the low-growth alternative, and the debt/GDP ratio is almost 5 percentage points higher. By 2008 the federal deficit is over $16 billion worse and the debt/GDP ratio over 10 percentage points higher. These impacts are severe and worrisome, but it is also worth noting that even in this low growth alternative the debt/GDP ratio still peaks then begins to fall (after 1995) and the deficit/GDP ratio falls at least until after the year 2000. In short, the federal fiscal situation is not sitting so precariously that a significantly lower growth rate than in the base would cause a deficit/debt "runaway." But if the fiscal objective is to remove the federal deficit by the late 1990s, then, naturally, a lower-trend growth path than in the

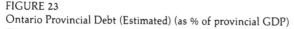

FIGURE 23
Ontario Provincial Debt (Estimated) (as % of provincial GDP)

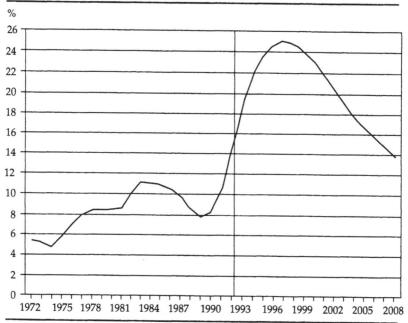

base will require some change in federal fiscal policy from what has been assumed.

On the aggregate provincial level there is also a severe impact of lower growth on deficits. In dollar terms, the impacts are just slightly larger than for the federal sector, with the deficit almost $10 billion worse in 2000 and almost $23 billion worse in 2008. Note that the provincial transfers to municipalities and hospitals are set in the model so that the modest surpluses of these sectors do not change from the base case. The provinces are therefore picking up in their deficits any deficit problems in the municipalities and hospitals caused by low growth. Also, the federal/provincial split of the worsening deficits results in part from the important assumption that federal transfers to the provinces are in proportion to nominal GDP. Under an alternative of lower growth, therefore, federal transfers are reduced relative to the base case. Were federal nominal transfers to the provinces to be held at base-case levels, the federal deficit and debt impacts would have been more severe and the provincial results accordingly less so.

TABLE 17
Canada Alternative, Lower Trend Growth: Summary of Projection

	1993	1994	1995	1996	1997	1998	1999	2000	2001	2002
Real gross domestic product (% growth)	2.3	3.4	4.3	4.1	3.5	3.3	3.1	3.2	2.9	2.9
Expenditure on personal consumption	1.1	1.6	3.3	2.9	2.6	2.7	2.6	3.1	3.0	2.7
Expenditure by governments	1.2	0.8	1.6	1.8	1.9	2.0	2.0	2.0	2.1	2.2
Investment expenditure	0.2	6.5	6.9	7.3	5.1	5.6	5.1	4.6	3.1	4.1
Exports	7.4	6.7	5.8	5.6	4.2	3.6	3.1	3.7	3.1	3.2
Imports	5.5	3.9	4.0	4.0	2.9	3.5	3.0	3.7	2.8	3.2
Inflation rate (CPI)	1.9	1.6	1.1	1.4	1.5	1.8	2.2	2.3	2.5	2.7
Unemployment rate	11.3	10.8	10.1	9.6	8.9	8.3	7.6	7.4	7.3	7.2
Employment (% change)	1.3	3.0	3.1	2.6	2.6	2.4	2.3	1.8	1.5	1.3
Finance Company 90-day paper rate	5.1	4.6	4.7	4.5	4.6	5.3	5.8	5.8	5.8	5.9
Labour productivity, private (% change)	0.0	0.0	0.0	0.0	0.0	0.0	0.0	0.0	0.0	0.0
Real capital stock (% change)	2.6	2.6	3.0	3.4	3.8	4.0	4.2	4.3	4.2	4.1
Total government balance (NA basis) ($ bill)	−51.9	−44.8	−39.3	−32.3	−27.3	−23.1	−19.9	−18.3	−18.3	−16.9
Balance as % of GDP	−7.3	−6.0	−5.0	−3.9	−3.2	−2.6	−2.1	−1.8	−1.7	−1.5
Debt as % of GDP	58.0	62.0	64.3	65.3	65.7	65.4	64.5	63.1	61.7	60.0
Federal balance (NA basis) ($ bill)	−30.2	−25.7	−23.1	−18.9	−16.0	−14.2	−13.7	−11.8	−10.8	−8.9
Federal balance as % of GDP	−4.3	−3.5	−3.0	−2.3	−1.9	−1.6	−1.4	−1.2	−1.0	−0.8
Federal debt as % of GDP	50.9	52.5	53.0	52.8	52.4	51.6	50.6	49.3	47.9	46.3
Provincial balance (NA basis) ($ bill)	−21.9	−19.2	−16.3	−13.5	−12.0	−10.2	−7.9	−8.7	−10.2	−11.4

	2003	2004	2005	2006	2007	2008
Real gross domestic product (% growth)	2.9	2.7	2.5	2.3	2.1	2.0
Expenditure on personal consumption	3.1	2.9	2.7	2.5	2.4	2.3
Expenditure by governments	2.2	2.3	2.2	2.6	2.4	2.2
Investment expenditure	2.5	2.2	1.7	1.1	1.0	0.7
Exports	2.9	2.6	2.4	2.0	1.8	1.6
Imports	2.5	2.4	2.2	1.6	1.6	1.5
Inflation rate (CPI)	2.8	3.0	3.1	3.2	3.3	3.3
Unemployment rate	7.2	7.1	7.0	7.0	7.0	7.0
Employment (% change)	1.2	1.0	1.0	0.8	0.7	0.7
Finance Company 90-day paper rate	5.9	5.8	5.8	5.9	5.8	5.8
Labour productivity, private (% change)	0.0	0.0	0.0	0.0	0.0	0.0
Real capital stock (% change)	4.0	3.7	3.5	3.2	2.9	2.6
Total government balance (NA basis) ($ bill)	−17.3	−19.3	−21.2	−23.6	−26.2	−29.0
Balance as % of GDP	−1.5	−1.6	−1.6	−1.7	−1.8	−1.9
Debt as % of GDP	58.3	56.7	55.4	54.3	53.3	52.6
Federal balance (NA basis) ($ bill)	−8.5	−9.4	−10.4	−11.5	−12.7	−14.0
Federal balance as % of GDP	−0.7	−0.8	−0.8	−0.8	−0.9	−0.9
Federal debt as % of GDP	44.5	42.9	41.5	40.2	39.0	38.0
Provincial balance (NA basis) ($ bill)	−12.6	−14.1	−15.7	−17.6	−19.6	−21.8

TABLE 18
Canada Alternative, Lower Trend Growth, Change from Base Projection: Summary of Impacts (% change)[a]

	1993	1994	1995	1996	1997	1998	1999	2000	2001	2002
Real gross domestic product	-0.3	-1.0	-1.5	-2.0	-2.7	-3.5	-4.3	-4.8	-5.3	-5.5
Expenditure on personal consumption	-0.2	-0.7	-1.1	-1.5	-2.1	-2.6	-3.2	-3.6	-3.9	-4.1
Expenditure by governments	0.0	0.0	0.0	0.0	0.0	0.0	0.0	0.0	0.0	0.0
Investment expenditure	-0.9	-3.0	-4.1	-5.2	-7.0	-8.7	-10.3	-11.2	-12.3	-12.8
Exports	-0.9	-3.0	-4.1	-5.2	-7.0	-8.7	-10.3	-11.2	-12.3	-12.8
Imports	-0.9	-3.0	-4.1	-5.2	-7.0	-8.7	-10.3	-11.2	-12.3	-12.8
Inflation rate (CPI)[a]	0.0	0.0	0.0	0.0	0.0	0.0	0.0	0.0	0.0	0.0
Unemployment rate[a]	0.0	0.0	0.0	0.0	0.0	0.0	0.0	0.0	0.0	0.0
Finance Company 90-day paper rate[a]	0.0	0.0	0.0	0.0	0.0	0.0	0.0	0.0	0.0	0.0
Productivity change (GDP/employee)	-0.2	-1.0	-1.5	-2.0	-2.7	-3.4	-4.2	-4.7	-5.2	-5.4
Real capital stock (% change)	0.0	-0.2	-0.6	-1.0	-1.6	-2.4	-3.2	-4.2	-5.1	-6.0
Total government balance (NA basis) ($ bill)[a]	-0.7	-2.7	-4.2	-5.9	-8.7	-11.8	-15.2	-18.0	-20.9	-23.2
Balance as % of GDP[a]	-0.1	-0.4	-0.6	-0.8	-1.1	-1.4	-1.6	-1.8	-2.0	-2.1
Debt as % of GDP[a]	0.2	1.0	1.8	2.8	4.1	5.7	7.4	9.0	10.8	12.3
Federal balance (NA basis) ($ bill)[a]	-0.3	-1.0	-1.6	-2.3	-3.5	-4.8	-6.2	-7.5	-8.7	-9.8
Balance as % of GDP[a]	0.0	-0.2	-0.3	-0.3	-0.4	-0.6	-0.7	-0.8	-0.8	-0.9
Debt as % of GDP[a]	0.2	0.7	1.2	1.7	2.4	3.2	4.1	4.9	5.7	6.4
Provincial government balance (NA basis) ($ bill)[a]	-0.4	-1.6	-2.5	-3.4	-4.9	-6.6	-8.4	-9.7	-11.3	-12.4

	2003	2004	2005	2006	2007	2008
Real gross domestic product	-5.8	-6.0	-6.3	-6.5	-6.8	-7.0
Expenditure on personal consumption	-4.3	-4.4	-4.5	-4.6	-4.8	-4.9
Expenditure by governments	0.0	0.0	0.0	0.0	0.0	0.0
Investment expenditure	-13.4	-14.0	-14.7	-15.4	-16.1	-16.9
Exports	-13.4	-14.0	-14.7	-15.4	-16.1	-16.9
Imports	-13.4	-14.0	-14.7	-15.4	-16.1	-16.9
Inflation rate (CPI)[a]	0.0	0.0	0.0	0.0	0.0	0.0
Unemployment rate[a]	0.0	0.0	0.0	0.0	0.0	0.0
Finance Company 90-day paper rate[a]	0.0	0.0	0.0	0.0	0.0	0.0
Productivity change (GDP/employee)	-5.7	-5.9	-6.2	-6.4	-6.7	-6.9
Real capital stock (% change)	-6.9	-7.7	-8.5	-9.2	-9.9	-10.6
Total government balance (NA basis) ($ bill)[a]	-25.7	-28.3	-31.2	-34.5	-37.9	-41.7
Balance as % of GDP[a]	-2.2	-2.2	-2.3	-2.5	-2.6	-2.7
Debt as % of GDP[a]	13.9	15.4	17.0	18.6	20.3	22.0
Federal balance (NA basis) ($ bill)[a]	-10.8	-11.7	-12.8	-13.9	-15.2	-16.5
Balance as % of GDP[a]	-0.9	-0.9	-1.0	-1.0	-1.0	-1.1
Debt as % of GDP[a]	7.0	7.6	8.3	8.9	9.6	10.2
Provincial government balance (NA basis) ($ bill)[a]	-13.7	-15.1	-16.8	-18.6	-20.6	-22.7

[a]indicates change in levels.

FIGURE 24
Real GDP Growth

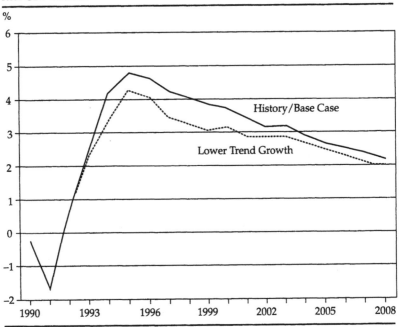

Ontario

The low-growth alternative for Ontario is summarized in Tables
19 and 20 and in Figures 27, 28, and 29. As for Canada, Table 19
shows key indicators for the Ontario economy under the alternative
and Table 20 shows changes from the base case.

The average Ontario growth rate is just over 0.7 per cent per
year lower than in the base case and the fiscal implications are relatively severe. By the year 2000, the Ontario provincial deficit is
about $4 billion worse than in the base case and the provincial
debt/GDP ratio is worse by either 4.5 or 5 percentage points, depending on the particular measure used. Naturally, the damage
worsens steadily thereafter. By 2008 the deficit is up about $9 billion
and the debt/GDP ratio is over 11 percentage points higher. However, despite this deterioration, the deficit/GDP ratio still falls
through the scenario, and the provincial debt/GDP ratio still peaks
(in 2000) and comes down very slowly thereafter. Again, as for Can-

FIGURE 25
Federal Deficit (as % of GDP)

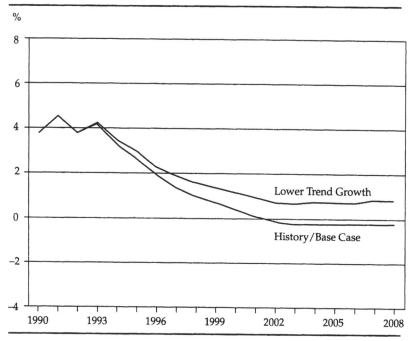

ada as a whole, the low trend growth alternative does not lead to a debt and deficit explosion. But Figure 29 does indicate that even lower trend growth than in the alternative (which would be considered possible, but unlikely) would push the provincial debt/GDP into an inexorable upward path unless provincial fiscal policy were adjusted. And, as in the federal case, if the fiscal objective is a zero deficit by the late 1990s or soon after, then with lower trend growth some combination of spending cuts or additional taxes would be required.

Alternative 2: Interrupted Recovery

The interrupted recovery alternative is a bit more complex than lower trend growth. No change from the base case in the 1993–95 period is assumed. But, in 1996, a world slow-down begins that spills over to Canada. Assuming that the world slow-down is caused by some kind of political or economic crisis or that it results from

FIGURE 26
Federal Debt (as % of GDP)

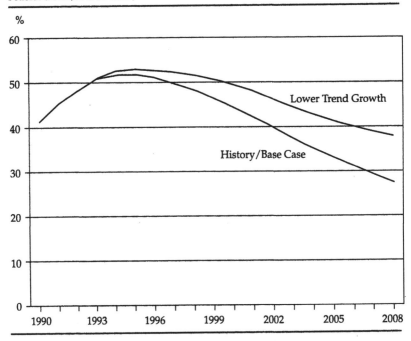

an attempt to halt resurgent inflation, I also assume a 1-percentage-point rise in world real interest rates – which is immediately passed through to Canadian interest rates. In Canada I assume an additional crisis – whether because of the constitution or because of a loss of confidence in Canada by the world financial community – together with a determination to resist any new inflationary pressures in the emerging recovery. As a result, the world downturn and the Canadian crisis lead to very little depreciation of the Canadian dollar but, instead, to still further increases in interest rates. I assume Canadian rates rise 1 to 1.5 percentage points above world rates over a sustained two-year period. (Naturally, rates would likely rise more than this for briefer intervals in a crisis.) Therefore, the total rise in Canadian short and long rates reaches 2.5 percentage points in 1997.

Higher real rates, a world slow-down, and a loss of confidence induce another recession: real growth is only 2.6 per cent in 1996 (well below potential) and zero in 1997. It is true that this assumed

FIGURE 27
Ontario Real GDP Growth

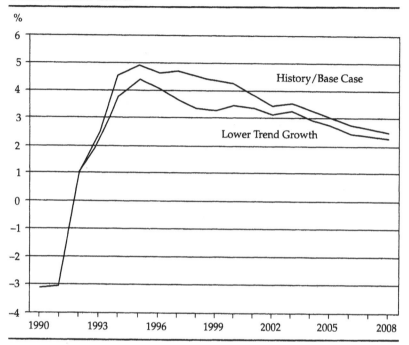

recession is not as bad as those of 1981–82 or 1990–91, but it is more serious than any other recession in the 1960s and 1970s, and it comes upon an economy with an already large output gap and not nearly as far along in recovery as was the economy in 1989. A new output gap of about 6 per cent is opened (on top of a pre-existing gap of from 3 to 4 per cent) and the unemployment rate climbs back above 11 per cent.

But the lesson of economic history is that crises and recessions end and economies recover and adjust. I assume that recovery from the "next" recession proceeds very gradually from 1998 through 2005, leaving the economy 1 per cent below base through 2008 because of a lower capital stock. The unemployment rate falls back to base levels in 2005. The period of additional sustained output gap and lower inflation permanently lowers inflation expectations and puts the inflation path lower than in the base case and, as a result, nominal (but not real) interest rates can gradually fall below

FIGURE 28
Ontario Provincial Deficit (as % of provincial GDP)

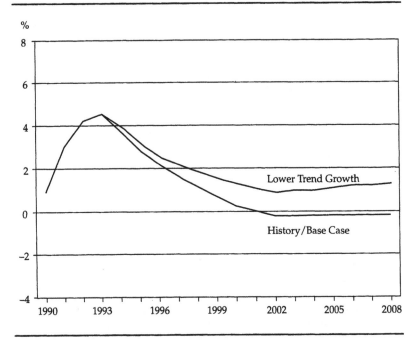

base levels too and the Canadian dollar can appreciate relative to the base in the longer term.

Canada

The interrupted recovery alternative for Canada is summarized in Figures 30 to 32 and Tables 21 and 22. Table 21 presents this alternative's indicators in levels form while Table 22 shows changes from the base case.

The combination of low growth, higher interest rates, and higher unemployment has an immediate and large effect on both the federal and total provincial balances. The federal deficit is worsened by over $20 billion in the 1997–99 period but improves again with the recovery. At its best point, in 2005, the federal deficit is only $5 billion worse than in the base, but then the deficit worsens still more as the higher debt load built up over the recession must be serviced. Nonetheless, the federal deficit as a share of GDP is held well under

FIGURE 29
Estimated Ontario Provincial Debt (as % of provincial GDP)

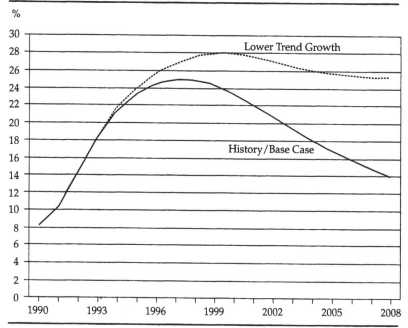

1 per cent and the debt/GDP ratio still declines, although from a higher peak and at a slower rate.

The deficit of the combined provincial sector (which must also cover any deficits at the local and hospital level) does not worsen as seriously as the federal deficit during the recession itself. One major reason for this is that its outstanding debt level is lower and therefore the real interest rate rise has less of an impact on expenditures. However, as the recovery takes place and real rates fall back to base-case levels, the much higher proportion of current and capital spending at the provincial (and local and hospital) levels – all of which is assumed to grow at the same rate as in the base – tells against the provincial deficit. After 2000, the impact on the provincial deficit in dollar terms is greater than on the federal deficit and remains so through 2008.

Ontario

Because my assumed next recession hits especially hard on trade

TABLE 19
Ontario Alternative, Lower Trend Growth: Summary of Projection

	1993	1994	1995	1996	1997	1998	1999	2000	2001	2002
Real provincial product (% change)	2.2	3.8	4.4	4.1	3.7	3.4	3.3	3.5	3.4	3.2
Consumption	0.9	1.7	2.7	2.5	2.4	2.7	2.8	2.7	2.9	2.8
Government	1.6	1.1	1.5	1.7	1.8	1.9	1.9	1.9	2.1	2.2
Private investment	-0.7	7.1	8.0	8.4	5.6	6.0	5.4	5.0	4.3	4.9
Exports	9.7	7.1	5.7	4.8	3.5	2.3	2.3	3.2	3.5	3.4
Imports	8.2	5.5	4.2	3.9	2.4	2.0	2.0	2.6	3.1	3.3
Unemployment rate (%)	10.6	10.2	9.5	8.9	8.3	7.7	7.0	6.5	6.2	5.9
Labour productivity (% change)	-0.1	0.6	0.8	1.1	0.7	0.8	0.8	1.3	1.5	1.6
Consolidated government balance ($ bill)	-13.7	-10.5	-7.6	-4.8	-2.4	-0.8	0.2	2.3	3.9	5.9
Federal balance in Ontario (NA basis) ($ bill)	-3.8	-1.5	-0.3	1.3	2.7	3.4	3.4	4.2	4.9	6.2
Provincial government balance (NA basis) ($ bill)	-13.1	-11.8	-9.8	-8.5	-7.6	-7.0	-6.1	-5.1	-4.5	-4.1
Provincial balance as % of GDP	-4.6	-4.0	-3.2	-2.6	-2.2	-1.9	-1.6	-1.3	-1.1	-0.9
Ratio: Provincial debt (accumulated NA deflator)/GDP (%)	18.4	21.8	24.1	25.7	26.8	27.6	28.0	28.0	27.6	27.1
Provincial government balance (public accounts) ($ bill)	-11.9	-10.8	-8.8	-7.5	-6.6	-5.9	-5.1	-4.1	-3.5	-3.1
Provincial balance (public accounts) as % of GDP	-4.2	-3.7	-2.8	-2.3	-1.9	-1.7	-1.4	-1.0	-0.8	-0.7
Ratio: Provincial debt (public accounts)/GDP (%)	24.9	27.5	29.0	29.9	30.5	30.7	30.6	30.1	29.3	28.4

	2003	2004	2005	2006	2007	2008
Real provincial product (% change)	3.3	3.0	2.8	2.5	2.4	2.3
Consumption	3.5	3.2	2.8	2.5	2.3	2.3
Government	2.3	2.3	2.2	2.6	2.5	2.3
Private investment	3.4	2.9	2.4	1.8	1.5	1.2
Exports	3.1	2.7	2.4	2.4	2.3	2.4
Imports	3.0	2.5	2.1	2.1	2.0	2.1
Unemployment rate (%)	5.5	5.4	5.4	5.4	5.4	5.4
Labour productivity (% change)	1.6	1.8	1.8	1.6	1.5	1.4
Consolidated government balance ($ bill)	6.4	6.3	6.1	5.9	5.6	5.2
Federal balance in Ontario (NA basis) ($ bill)	6.9	7.1	7.3	7.4	7.5	7.7
Provincial government balance (NA basis) ($ bill)	-4.5	-5.1	-5.8	-6.5	-7.2	-8.1
Provincial balance as % of GDP	-1.0	-1.0	-1.1	-1.2	-1.2	-1.3
Ratio: Provincial debt (accumulated NA deflator)/GDP (%)	26.5	26.0	25.7	25.5	25.3	25.3
Provincial government balance (public accounts) ($ bill)	-3.5	-4.1	-4.8	-5.5	-6.2	-7.0
Provincial balance (public accounts) as % of GDP	-0.8	-0.8	-0.9	-1.0	-1.1	-1.2
Ratio: Provincial debt (public accounts)/GDP (%)	27.6	26.9	26.4	26.0	25.7	25.5

TABLE 20
Ontario Alternative, Lower Trend Growth, Change from Base: Summary of Impacts (% change)[a]

	1993	1994	1995	1996	1997	1998	1999	2000	2001	2002
Real provincial product (% change)	-0.2	-1.0	-1.5	-2.0	-3.0	-4.0	-5.0	-5.8	-6.3	-6.5
Consumption	-0.2	-0.7	-1.1	-1.4	-2.1	-2.8	-3.5	-4.1	-4.4	-4.6
Government	0.0	0.0	0.0	0.0	0.0	0.0	0.0	0.0	0.0	0.0
Private investment	-0.8	-2.8	-4.0	-5.0	-7.3	-9.4	-11.5	-12.8	-13.6	-14.0
Exports	-0.8	-2.8	-4.0	-5.0	-7.3	-9.4	-11.5	-12.8	-13.6	-14.0
Imports	-0.8	-2.8	-4.0	-5.0	-7.3	-9.4	-11.5	-12.8	-13.6	-14.0
Unemployment rate[a]	0.0	0.0	0.0	0.0	0.0	0.0	0.0	0.0	0.0	0.0
Labour productivity	-0.2	-1.0	-1.5	-2.0	-3.0	-4.0	-5.0	-5.8	-6.3	-6.5
Consolidated government balance ($ bill)[a]	-0.3	-1.0	-1.5	-2.2	-3.5	-5.1	-6.8	-8.4	-9.8	-10.9
Federal balance in Ontario (NA basis) ($ bill)[a]	-0.1	-0.5	-0.8	-1.1	-1.8	-2.6	-3.5	-4.3	-4.9	-5.5
Provincial government balance (NA basis) ($ bill)[a]	-0.1	-0.5	-0.7	-1.0	-1.6	-2.3	-3.1	-3.9	-4.5	-5.0
Provincial balance as % of GDP[a]	-0.1	-0.2	-0.3	-0.4	-0.5	-0.7	-0.9	-1.0	-1.1	-1.1
Ratio: Provincial debt (accumulated NA deflator)/GDP (%)	0.1	0.4	0.7	1.1	1.8	2.6	3.6	4.5	5.4	6.3
Provincial government balance (public accounts) ($ bill)[a]	-0.1	-0.5	-0.7	-1.0	-1.6	-2.3	-3.1	-3.9	-4.5	-5.0
Provincial balance (public accounts) as % of GDP[a]	-0.1	-0.2	-0.3	-0.3	-0.5	-0.7	-0.9	-1.0	-1.1	-1.1
Ratio: Provincial debt (public accounts)/GDP (%)[a]	0.1	0.5	0.9	1.4	2.1	3.0	4.0	5.0	5.9	6.7

	2003	2004	2005	2006	2007	2008
Real provincial product (% change)	−6.8	−7.0	−7.3	−7.5	−7.8	−8.0
Consumption	−4.8	−4.9	−5.1	−5.2	−5.4	−5.5
Government	0.0	0.0	0.0	0.0	0.0	0.0
Private investment	−14.4	−14.9	−15.4	−16.0	−16.5	−17.1
Exports	−14.4	−14.9	−15.4	−16.0	−16.5	−17.1
Imports	−14.4	−14.9	−15.4	−16.0	−16.5	−17.1
Unemployment rate[a]	0.0	0.0	0.0	0.0	0.0	0.0
Labour productivity	−6.8	−7.0	−7.3	−7.5	−7.8	−8.0
Consolidated government balance ($ bill)[a]	−12.1	−13.3	−14.6	−16.1	−17.7	−19.5
Federal balance in Ontario (NA basis) ($ bill)[a]	−6.1	−6.6	−7.2	−7.9	−8.6	−9.4
Provincial government balance (NA basis) ($ bill)[a]	−5.5	−6.1	−6.7	−7.4	−8.2	−9.0
Provincial balance as % of GDP[a]	−1.2	−1.2	−1.3	−1.3	−1.4	−1.5
Ratio: Provincial debt (accumulated NA deflator)/GDP (%)	7.1	7.9	8.8	9.6	10.5	11.4
Provincial government balance (public accounts) ($ bill)[a]	−5.5	−6.1	−6.7	−7.4	−8.2	−9.0
Provincial balance (public accounts) as % of GDP[a]	−1.1	−1.2	−1.3	−1.3	−1.4	−1.4
Ratio: Provincial debt (public accounts)/GDP (%)[a]	7.6	8.4	9.2	10.1	11.0	11.9

[a]indicates change in levels.

TABLE 21
Canada Alternative, Interrupted Recovery: Summary of Projection

	1993	1994	1995	1996	1997	1998	1999	2000	2001	2002
Real gross domestic product (% growth)	2.5	4.2	4.8	2.6	0.0	4.6	4.7	4.6	4.3	4.0
Expenditure on personal consumption	1.3	2.2	3.7	2.0	0.0	2.4	3.6	4.3	4.2	3.7
Expenditure by governments	1.2	0.8	1.6	1.8	1.9	2.0	2.0	2.0	2.1	2.2
Investment expenditure	1.0	8.8	8.2	5.6	0.6	6.4	8.7	7.6	6.1	6.2
Exports	8.3	8.9	7.0	2.9	-1.7	6.7	6.7	6.4	5.8	5.2
Imports	6.5	6.1	5.2	3.1	-0.7	2.7	5.9	6.5	5.7	5.3
Inflation rate (CPI)	1.9	1.5	1.1	1.1	1.2	1.3	1.6	1.6	1.8	2.0
Unemployment rate	11.3	10.8	10.1	10.4	11.4	10.2	9.1	8.6	8.2	7.8
Finance Company 90-day paper rate	5.1	4.6	4.7	6.5	7.1	6.8	6.8	6.0	5.5	5.4
Labour productivity, private (% change)	0.0	0.0	0.0	0.0	0.0	0.0	0.0	0.0	0.0	0.0
Real capital stock (% change)	2.6	2.9	3.3	3.8	3.8	3.6	4.1	4.7	4.9	5.0
Exchange rate (U.S.$/Cdn$)	0.777	0.768	0.778	0.788	0.794	0.804	0.813	0.824	0.834	0.844
Total government balance (NA basis) ($ bill)	-51.2	-42.1	-35.0	-37.6	-51.1	-46.0	-39.4	-33.4	-26.7	-19.3
Balance as % of GDP	-7.2	-5.6	-4.4	-4.6	-6.1	-5.2	-4.2	-3.4	-2.5	-1.7
Debt as % of GDP	57.8	61.0	62.4	64.6	69.3	71.0	71.4	70.9	69.7	67.9
Federal balance (NA basis) ($ bill)	-29.9	-24.7	-21.5	-24.3	-32.9	-30.8	-28.0	-22.4	-16.1	-9.5
Federal balance as % of GDP	-4.2	-3.3	-2.7	-3.0	-3.9	-3.5	-3.0	-2.3	-1.5	-0.9
Federal debt as % of GDP	50.7	51.8	51.8	52.7	55.6	56.2	56.1	55.4	54.1	52.2
Provincial balance (NA basis) ($ bill)	-21.5	-17.6	-13.8	-13.4	-18.5	-16.1	-12.8	-12.8	-13.1	-13.0

	2003	2004	2005	2006	2007	2008
Real gross domestic product (% growth)	4.0	3.4	3.0	2.6	2.4	2.2
Expenditure on personal consumption	4.1	3.8	3.3	2.8	2.6	2.4
Expenditure by governments	2.2	2.3	2.2	2.6	2.4	2.2
Investment expenditure	4.7	3.8	2.9	1.9	1.8	1.5
Exports	4.9	4.0	3.6	2.8	2.6	2.4
Imports	4.6	4.2	3.5	2.6	2.4	2.3
Inflation rate (CPI)	2.1	2.3	2.3	2.4	2.5	2.5
Unemployment rate	7.5	7.2	7.0	7.0	7.0	7.0
Finance Company 90-day paper rate	5.2	5.2	5.1	5.2	5.2	5.1
Labour productivity, private (% change)	0.0	0.0	0.0	0.0	0.0	0.0
Real capital stock (% change)	5.1	4.9	4.6	4.3	3.9	3.6
Exchange rate (U.S.$/Cdn$)	0.854	0.863	0.872	0.880	0.889	0.897
Total government balance (NA basis) ($ bill)	-13.5	-11.0	-9.6	-10.4	-11.7	-13.1
Balance as % of GDP	-1.1	-0.9	-0.7	-0.8	-0.8	-0.9
Debt as % of GDP	65.4	62.9	60.6	58.5	56.6	55.0
Federal balance (NA basis) ($ bill)	-5.1	-3.4	-2.7	-3.2	-4.0	-4.9
Federal balance as % of GDP	-0.4	-0.3	-0.2	-0.2	-0.3	-0.3
Federal debt as % of GDP	49.8	47.5	45.4	43.5	41.8	40.2
Provincial balance (NA basis) ($ bill)	-12.4	-12.3	-12.4	-13.5	-14.7	-16.0

TABLE 22
Canada Alternative, Interrupted Recovery, Change from Base Projection (% change)[a]

	1993	1994	1995	1996	1997	1998	1999	2000	2001	2002
Real gross domestic product	0.0	0.0	0.0	-2.0	-6.0	-5.5	-4.7	-4.0	-3.2	-2.5
Expenditure on personal consumption	0.0	0.0	0.0	-1.2	-4.3	-5.1	-4.8	-4.0	-3.3	-2.5
Expenditure by governments	0.0	0.0	0.0	0.0	0.0	0.0	0.0	0.0	0.0	0.0
Investment expenditure	0.0	0.0	0.0	-2.7	-8.7	-9.6	-8.2	-6.6	-5.1	-3.6
Exports	0.0	0.0	0.0	-3.6	-10.8	-9.9	-8.4	-7.0	-5.7	-4.4
Imports	0.0	0.0	0.0	-2.0	-7.3	-9.6	-8.7	-7.2	-5.7	-4.3
Inflation rate (CPI)[a]	0.0	0.0	0.0	-0.3	-0.3	-0.5	-0.6	-0.7	-0.7	-0.7
Unemployment rate[a]	0.0	0.0	0.0	0.8	2.5	1.9	1.5	1.2	0.9	0.6
Finance company 90-day paper rate[a]	0.0	0.0	0.0	2.0	2.5	1.5	1.0	0.3	-0.3	-0.5
Productivity change (GDP/employee)	0.0	0.0	0.0	-0.8	-2.3	-2.5	-2.3	-1.9	-1.6	-1.3
Real capital stock (% change)	0.0	0.0	0.0	-0.1	-0.7	-1.8	-2.7	-3.3	-3.6	-3.7
Exchange rate (U.S.$/Cdn$)	0.0	0.0	0.0	0.0	-0.3	-0.2	0.0	0.5	0.9	1.4
Total government balance (NA basis) ($ bill)[a]	0.0	0.0	0.1	-11.2	-32.5	-34.7	-34.8	-33.0	-29.3	-25.6
Balance as % of GDP[a]	0.0	0.0	0.0	-1.4	-4.0	-4.0	-3.8	-3.3	-2.8	-2.3
Debt as % of GDP[a]	0.0	0.0	0.0	2.1	7.7	11.3	14.3	16.9	18.8	20.2
Federal balance (NA basis) ($ bill)[a]	0.0	0.0	0.0	-7.8	-20.4	-21.4	-20.6	-18.1	-14.0	-10.4
Balance as % of GDP[a]	0.0	0.0	0.0	-1.0	-2.5	-2.5	-2.2	-1.9	-1.3	-0.9
Debt as % of GDP[a]	0.0	0.0	0.0	1.6	5.6	7.9	9.6	11.0	11.9	12.3
Provincial government balance (NA basis) ($ bill)[a]	0.0	0.0	0.1	-3.2	-11.4	-12.5	-13.3	-13.9	-14.1	-14.0

	2003	2004	2005	2006	2007	2008
Real gross domestic product	-1.7	-1.3	-1.0	-1.0	-1.0	-1.0
Expenditure on personal consumption	-1.7	-1.0	-0.6	-0.4	-0.4	-0.3
Expenditure by governments	0.0	0.0	0.0	0.0	0.0	0.0
Investment expenditure	-2.3	-1.5	-1.1	-1.1	-1.2	-1.3
Exports	-3.3	-2.6	-2.3	-2.3	-2.4	-2.5
Imports	-2.9	-1.9	-1.4	-1.2	-1.3	-1.4
Inflation rate (CPI)[a]	-0.7	-0.7	-0.7	-0.8	-0.8	-0.8
Unemployment rate[a]	0.3	0.1	0.0	0.0	0.0	0.0
Finance company 90-day paper rate[a]	-0.7	-0.7	-0.7	-0.7	-0.7	-0.7
Productivity change (GDP/employee)	-1.1	-1.0	-0.9	-0.9	-0.9	-0.9
Real capital stock (% change)	-3.6	-3.3	-3.0	-2.7	-2.5	-2.3
Exchange rate (U.S.$/Cdn$)	1.9	2.4	2.9	3.4	4.0	4.5
Total government balance (NA basis) ($ bill)[a]	-21.9	-20.1	-19.6	-21.3	-23.4	-25.8
Balance as % of GDP[a]	-1.8	-1.6	-1.5	-1.5	-1.6	-1.6
Debt as % of GDP[a]	21.0	21.6	22.2	22.9	23.6	24.4
Federal balance (NA basis) ($ bill)[a]	-7.4	-5.7	-5.1	-5.6	-6.5	-7.5
Balance as % of GDP[a]	-0.6	-0.4	-0.4	-0.4	-0.4	-0.5
Debt as % of GDP[a]	12.3	12.2	12.2	12.2	12.3	12.4
Provincial government balance (NA basis) ($ bill)[a]	-13.4	-13.3	-13.4	-14.5	-15.7	-16.9

[a]indicates change in levels

FIGURE 30
Real GDP Growth

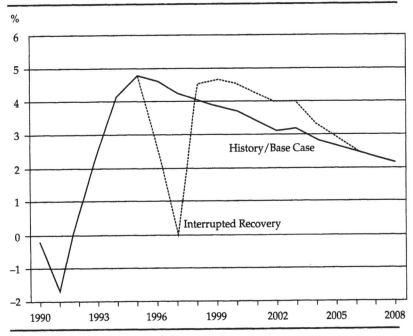

and investment, real impacts are somewhat more severe for Ontario than for Canada as a whole. Ontario real growth declines 2.4 per cent from base in 1996 (versus 2 per cent for Canada) and 6.5 per cent from base in 1997 (versus 6 per cent for Canada). But the Ontario economy is also assumed to recover most of this extra lost ground in the following years. The recession assumed is, for Ontario, much less serious than that of 1990 to 1992 and therefore I would also expect the fiscal implications to be less serious too. But note that, when this "next" recession hits, the Ontario economy is only partway along its recovery from the 1990–92 recession and the absolute levels of the output gap and the unemployment rate reached in this next recession are very high. For example, the Ontario unemployment rate reaches over 11 per cent in 1997, above even its peak in the early 1990s.

The Ontario interrupted recovery alternative is depicted in Figures 33 to 35 and Tables 23 and 24.

The impact on the Ontario provincial deficit of my assumed 1996–

FIGURE 31
Federal Deficit (as % of GDP)

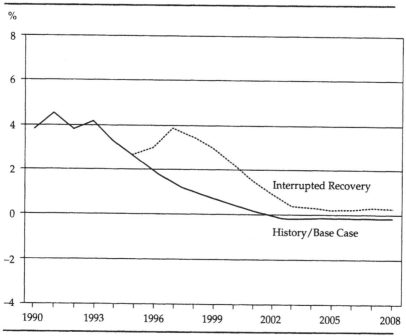

97 recession reaches about $5 billion in the late 1990s, or just over an additional 1 per cent of GDP. One major reason Ontario is less severely affected than the federal government, or even some other provinces, is that its proportional debt load is lower coming into the recession and the impact of higher real interest rates is not as great. By the same token, there is less recovery in the deficit when interest rates come down again after 1998. Therefore, the build-up of debt and other expenditures and loss of some tax revenues lingers on, such that the provincial deficit never fully recovers with the economy (although the deficit/GDP ratio does fall back some-what). The debt/GDP profile is raised by the assumed recession, but it still peaks and falls after the turn of the century at a more gradual pace than in the base case.

The lesson of this alternative is that a severe disruption in the recovery of the Ontario economy would not put the Ontario fiscal situation out of control, but that it would require some additional fiscal adjustments (lower expenditures than in the base case, or

FIGURE 32
Federal Debt (as % of GDP)

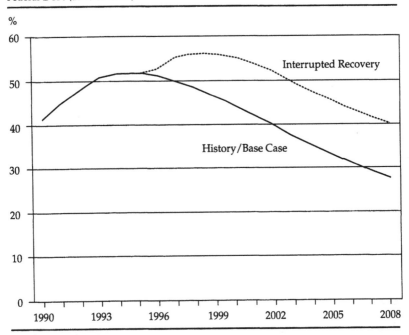

higher taxes) in the recovery phase to put the deficit and debt paths
back on a reasonable track.

Conclusions

This paper has attempted to present a picture of the economic future
of the Ontario economy, together with two more pessimistic alternatives. When a painting is put on display, it should normally
be left to gallery-goers to reach their own conclusions – both about
whether the painting is any good or not and about what the painting
says to them. That should also be the case with the readers of this
paper, but I make bold to offer a few tentative conclusions of my
own.

Canada and Ontario can be expected to enjoy a period of sustained
high growth through the remainder of the 1990s and beyond. This
growth will be based on an underlying potential growth above 3
per cent, combined with growth needed to close an output gap that

FIGURE 33
Ontario Real GDP Growth

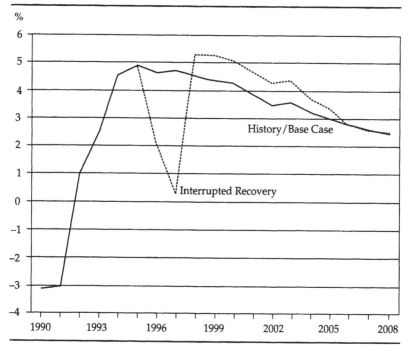

may be over 10 per cent for Canada, and more for Ontario. A series of years with non-inflationary growth above 4 per cent might reasonably be expected. This growth will be led by business investment, housing, and net exports, with consumption growth on average below that of GDP. Corporate incomes might be expected to rise relative to wage incomes, moving in the direction of more long-run average shares for each income category.

It is clear that both the federal government and the Ontario provincial government face significant fiscal pressures in the form of high deficits for some years to come. But at the same time, the problem is fully controllable, if not fully under control. For the federal government especially, recovery from the 1990–92 recession, together with sustained but not Draconian restrictions on expenditure, should erase most of the deficit by the late 1990s. The ratio of federal debt to GDP – the primary indicator of fiscal well-being – starts to decline even sooner.

It also appears that the problem is more serious at the Ontario

TABLE 23
Ontario Alternative, Interrupted Recovery: Summary of Projection

	1993	1994	1995	1996	1997	1998	1999	2000	2001	2002
Real provincial product (% change)	2.5	4.6	4.9	2.1	0.3	5.3	5.3	5.1	4.7	4.3
Consumption	1.1	2.3	3.1	1.5	-0.6	1.5	4.0	4.3	4.4	4.1
Government	1.6	1.1	1.5	1.7	1.8	1.9	1.9	1.9	2.1	2.2
Private investment	0.1	9.4	9.3	6.4	0.7	5.2	10.0	9.4	7.8	7.5
Exports	10.6	9.3	6.9	2.5	-0.6	5.8	6.0	6.1	5.8	5.0
Imports	9.1	7.7	5.5	2.9	-1.1	1.2	5.5	6.1	6.0	5.5
Unemployment rate (%)	10.6	10.2	9.5	9.8	11.1	9.8	8.7	7.8	7.2	6.6
Labour productivity (% change)	0.1	1.3	1.3	0.6	0.6	1.7	2.0	2.2	2.3	2.1
Consolidated government balance ($ bill)	-13.5	-9.6	-6.2	-7.5	-11.8	-9.3	-6.5	-2.0	2.2	6.4
Federal balance in Ontario (NA basis) ($ bill)	-3.7	-1.1	0.4	-1.1	-3.9	-2.6	-1.5	0.9	3.5	6.2
Provincial government balance (NA basis) $ bill)	-12.9	-11.3	-9.1	-8.5	-9.3	-8.5	-7.1	-5.6	-4.6	-3.9
Provincial balance as % of GDP	-4.6	-3.8	-2.9	-2.6	-2.8	-2.4	-1.9	-1.4	-1.1	-0.9
Ratio: Provincial debt (accumulate NA deflator)/GDP (%)	18.4	21.4	23.4	25.4	27.7	28.6	28.9	28.7	28.2	27.5
Provincial government balance (public accounts) ($ bill)	-11.8	-10.3	-8.1	-7.5	-8.3	-7.4	-6.1	-4.6	-3.5	-2.8
Provincial balance (public accounts) as % of GDP	-4.2	-3.5	-2.6	-2.3	-2.5	-2.1	-1.6	-1.1	-0.8	-0.6
Ratio: Provincial debt (public accounts)/GDP (%)	24.8	27.0	28.1	29.6	31.7	32.0	31.6	30.9	29.9	28.8

	2003	2004	2005	2006	2007	2008
Real provincial product (% change)	4.4	3.8	3.4	2.8	2.6	2.5
Consumption	4.9	4.4	3.7	2.9	2.6	2.5
Government	2.3	2.3	2.2	2.6	2.5	2.3
Private investment	5.8	4.8	3.7	2.5	2.1	1.9
Exports	4.6	3.8	3.3	3.0	2.9	3.1
Imports	5.1	4.2	3.4	2.9	2.6	2.8
Unemployment rate (%)	5.8	5.5	5.4	5.4	5.4	5.4
Labour productivity (% change)	1.9	2.3	2.2	1.9	1.8	1.7
Consolidated government balance ($ bill)	9.3	10.8	11.8	12.2	12.3	12.3
Federal balance in Ontario (NA basis) ($ bill)	8.3	9.3	10.0	10.4	10.6	10.9
Provincial government balance (NA basis) ($ bill)	-3.9	-4.1	-4.6	-5.3	-6.2	-7.2
Provincial balance as % of GDP	-0.8	-0.8	-0.9	-1.0	-1.1	-1.2
Ratio: Provincial debt (accumulate NA deflator)/GDP (%)	26.7	26.0	25.4	25.1	25.0	24.9
Provincial government balance (public accounts) ($ bill)	-2.9	-3.1	-3.6	-4.3	-5.2	-6.2
Provincial balance (public accounts) as % of GDP	-0.6	-0.6	-0.7	-0.8	-0.9	-1.0
Ratio: Provincial debt (public accounts)/GDP (%)	27.7	26.8	26.1	25.6	25.2	25.1

TABLE 24
Ontario Alternative, Interrupted Recovery, Change from Base Projection (% change)[a]

	1993	1994	1995	1996	1997	1998	1999	2000	2001	2002
Real provincial product (% change)	0.0	0.0	0.0	-2.4	-6.5	-5.8	-5.0	-4.2	-3.5	-2.7
Consumption	0.0	0.0	0.0	-1.4	-4.9	-6.7	-6.3	-5.4	-4.4	-3.4
Government	0.0	0.0	0.0	0.0	0.0	0.0	0.0	0.0	0.0	0.0
Private investment	0.0	0.0	0.0	-3.0	-9.7	-12.4	-10.6	-8.3	-6.2	-4.3
Exports	0.0	0.0	0.0	-3.3	-9.4	-8.5	-7.3	-6.1	-5.0	-3.9
Imports	0.0	0.0	0.0	-2.1	-7.7	-10.5	-9.5	-7.8	-6.1	-4.6
Unemployment rate[a]	0.0	0.0	0.0	0.9	2.8	2.1	1.7	1.3	1.0	0.7
Labour productivity	0.0	0.0	0.0	-1.0	-2.1	-2.3	-2.1	-2.0	-1.8	-1.5
Consolidated government balance ($ bill)[a]	0.0	-0.1	-0.1	-4.9	-13.0	-13.7	-13.5	-12.7	-11.4	-10.4
Federal balance in Ontario (NA basis) ($ bill)[a]	0.0	-0.1	-0.1	-3.5	-8.3	-8.7	-8.4	-7.6	-6.4	-5.5
Provincial government balance (NA basis) ($ bill)[a]	0.0	0.0	0.0	-1.0	-3.3	-3.8	-4.1	-4.3	-4.6	-4.7
Provincial balance as % of GDP[a]	0.0	0.0	0.0	-0.4	-1.1	-1.2	-1.1	-1.1	-1.1	-1.0
Ratio: Provincial debt (accumulate NA deflator)/GDP (%)	0.0	0.0	0.0	0.8	2.7	3.6	4.5	5.3	6.0	6.7
Provincial government balance (public accounts) ($ bill)[a]	0.0	0.0	0.0	-1.0	-3.3	-3.8	-4.1	-4.3	-4.5	-4.7
Provincial balance (public accounts) as % of GDP[a]	0.0	0.0	0.0	-0.4	-1.1	-1.2	-1.1	-1.1	-1.1	-1.0
Ratio: Provincial debt (public accounts)/GDP (%)[a]	0.0	0.0	0.0	1.0	3.3	4.3	5.0	5.8	6.5	7.1

	2003	2004	2005	2006	2007	2008
Real provincial product (% change)	-2.0	-1.5	-1.2	-1.2	-1.2	-1.2
Consumption	-2.2	-1.2	-0.6	-0.3	-0.2	-0.2
Government	0.0	0.0	0.0	0.0	0.0	0.0
Private investment	-2.5	-1.3	-0.6	-0.5	-0.6	-0.6
Exports	-3.1	-2.6	-2.3	-2.4	-2.5	-2.6
Imports	-3.1	-2.0	-1.4	-1.2	-1.3	-1.3
Unemployment rate[a]	0.3	0.1	0.0	0.0	0.0	0.0
Labour productivity	-1.4	-1.3	-1.2	-1.2	-1.2	-1.2
Consolidated government balance ($ bill)[a]	-9.2	-8.8	-8.9	-9.9	-11.0	-12.3
Federal balance in Ontario (NA basis) ($ bill)[a]	-4.7	-4.4	-4.5	-5.0	-5.6	-6.2
Provincial government balance (NA basis) ($ bill)[a]	-4.8	-5.1	-5.5	-6.3	-7.2	-8.2
Provincial balance as % of GDP[a]	-1.0	-1.0	-1.0	-1.1	-1.2	-1.3
Ratio: Provincial debt (accumulate NA deflator)/GDP (%)	7.3	7.9	8.5	9.3	10.1	11.0
Provincial government balance (public accounts) ($ bill)[a]	-4.8	-5.1	-5.5	-6.3	-7.2	-8.2
Provincial balance (public accounts) as % of GDP[a]	-1.0	-1.0	-1.0	-1.1	-1.2	-1.3
Ratio: Provincial debt (public accounts)/GDP (%)[a]	7.7	8.3	8.9	9.7	10.5	11.4

[a]indicates change in levels

FIGURE 34
Ontario Provincial Debt (Estimated) (as % of provincial GDP)

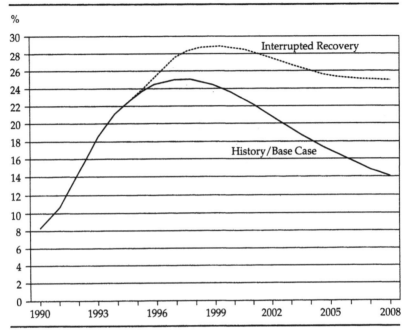

provincial level than for the federal government, but that the problem is again controllable. For the provincial government I find that some tax increases are required together with credible and sustained expenditure restraint to put the deficit on a firm downward path and, ultimately, to reduce the ratio of debt to GDP. Note that the requirement of expenditure restraint extends to the municipalities and hospitals, as their deficits are, in the end, the responsibility of the province. The tax increases and spending cuts in the Ontario budget of May 1993 and the following "Social Contract" effort give us all the more reason to conclude that the provincial fiscal situation is in the process of being effectively controlled.

The alternative simulations show that the fiscal paths for both the federal and provincial governments are, of course, sensitive to any further economic disruptions in the 1990s and to disappointments in the underlying growth paths the economies can achieve. But the fiscal paths do not appear to be balanced on knife edges: the relatively severe alternatives I examined certainly worsened the debt/GDP profiles of both the federal and Ontario governments, but they did not send them spinning off into exponential growth and ultimate catastrophe – and this was before any discretionary fiscal corrections.

Several important challenges to the fiscal and tax systems can be seen emerging from this picture of the economy. Obviously, under strong deficit pressure, the tax system will need to be as efficient as possible. This will prove especially so if more research shows that growth in the underground economy is responsible for eroding the tax base in the early 1990s. This will lead to strong emphasis on tax enforcement and enforceable taxes.

A theme of my projections is that the federal deficit problem, owing to debt and deficit dynamics and the relatively higher spending pressures facing the sub-federal governments, can be more easily and swiftly solved than that of the provinces. Will or should this lead to increased federal transfers to provinces, or to transfers of tax powers, or to increased federal spending in areas of provincial responsibilities?

Inflation will continue to be a preoccupation of the Bank of Canada and the federal government, but indirect taxes for environmental or revenue purposes can exert strong inflationary pressures. My projection shows that some indirect tax increases can be accommodated, but excess reliance on indirect tax hikes for revenue purposes (as in the late 1980s)[11] would force anti-inflationary restriction of monetary policy that could hobble growth and revenues. Indirect-tax increases for environmental or other purposes should be offset by indirect-tax reductions elsewhere to neutralize any inflationary effect.

Because consumption will be to some extent a lagging spending sector in the recovery, revenue from consumption-based taxes (such as the GST or a harmonized RST) cannot be expected to match nominal GDP growth. This does not argue against such taxes, but only that these revenue consequences need to be recognized in sound fiscal planning.

Notes

1 The Institute for Policy Analysis at the University of Toronto developed its first, medium-term projection for the Ontario economy in 1977 (see David K. Foot et al. 1977). Researchers at the Institute have been build-

ing macroeconometric models and applying them to problems of policy analysis and economic projection since the late 1960s.

2 For detailed descriptions of the models, see D. Peter Dungan and Gregory Jump (1992) mimeo; and D. Peter Dungan (1992) mimeo.

3 The population projections are taken from *Population Projections for Canada, Provinces and Territories: 1989–2011* (Ottawa: 1990). Population projection 3 is used, based on average fertility of 1.7 children per woman and average immigration of 200,000 per year.

4 See D. Peter Dungan, Richard G. Harris, and Thomas A. Wilson (1991, 417–57).

5 This section is a brief overview of the projection results for Canada, intended as background to the more detailed description of the projection for Ontario in the fourth section, below. For more detail on a national projection developed slightly earlier than the projection here, see D. Peter Dungan, Steve Murphy, and Thomas Wilson (1993).

6 My measure of the output gap versus those of 1989 levels off at over 2.0 per cent, allowing for the possibility that the economy was in fact at excess capacity in that year or that potential growth has been overestimated.

7 Spending and tax categories in the model have not been adjusted for the substitution of child-care credits in the place of family allowances, to take place at the beginning of 1993. This substitution will cause a one-time reduction in transfers and in personal income tax revenues that will largely balance.

8 As it is in my projection, the pension plans run almost no net surplus through the 1990s – which is a doubtful result. Their payouts may have been over-projected in this period, or it is possible that still greater increases in the pension-plan contribution rates will be required.

9 In my debt measures for the federal, provincial, and consolidated government accounts, I have used accumulated NIA measures as these are the most easily calculated within the model and, in my view, give the best picture of government debts in relation to GDP and other NIA income measures. Public accounts measures of federal debt and total debts are uniformly higher than accumulated NIA deficit measures, but they can be expected to move in much the same trajectories in the next decade. All the debt measures so far mentioned are gross debts. No attempt has been made in any of these calculations to value the stocks of government assets (which include port facilities, airports, highways, and hospitals).

10 The provincial debt stock used in the model is the accumulated stock of provincial income-account deficits. It will vary from the total debt on a

public accounts basis published by the Ontario Ministry of Finance. The rough projection for the debt/GDP and deficit on the public accounts basis is shown in Table 8.

11 For an analysis of the various sources of the recession see Thomas Wilson, Peter Dungan, and Steve Murphy (1993).

Bibliography

Dungan, D. Peter, Richard G. Harris, and Thomas A. Wilson. 1991. "Symposium – The Canada–U.S. Free Trade Agreement." *Journal of Policy Modeling*, 13 (3): 417–57

Dungan, D. Peter. 1992. *The FOCUS-Ontario Model*, Version 92A. Institute for Policy Analysis. Mimeo

Dungan, D. Peter, and Gregory Jump. 1992. *FOCUS: Forecasting and User Simulation Model of the Canadian Economy*, Version 92A. Institute for Policy Analysis. Mimeo

Dungan, Peter, Steve Murphy, and Thomas Wilson. 1993. "Outlook for the Canadian Economy: National Projection through 2015." *PEAP Policy Study 93-4*, August. Institute for Policy Analysis. Toronto: University of Toronto Press

Foot, David K., James E. Pesando, John A. Sawyer, and John W.L. Winder. 1977. *The Ontario Economy 1977–1987*. Toronto: Ontario Economic Council

Statistics Canada. 1990. *Population Projections for Canada, Provinces and Territories: 1989–2011*. Cat. No. 91–520. Ottawa: Queen's Printer

Wilson, Thomas, Peter Dungan, and Steve Murphy. 1993. "The Sources of the Recession in Canada: 1989–1992." *Policy and Economic Analysis Program Policy Study 93-2*, May. Institute for Policy Analysis. Toronto: University of Toronto Press

4 Pensions, Deficits, and Ageing: Impacts for Ontario's Residents

BRIAN B. MURPHY and MICHAEL C. WOLFSON

Introduction

Canada, like many other countries, is experiencing a significant ageing of its population. The "baby boom" was reflected in a peak of 3.9 in the fertility rate in the mid-1960s and was followed by a "baby bust" with a sharp drop in fertility to 1.7 by the early 1970s.[1] Fertility has remained roughly constant since that time. However, as has been pointed out in a recent IMF study (Heller, Hemming, and Hohnert 1986) of seven major industrialized countries, Canada has the lowest expected public-sector costs associated with an ageing population. Subsequently, Fellegi (1988) and Murphy and Wolfson (1991) have undertaken more detailed projections of the impacts of an ageing population structure.

The main focus of this paper is the projected public-sector costs of the major cash-transfer programs in Ontario and Canada, in conjunction with income and sales tax revenues. These projected tax and transfer flows will be analysed in relation to various scenarios for demographic change, labour-force participation rates, economic growth, and structural aspects related principally to indexing provisions. The conventional wisdom is that the expected ageing of the population will have a major adverse impact on the public-sector cost/revenue balance, a theme of recurring attention in the national press (for example, Beauchesne 1993; Gault 1993). However, by analysing demographic changes in relation to economic growth, and program and taxation structures, it becomes apparent that population ageing is not always the most important factor.

This paper is an update and extension of parts of our previous analysis mentioned above. The current analysis focuses on Ontario and differs from the earlier study in three ways. First, the projected time periods are closer (2001 and 2011 versus 2016 and 2036). Also, a scenario using Ontario-dominated migration patterns has been added. Second, due to difficulties in obtaining accurate provincial-level data on health and education use and costs, in-kind transfers are not examined. Third, we have added two scenarios that simulate different economic growth assumptions.

The paper takes as its starting point estimates of government taxes and transfers in 1988. These results are compared with various projections for the years 1993 and 2011. While our earlier analysis (Murphy and Wolfson 1991) examined the years in which the leading and trailing edge of Canada's baby boom cohort will reach age 65 (that is, as far ahead as 2036), this analysis focuses on the next one or two decades. Moreover, results for the province of Ontario are highlighted and then compared with results for Canada.

Public Sector Taxes and Programs

Two main groups of public-sector activities will be explicitly analysed for both the federal and Ontario provincial governments – taxes bearing more or less directly on households, and major cash transfers.

Taxes considered in this analysis are personal income taxes (both federal and provincial), payroll taxes used to fund the public contributory pension system (the Canada and Quebec pension plans or C/QPP) and unemployment insurance (UI), and the federal and provincial sales taxes borne by households. Taxes such as the GST, to the extent that they are levied at intermediate levels in the production process, are assumed to be shifted forward to consumers.

The major cash transfers are the public pension programs, unemployment insurance, child benefits, and welfare. The public pension programs consist of several tiers: earnings-related pensions (the C/QPP); the federal old-age demogrant – old-age security (OAS); and a guaranteed annual income benefit received by about half of the over-65 population – the guaranteed income supplement (GIS). Child benefits consist mainly of a tax credit in respect of children under age 18 called the child tax benefit. Effective 1 January 1993, this program replaced family allowances, the refundable child tax credit, and the non-refundable child tax credit for dependent children in the income tax system. Unemployment insurance in Canada, operated by the federal government, is a very large program compared with those of other OECD countries. Finally, welfare, or social assistance benefits, constitute the "social safety net" income support program of last resort. Neither of these programs provides significant benefits to the elderly. However, they do tend to provide relatively more benefits to younger families, owing to the higher unemployment rates and incidence of single parenthood at young ages. Thus, population ageing might be expected to have some effects on the projected costs of these programs.

The federal government is responsible for most of the above-mentioned programs. Provincial income taxes are largely based on a percentage of federal tax payable. Recently, Ontario and several other provinces have implemented a number of tax credit programs, some of which will be sensitive to changes in age structure and family composition. In 1978, Ontario had only two tax credits, the property tax credit and political contribution tax credit. By 1993 at least five new programs had been added, including a grant for seniors that is being phased into a tax credit for seniors, as well as a dependant-based tax reduction. Provincial cash transfers are largely made up of social assistance payments under the Canada assistance plan (CAP). Changes to the federal/provincial cost-sharing rules have increased Ontario's proportion of CAP costs to over 70 per cent in 1993 from 50 per cent in 1988. (Other provincial transfers such as workers' compensation are not analysed explicitly, but are included.)

The Simulation Approach

The projections that underlie this analysis are based on Statistics Canada's Social Policy Simulation Database and Model (SPSD/M). This is a publicly accessible PC-based microsimulation model of the principal federal and provincial taxes and cash-transfer programs. The version used for this analysis is based on a detailed income distribution microdata file for 1988. (See Bordt et al. 1990 or Wolfson et al. 1990, for a fuller description.)

The SPSD/M does not account for all taxes or transfers. Absent are corporate income taxes, municipal-level taxes, and in-kind publicly provided benefits in areas such as health, education, housing, and transportation. (Projections of health and education costs were included in Murphy and Wolfson 1991.) In the 1988 release of the

SPSD/M, the model accurately accounted for over 60 per cent of the national accounts estimate of total federal and provincial direct and indirect taxes, and virtually 100 per cent of the cash transfers were covered. Of these major cash transfers, about 80 per cent are explicitly modelled, with the remainder coming from survey data (for example, workers' compensation).

Two main procedures have been used to construct the projections that underlie this analysis. First, the effects of changing population and labour-force participation are simulated by adjusting survey weights. The starting point is the 1988 population sample microdata file, the Social Policy Simulation Database or SPSD. It is reweighted to reflect the individual population age structure by province, sex, and five-year age groups as given by each of Statistics Canada's four standard demographic projections – one low, two middle, and one high population-growth scenario – for the two target years, 2001 and 2011 (Statistics Canada 1990). A detailed list of assumptions underlying the specific scenarios appears in Appendix A.

In addition to these four demographic scenarios, additional scenarios have been constructed to take account of projected changes in labour-force participation. Five-year age- and sex-specific labour-force participation rates for the years 2000 and 2020 have been drawn from the chief actuary of Canada's most recent projections for purposes of his triennial actuarial valuation of the CPP (Government of Canada 1992). For this analysis, labour-force participation is defined as having non-zero wages, salaries, or self-employment earnings in a year. These scenarios are particularly important because of the expected continuing increase in female labour-force participation.

Given these projected population counts and labour-force participation rates, an iterative approach to reweighting the SPSD sample is used that preserves the integrity of household weights, while at the same time assuring that distributions of individuals by age, sex, province, and labour-force participation match the desired control totals.[2] This reweighting process allows us to estimate tax revenues, program costs, and income distributions for various hypothetical scenarios, for example, where 1993 tax and program structures remained fixed but the population size and age structure, as well as labour-force participation rates, match these specific projection scenarios.

The second step is to take account of legislated changes in tax and program structures for future years (for example, indexing).

This step makes use of the explicit capability of the Social Policy Simulation Model (SPSM) to model these taxes and cash-transfer programs for the households on the (reweighted) Social Policy Simulation Database (SPSD).

A key question here is what is the role of indexing provisions in the personal income tax system, associated refundable tax credits, and cash transfers. Legislation has tied government taxes received from the household sector, as well as cash transfers paid to this sector, to price or wage indices. The C/QPP and unemployment insurance programs and payroll tax ceilings are effectively wage indexed, and the other old-age transfers programs (OAS and GIS) are indexed to the Consumer Price Index (CPI). Recent legislative changes have amended the indexing of the federal and provincial tax brackets, refundable income tax, non-refundable personal tax credits, and thresholds for the repayment of OAS transfers by upper-income individuals to a rate equal to the CPI minus 3 percentage points.[3] Social Assistance benefit levels are not formally indexed but have been updated from time to time. The overall trend is that nominal benefit levels have increased at a lower rate than inflation; though, recently, overall program costs have increased much faster, owing to increasing case-loads associated with the recession.

Given the significance of these indexing provisions and updating policies, it is important to explore the sensitivity of the results in alternative scenarios with respect to inflation and per capita economic growth. For this purpose, three economic growth scenarios will be explored. Specifically, these scenarios assume annual inflation rates of 2, 3.5, and 5 per cent, with corresponding nominal annual rates of increase in average wages of 3, 4.8, and 6.5 per cent, respectively. Thus, real per capita economic growth (measured by average annual growth rates in real average wages) is explored assuming either 1, 1.3, or 1.5 per cent growth rates. The 1.3 per cent, or "middle" figure is the main assumption used by the chief actuary (Government of Canada 1992). A real growth rate of zero is also considered.

Another potentially significant factor for these projections is the continuing maturation of the C/QPP. The Canada and Quebec pension plans were introduced in 1966 with maximum benefits fully phased in by 1976. Thus, by 1988 (the year to which the underlying data refer), everyone aged 65 to 77 had full C/QPP benefits; those between ages 78 and 87 had partial benefits; and those over 87 had no benefits. By 2001, the first target year of the analysis, everyone aged 65 to 90 will be entitled to full C/QPP benefits; and by 2011 virtually all persons over 65 will be entitled to full benefits. Moreover, recent and projected continuing increases in female labour-force participation will entitle more women to retirement benefits (and not just survivor benefits) in the future. This expected maturation of the C/QPP has been simulated by imputing retirement and survivors' benefits based in part on earnings distribution data from CPP administrative files. Corresponding to the projected increases in benefits payable from the C/QPP, combined employer and employee payroll taxes rates are currently legislated to increase from the 4 and 4.8 per cent rates in 1988 and 1993 to rates of 6.85 per cent and 9.1 per cent in 2001 and 2011, respectively.

Finally, it is important to note that the major aggregate results are being presented in the form typically preferred by actuaries; aggregate tax revenues and program costs are expressed as percentages of aggregate labour income (wages, salaries, and self-employment income) – or aggregate wages for short. In this way, the analysis avoids presenting very large dollar numbers that reflect only inflation; and it allows the effects of real per capita economic growth to be placed in context.

Results

Projection Scenarios

In order to examine the factors mentioned above, we have developed a series of twelve projection scenarios. The assumptions underlying each scenario are set out in Table 1. We begin with results for the base year of the SPSD/M, 1988. The other scenarios then modify one or more of the sets of assumptions. The first of these is the formal tax/transfer program structure. This structure has already changed from the base year as a result of legislation enacted between 1988 and the present. Furthermore, many changes in structure for 2011 can be anticipated from the implicit operation of currently legislated indexing provisions and other legislated changes (for example, C/QPP contribution rates, phasing in of transfer programs). The second group of assumptions refers to projected demographic changes, and is based on Statistics Canada's standard four demographic scenarios. These are varied in the third through sixth scenarios, and then a "middle" assumption is used for all subsequent scenarios.[4] The third group of assumptions relates to the labour-force participation rate changes projected by the chief actuary for either 2000 or 2020. (No detailed projections were published for 2011; and these two years provide a measure of sensitivity analysis.) The next-to-last set of assumptions refers to the maturation of the C/QPP; and the last three scenarios explore alternative economic growth assumptions affecting the structure of the tax/transfer system.

In all but the last three scenarios, economic variables are held fixed at their current levels. The reweighting of the underlying sample to reflect projected changes in age structure to 2011, for example, is done without changing the dollar levels of pensions, income taxes, and other dollar-denominated variables. It is important to note that such hypothetical 2011 scenarios do not represent constant dollars in the usual sense. Rather, dollar magnitudes are held at their same relative position with respect to average wages. In effect, these "relative" scenarios (3–9) assume that public (as well as private) pensions, taxes, and such are indexed to average wages. To the extent that over the long term average wages grow faster than prices, this relative indexing scenario implicitly assumes that pensions, for example, are indexed at a higher rate than prices, such that they stay at exactly the same fraction of the average wage as they are at present.

The last three scenarios then add the effects of legislated indexing of the tax/transfer system under three different sets of inflation and real per capita economic growth assumptions. All three of these scenarios build on the middle population-growth scenario and participation rates from the year 2000. The annual economic growth rates shown in the table are assumed for all years after 1995. From 1988 to 1992 we have used actual growth rates, and for 1993 to 1995 we have used recent forecasts of the three growth factors (Conference Board of Canada 1992). For the C/QPP and unemployment insurance, the "indexing" scenarios are essentially no different from the previous ones (that is, with real per capita income growth rates effectively zero) because these programs are explicitly wage indexed. (Consider, for example, the "years maximum pensionable earnings" in the C/QPP; the major exception is that C/QPP benefits are price- rather than wage-indexed once they come into play.) However, for cash transfers and many aspects of the income tax system, the CPI consumer price index (CPI) or CPI-3 indexing provisions apply.

TABLE 1
Summary of Alternative Projection Scenarios

	Base		Results for 2011									
			Population growth				Labour force participation		CPP	Legislated indexation and economic growth		
Scenario number	1988	1993	Low	Ont	Mid	High	2000	2020	CPP	Low	Mid	High
	1	2	3	4	5	6	7	8	9	10	11	12
Tax/transfer program Structure (excluding C/QPP)	1988	1993	↑	↑	↑	↑	↑	↑	↑	2011	↑	↑
C/QPP program structure	1988	↑	↑	↑	↑	↑	↑	↑	2011	↑	↑	↑
Demographic projection year	1988	↑	2011	↑	↑	↑	↑	↑	↑	↑	↑	↑
Growth/migration		↑	Low	Ont	Mid	High	Mid	↑	↑	↑	↑	↑
Labour force participation	1988	↑	↑	↑	↑	↑	2000	2020	2000	↑	↑	↑
Annual inflation (%)	None	3.9[a]	↑	↑	↑	↑	↑	↑	↑	2.0	3.5	5.0
Real annual per capita economic growth (%)	None	0.3[b]	↑	↑	↑	↑	↑	↑	↑	1.0	1.3	1.5

[a] Average annual rates from 1988 to 1993.
[b] An alternative interpretation is that these scenarios assume zero real growth, and either zero inflation or full CPI indexing.

One way to think of these economic scenarios is as follows: dollar items are indexed forward by either the wage index, the CPI, or CPI-3, as appropriate; then all are deflated back to the present (that is, to 1988) by the wage index. Mechanically, however, this is simply equivalent to holding the wage-indexed items constant (as with all dollar variables in the previous scenarios), deflating the CPI-indexed amounts by the real per capita wage growth rate, and deflating the CPI-3-indexed amounts by the real per capita wage growth rate plus 3 percentage points. For example, following the actuarial report for the CPP (Government of Canada 1992), we assume the same long-run growth rate of real per capita wages, 1.3 per cent per annum. Thus, CPI indexing is equivalent to deflating the CPI indexed amounts by 1.3 per cent per annum, and deflating amounts such as tax brackets, which are indexed to CPI-3 by 4.3 per cent per annum. As might be expected, these indexing differences can have sizeable impacts when cumulated over two decades.

Impacts of Population Changes on Dependency Ratios

As a precursor to discussing the basic projection results for the public sector, it is useful to consider a few of the more directly measurable impacts of changing population size and structure. One widely used indicator is the dependency ratio. The usual "demographic" dependency ratio is the number of individuals not in the 20-to-64 age range divided by the number of those who are. Given the importance of projected changes in female labour-force participation, it is also informative to consider an alternative "labour force" dependency ratio – the ratio of those not in the paid labour force to those who are.[5]

The results for the first, second, and fourth population-growth scenarios for Canada and Ontario are shown in Figure 1. The top set of three curves (two solid, one dashed with no shading) shows the spread in Canadian labour-force dependency ratios if 1988 age- and sex-specific labour-force participation rates are held fixed and only the population age/sex structure is projected. The bottom three curves show the corresponding patterns for Ontario dependency rates. The superimposed shaded shapes incorporate an adjustment to reflect the chief actuary's labour-force participation projection for the years 2000 and 2020 – the closest published projection years to our target years of 2001 and 2011 (Government of Canada 1988). This spread applies only to the middle demographic scenario (5).

FIGURE 1
"Labour Force" Dependency Ratios for Alternative Demographic Growth Scenarios, Canada and Ontario

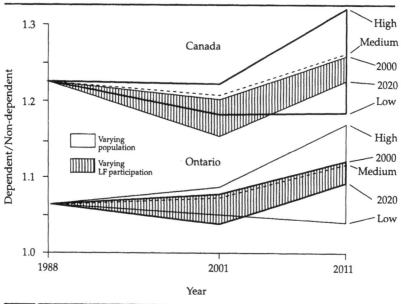

These results clearly show the importance of labour-force participation when thinking about future dependency burdens (as already noted in Falkingham 1987 and Fellegi 1988). In terms of labour-force dependency ratios, the effects of population ageing are substantially offset by increased numbers of women in the paid labour force in 2011. For Canada overall the present ratio is about 1.23 non-participants per labour-force participant, while in Ontario it is considerably lower, at about 1.07. The much lower rate in Ontario is due mainly to higher labour-force participation rates – 75.7 per cent of the 18-to-64 age group in Ontario compared with 70.8 per cent for Canada overall.

Depending on the demographic scenario (but holding 1988 participation rates fixed), these ratios are projected to range from remaining about constant over the next two decades to increasing by about 10 per cent (that is, 0.1 dependants per labour-force participant). Taking the middle demographic scenario, the labour-force dependency ratio is projected to increase by about 5 per cent.

The impact of the chief actuary's labour-force participation scenarios tends to offset the demographic effects, leading to about a 3 per cent decrease in this form of dependency ratio (given the medium-case scenario, demographic changes).

Recall that we shall express the costs of public programs and tax revenues as proportions of aggregate wages. In the set of projection scenarios we are considering, there are four factors that will affect this aggregate wage denominator in turn: labour-force participation rates, population structure, population size, and real per capita economic growth. (See Appendix A for the wage denominator for each of the scenarios.)

Ontario's Public Finances

The taxes and transfers considered in this study make up a significant proportion of both Canada's and Ontario's public finances. With the exception of health and education costs, the remaining sources of revenue and expenditures of the federal and provincial governments not included in this analysis are not highly sensitive to changes in population age structure or other factors considered in the various scenarios. Thus, to a great extent, the changes in fiscal positions that may be attributed to demographic factors are included in the following section.

Ontario income tax revenues are closely tied to the federal system by using the same tax base. Also, a significant proportion of provincial cash-transfer programs are directly tied to federal programs (for example, GAINS-A based on Guaranteed Income Supplement (GIS)) while others are subject to unilateral federal modification (for example, Canada Assistance Plan (CAP)). Because of the interrelated nature of the two levels of government in the structure and delivery of these transfer programs they will be considered together in this section. First we examine the costs to federal and provincial governments, then the revenues, and finally – the real bottom line – the balance.

Table 2 shows the aggregate costs for Ontario of the major public-sector cash-transfer programs under the various projection scenarios. They are all expressed as percentages of aggregate wages. For example, in the first column with the 1988 status quo scenario, federal OAS pensions for Ontario residents are the single largest program at 2.9 per cent of Ontario aggregate wages.

These cash-transfer programs have been identified using a some-

TABLE 2
Cash Transfer Program Costs as Percentages of Aggregate Wages, Ontario Residents

| | Base | | Results for 2011 | | | | | | | | | |
| | | | Population growth | | | | Labour force participation | | CPP | Legislated indexation and economic growth | | |
Program	1988 1	1993 2	Low 3	Ont 4	Mid 5	High 6	2000 7	2020 8	9	Low 10	Mid 11	High 12
Total cash transfers	11.9	11.9	13.8	13.7	13.8	13.9	13.8	13.8	14.5	12.5	12.1	11.6
Federal transfers	10.7	10.6	12.4	12.3	12.4	12.5	12.4	12.4	13.2	11.6	11.3	10.8
Total elderly	6.5	6.5	8.8	8.5	8.6	8.5	8.6	8.6	9.4	8.4	8.2	8.1
C/QPP	2.6	2.6	3.4	3.3	3.3	3.3	3.4	3.4	4.7	4.7	4.7	4.7
OAS	2.9	2.9	3.9	3.8	3.9	3.8	3.9	3.9	3.8	3.1	3.0	2.9
GIS/SPA	1.0	1.0	1.4	1.4	1.4	1.4	1.4	1.4	1.0	0.7	0.6	0.6
Child tax benefit[a]	1.1	1.0	0.6	0.8	0.8	0.8	0.8	0.8	0.7	0.4	0.3	0.1
Sales tax credit	0.1	0.5	0.5	0.5	0.5	0.5	0.5	0.5	0.5	0.3	0.2	0.1
Other transfers	3.0	2.7	2.6	2.6	2.6	2.6	2.6	2.5	2.5	2.5	2.5	2.5
Unemployment	1.7	1.6	1.4	1.5	1.5	1.5	1.4	1.4	1.4	1.4	1.4	1.4
Social assistance	0.6	0.4	0.3	0.3	0.3	0.3	0.3	0.3	0.3	0.3	0.3	0.3
Other	0.7	0.7	0.8	0.8	0.8	0.8	0.8	0.8	0.8	0.8	0.8	0.8
Ontario transfers	1.3	1.3	1.4	1.4	1.4	1.4	1.4	1.4	1.3	0.9	0.9	0.8
Social assistance	0.6	0.8	0.8	0.8	0.8	0.8	0.8	0.7	0.8	0.8	0.8	0.8
Other	0.7	0.5	0.6	0.6	0.6	0.6	0.6	0.6	0.5	0.2	0.1	0.1

[a] In 1988, this figure is the sum of federal family allowances and the federal child tax credit, which were subsequently transformed into the Child Tax Benefit in 1993.

what different classification system in order to present a clearer picture of the main trends. Specifically, refundable income tax credits that are legally provided under the Income Tax Act are shown separately as cash-transfer programs. In structure they are virtually identical to the Guaranteed Income Supplement (GIS) program for the elderly; conceptually, they could be considered expenditure programs just as easily as income tax provisions. If they were netted from income taxes (the current public accounts treatment and national accounts treatment prior to 1990,[6]) their important roles would be obscured. Similarly the repayment of the OAS demogrant by higher-income recipients (the so-called "clawback") has been shown explicitly in the next table on taxation, rather than having it included in income taxes, or having it netted against total OAS program expenditures.

Also, the Canada and Quebec pension plans (C/QPP) are shown as federal in this table, as are the associated payroll taxes in the next table. However, the federal-provincial aspect of these programs is considered further below.

Legislated changes from 1988 to 1993 are most noticeable for the refundable sales tax credit (STC), which, in conjunction with the introduction of the GST, increases from 0.1 to 0.5 per cent of aggregate wages. Unemployment insurance declines from 1.7 to 1.6 per cent. This is clearly unrealistic; it reflects the fact that the scenario in the second column only changes the tax/transfer program structures. It does not project the underlying database, in particular to take account of the increase in the unemployment rate from 1988 to 1993. While this is unreasonable if the objective were to analyse 1993, it is not so unreasonable for projections out to 2001 or 2011. In these cases, the implicit assumption is that the unemployment rate one or two decades hence will be similar to the unemployment rate in 1988.

Ontario transfers as a whole remain constant across the first two columns because of offsetting changes in the components. The increase in social assistance is a result of the increased provincial share of total Ontario Canada Assistance Plan payments mentioned earlier. The decrease in "other" is because of the gradual discontinuation of the sales tax grant and property tax grant for seniors by 1993. In 1992 a new system of tax credits for seniors with an unindexed benefit structure was introduced in its place. Recall that the 1993 figures are again unrealistic because no attempt has been made to model the impact of the most recent recession.

The next four columns leave the tax/transfer structure as legislated for 1993, and the database (for example, the unemployment rate) as in 1988. The only change from scenario 2 is to reweight the population to reflect Statistics Canada's four standard demographic projections to 2011 for individuals by age, sex, and province. The first and fourth demographic scenarios correspond to low and high population growth, respectively, through a combination of fertility rate and immigration assumptions. (Appendix A gives the complete set of assumptions.) The middle two projections assume intermediate population growth and differ mainly with respect to interprovincial migration patterns.

As expected, low population growth is associated with higher costs of programs directed to seniors in Ontario (OAS, GIS, and C/QPP), and somewhat lower costs for programs directed to children (child tax benefit). The impacts at the federal level for Ontario residents amount to an increase compared with the present (that is, scenario two) of almost 2 percentage points of aggregate wages, but do not vary significantly between demographic projection scenarios. For the transfers provided by Ontario, the differences are negligible.

The next two columns (scenarios 7 and 8) show the impacts of increased female labour-force participation. There is a slight increase in CPP benefits with a corresponding drop in unemployment insurance and social assistance. The impacts are relatively small, indicating that even though the percentage increase in numbers of women in paid work may appear substantial, in terms of aggregate wages the impact is much more modest.

The fourth-last column (scenario 9) highlights the expected impacts of maturation of the C/QPP, particularly in comparison with scenario 5 with the middle, population-growth assumptions. The direct impact of this scenario is on C/QPP program costs, which show about a 40 per cent increase by 2011 (that is, an increase from 3.3 to 4.7 per cent of aggregate wages). However, there is also an indirect impact because the income-testing provisions of the GIS include C/QPP benefits as income. Hence, there is an offsetting 30 per cent decrease in GIS costs (from 1.4 to 1 per cent of aggregate wages).

The maturation of the C/QPP is accompanied by a legislated increase that more than doubles the associated payroll taxes. The increased C/QPP benefits are included in taxable income, while the legislated increase in payroll taxes is tax deductible, and the reduction in GIS has no effect on taxes since GIS benefits are not taxable. As a result, there is also a 0.1 per cent net reduction in income tax revenues, shown in Table 3.

Finally, given the maturation of the C/QPP, the last three columns show the impacts of currently legislated indexing under three alternative economic scenarios. Other than for the wage-indexed programs, these scenarios have a dramatic impact. The C/QPP and UI, as already noted, are unaffected because their earnings-related character (and the explicit wage indexing of their respective earnings ceilings) makes them effectively wage indexed. Also, social assistance benefits have been implicitly assumed to keep pace with real average wages.

However, OAS benefits (before the clawback) fall as a percentage of average wages by about 20 per cent and GIS benefits fall by more than one-third. This is particularly serious for the poorer elderly, as will be shown below. Furthermore, the new child tax benefit falls to less than half its current value under low economic growth assumptions and almost vanishes under high growth. The CPI-3 indexing causes it to decline by more than three-quarters. Similarly "other" Ontario transfers (a mix of GAINS-A and refundable tax credits) virtually disappear due to a lack of indexation provisions.[7]

Table B1 in Appendix B gives the corresponding figures to those in Table 2 for the all-Canada population. They are slightly higher than the Ontario numbers[8] but follow the same trend. Notable is a shift with respect to the other provinces shown in Table B2. Other provincial transfers are largely made up of programs for the elderly in Ontario (seniors' tax credits and GIS top-ups). The tax credits are not explicitly indexed and thus, while small in overall terms, go from 137 per cent of the Canadian figure in scenario 1 to as low as 43 per cent in scenario 12. Also comparing the same scenarios, overall transfers to the elderly grow at the same rate in Ontario and in Canada. However, this overall constancy masks a relatively declining role for CPP in Ontario and a relatively growing role for GIS compared with all of Canada. CPP growth as a percentage of aggregate wages is 10 per cent slower in Ontario and GIS reduction is more rapid.

Projections of Major Components of Revenue

Table 3 is similar to Table 2 except that it focuses on most of the major sources of revenue readily identified with households – in-

TABLE 3
Major Tax Revenues as Percentages of Aggregate Wages, Ontario Residents

| | Base | | Population growth | | | | Results for 2011 | | | | | |
| | | | | | | | Labour force participation | | CPP | Legislated indexation and economic growth | | |
Program	1988 1	1993 2	Low 3	Ont 4	Mid 5	High 6	2000 7	2020 8	9	Low 10	Mid 11	High 12
Federal/provincial taxes	40.2	45.8	47.5	47.3	47.3	47.3	47.3	47.2	48.7	51.9	53.4	59.0
Federal taxes	26.4	30.5	31.4	31.3	31.3	31.3	31.3	31.2	33.0	35.0	36.0	39.8
Payroll taxes	5.5	7.1	6.9	6.9	6.9	6.9	6.9	7.0	8.9	8.9	8.9	8.9
C/QPP	2.4	3.0	2.9	2.9	2.9	2.9	2.9	2.9	4.9	4.9	4.9	4.9
UI	3.2	4.1	4.0	4.0	4.0	4.0	4.0	4.0	4.0	4.0	4.0	4.0
Income taxes	16.2	17.3	18.1	18.1	18.1	18.1	18.1	18.0	17.8	20.2	21.3	25.5
Income taxes	16.2	17.2	18.0	18.0	18.0	18.0	17.9	17.8	17.7	20.0	21.1	25.1
OAS repayments	0.0	0.1	0.1	0.1	0.1	0.1	0.1	0.1	0.1	0.2	0.2	0.4
Other	0.0	0.0	0.0	0.0	0.0	0.0	0.0	0.0	0.0	0.0	0.0	0.0
Commodity taxes	4.6	6.1	6.3	6.3	6.3	6.3	6.3	6.3	6.2	5.9	5.8	5.4
Provincial taxes	13.8	15.3	16.1	16.0	16.0	16.0	16.0	15.9	15.8	16.9	17.4	19.2
Income taxes	8.1	9.4	9.9	9.9	9.9	9.9	9.9	9.8	9.7	11.1	11.8	13.9
Commodity taxes	5.7	5.9	6.2	6.1	6.1	6.1	6.1	6.1	6.1	5.7	5.6	5.3

come, payroll, and sales taxes. Comparing the first two columns highlights the impacts of the major tax changes enacted between 1988 and 1993. These include increases in payroll taxes for unemployment insurance and C/QPP, legislated changes to income taxes as well as the effects of five years of partial de-indexing, and the introduction of the GST to replace the manufacturers' sales tax. (Recall that income tax is gross of the augmented refundable sales tax credit, the new refundable child tax benefit, and the former child tax credit, all of which were shown on the previous table.) For Ontario, changes include a 4 percentage point increase in the rate of personal income tax as a proportion of federal basic tax, and up to 50 per cent increases in gasoline, alcohol, and tobacco sales tax rates.

Overall, these tax structure changes by themselves would have resulted in a 4 percentage point (of aggregate wages) increase for the federal government in respect of Ontario residents (from 26.4 to 30.5 per cent), and a 1.5 percentage point increase for Ontario – that is, about a 10 per cent relative increase in revenues. In fact, this potential tax increase was more than offset over the past five years by the decline in the Ontario tax base associated with the recession.

Projected changes in the population to 2011 (scenario 2 vis-à-vis scenarios 3 through 6) are projected to raise federal and Ontario taxes for Ontario residents by about 0.8 and 0.7 percentage points, respectively. This is likely the result of population ageing moving the baby boom generation from its early years of labour-force participation to late middle-age at the peak of its earnings. Clearly, the impacts of these age-structure changes on revenues are small compared with the effects of the latest recession.

Furthermore, among themselves, the various demographic and labour-force participation scenarios (3 to 8) have relatively minor impacts on tax revenues, with 0.1 percentage point, or less, variation between scenarios.

With C/QPP maturation (scenario 9), the main impact is the legislated increase in payroll tax rates to 2011, and continuing beyond that time. These increases amount to about 2 percentage points of aggregate wages. With the deductibility of these payroll taxes, and the fact that payroll taxes tend to be paid by individuals in higher marginal tax brackets than those seniors receiving increased C/QPP benefits, income tax revenues decline overall by about 0.3 percentage points.

Finally, the last three scenarios show the impacts of the various indexing provisions. Indexing of basic personal credits and tax brackets to CPI-3 per cent creates a large "fiscal dividend." Over the two decades to 2011, income tax revenues in respect of Ontario residents increase by almost one-third as a share of the economy, from just over one-quarter (17.7 per cent federal plus 9.7 per cent Ontario in scenario 9) to almost 40 per cent (25.1 per cent federal plus 13.9 per cent Ontario in scenario 12) of aggregate wages. In addition, the benefit repayments from higher-income individuals receiving OAS have as much as a four-fold increase, since the threshold defining high income is indexed to CPI-3 per cent.

The increased income taxes and benefit repayments and the reduced cash transfers associated with the "indexation" scenario result in lower disposable income, which, in turn, is reflected in lower sales tax revenues. Federal GST and Ontario retail sales taxes for Ontario residents each decrease by almost 1 percentage point of aggregate wages, or relatively by about one-seventh in the "high" scenario.

These implications over the longer term of current legislated indexing provisions in the income tax and pension systems may not appear realistic. However, if they do not, it shows the likelihood that current indexing legislation will be amended.

Table B3 in Appendix B gives the corresponding figures for Table 3 for the provincial Canada population. Ontario residents show a similar position and similar trends for total taxes compared with the all-Canada situation.

The "Deficit"

Finally, Table 4 shows the net fiscal balance between the government and household sectors accounted for by the specific expenditure programs and taxes shown in the previous tables. This is the "bottom line" – the net effects of the flows of the various taxes and cash transfers on the fiscal position of the federal and Ontario governments in respect of Ontario residents. Note that for this table, C/QPP payroll taxes are shown separately. The difference between C/QPP taxes and benefit payouts is used by the CPP fund to purchase provincial government bonds (the QPP fund holds a more diversified portfolio). Thus the difference is best considered a provincial source of revenue.

The net fiscal balance shown here is total income, payroll, and sales taxes less cash transfers. This is not the same as the deficit, since only a portion of government expenditures and revenues are being considered, albeit a major proportion. However, to the extent that the remaining sources of revenue and expenditures of the federal and provincial governments are not sensitive to changes in population age structure or other factors considered in the various scenarios, then changes in the "net fiscal balance" shown in the first row of the table will equal changes in the joint federal/provincial deficit.

Starting by comparing the first two columns (but ignoring the impact of the recession on households' incomes or employment), the structural changes in the tax/transfer system over the past five years have the net effect of increasing government balances by 5.5 percentage points of aggregate wages, from 28.3 to 33.8.[9] About one-third of this change in the "structural deficit" (that is, the deficit exclusive of the impact of changes in the macro economy – 1.4 of the 5.5 percentage point increase shown in the table) accrued to Ontario. In comparison, the demographic scenarios in the next four columns have almost no impacts. Projected changes in female labour-force participation (shown in scenarios 7 and 8) also have a negligible net impact. The combined impact of these two factors, demographic ageing and labour-force participation changes, is only 0.4 percentage points.

The maturation of the C/QPP (shown in column 9), given a considerably larger increase in payroll taxes than in benefits, improves the net balances by almost 1 percentage point.

Most dramatically, the legislated indexing provisions examined in the last three scenarios improve the combined Ontario and federal government net balances by 5 to 13 percentage points of aggregate wages, depending on the economic growth scenario. This is a large increase. For the Ontario government, including funds from the CPP, the net increase in the fiscal balance (comparing scenarios 10 through 12 with scenario 2) is on the order of 2 percentage points of aggregate wages, or almost $3 billion in today's terms.

While the same general trends are found for Canada as a whole (see Table B5), the rate of growth of this surplus of taxes over cash transfers is higher for all Canada than for Ontario. Federal balances in Ontario increase at a slower rate than for Canada as a whole, while provincial surpluses rise faster in Ontario than in Canada overall.

TABLE 4
Net Fiscal Balances as Percentages of Aggregate Wages, Ontario Residents

	Base		Results for 2011										
			Population growth				Labour force participation				Legislated indexation and economic growth		
Program	1988 1	1993 2	Low 3	Ont 4	Mid 5	High 6	2000 7	2020 8	CPP 9	Low 10	Mid 11	High 12
Total	28.3	33.8	33.7	33.6	33.5	33.5	33.5	33.4	34.3	39.4	41.3	47.4
Federal (excl. C/QPP)	16.0	19.5	19.5	19.4	19.3	19.3	19.3	19.3	19.5	23.1	24.5	28.8
CPP/QPP	−0.3	0.4	−0.5	−0.4	−0.4	−0.4	−0.5	−0.4	0.3	0.3	0.3	0.3
Ontario	12.6	14.0	14.7	14.6	14.6	14.6	14.6	14.6	14.5	15.9	16.5	18.4

Distributional Impacts

The trends and factors considered in this analysis obviously affect more than government deficits. They can also have a profound effect on the distribution of income. Figures 2 and 3 show the distributional impacts of the status quo plus two of the projection scenarios on the disposable incomes of all families and elderly families, respectively.

In both figures, family income is shown along the horizontal axis in a somewhat different way from usual. First, each family's income was adjusted for family size and numbers of children based on an equivalence scale.[10] Next, the ratio of this adjusted income for each family to the median adjusted income over all families was computed. This ratio was used to rank families (including unattached individuals) along the horizontal axis. Disposable income – everything but in-kind transfers and sales taxes – is the concept used in all these calculations. The family unit is the census family, similar to the nuclear family; it includes spouses and never-married children living in the same dwelling.

Family income, adjusted for equivalent adult units and expressed as a proportion of the median, is a useful way of displaying income distributions for an analysis such as this. Instead of using nominal or constant dollars, it provides a measure for which comparisons over several decades have some chance of being meaningful. Furthermore, many analyses define a poverty or "low income" line as 50 per cent of (adjusted) median family income. If this definition is accepted, the incidence of low income can be simply read off the graphs as the proportion of families with incomes less than this threshold. Finally, there has recently been increased interest in the "disappearing middle class." The proportion of families with incomes between 75 and 150 per cent of adjusted median family income is a reasonable indicator of the size of the middle class (Wolfson 1989).

Figures 2 and 3 both examine the same three scenarios: the status quo (1988 population structure and market sources of income with 1993 tax/transfer program structures that correspond to scenario 2); and the 2011 structure, taking account of changes in labour-force participation rates and population age structure and C/QPP maturation (and payroll tax increases that correspond to scenario 9), and then including the effects of legislated indexing provisions with medium economic growth – scenario 11. (Appendix C gives the underlying percentages.)

Compared with the status quo, the second of these scenarios is

FIGURE 2
The Distribution of Disposable Income for All Unattached Individuals and Families
in Ontario under Three Projection Scenarios

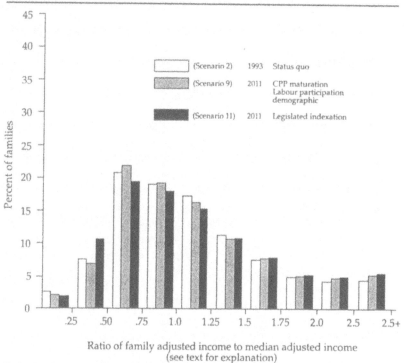

Ratio of family adjusted income to median adjusted income
(see text for explanation)

associated with a modest movement of people out of relative income
poverty; the proportion of families below 50 per cent of median
adjusted income is lower while the proportion between 50 and 100
per cent of median income increases by about the same amount.
Above the median, the effects are disequalizing. Proportions of families with incomes between 100 and 150 per cent of the median
fall, while proportions with income above 200 per cent increase.

The effects of the legislated indexing scenario are larger and move
in the opposite direction. Compared with the status quo (scenario
2), there is an overall 25 per cent increase in the proportion of
families with incomes below 50 per cent of the median, despite a
25 per cent decrease in the proportion of families with incomes
below 25 per cent of the median. Between 75 and 125 per cent
of the median, there is a decline in the proportion of families in
all the income ranges, which indicates a decline in the middle class.
Finally there is an increase in the proportion of families with high
incomes, particularly those over 250 per cent of the median.

Figure 2 thus suggests a strong regressive distributional impact associated with current tax/transfer indexing provisions compared with the current relative magnitudes of the relevant programs and taxes.

The impacts of these projected scenarios on the income distribution for the elderly is shown in Figure 3. To begin, it should be noted that the elderly have generally lower incomes, and are much more concentrated in the 50 to 100 per cent of adjusted median income range. As for all families, the second scenario shown in the graph (that is, scenario 9) has modest impacts. The main factor acting here is the maturation of the C/QPP. The effects of this scenario appear distributionally progressive.

However, the situation is more than reversed when account is taken of the legislated indexing provisions. There is more than a four-fold increase in the incidence of low income (less than 50 per cent of the median) among the elderly, rising to over one in six. At the same time, the proportion of elderly families with incomes between 75 and 175 per cent of adjusted median (all family) income falls by almost 10 percentage points – a significant drop in the number of middle-class elderly families.

These effects are due principally to the erosion of the non-earnings-related public pensions (OAS and GIS) relative to average wages since these programs are indexed to the CPI, unlike the C/QPP, which are effectively indexed to the growth in average wages. These distributional impacts are also associated with the CPI-3 per cent indexing of the "high-income" threshold for repayment of OAS benefits. It should be noted, however, that these results may illustrate a worst-case scenario. Other factors not included in this analysis, such as an increase in private pension plan coverage and other private sources of retirement income, could offset the significant relative declines in public pension benefits being projected, though evidence for such a possibility is at best weak.

Conclusions

This study has examined the relative quantitative importance of a range of factors pertinent to the ageing of Canada's population, and their effects on Ontario's residents. The factors examined include population growth and ageing, increasing female labour-force

FIGURE 3
The Distribution of Disposable Income for Elderly Individuals and Families in
Ontario under Three Projection Scenarios

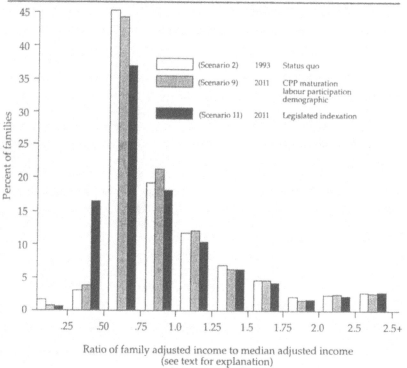

Ratio of family adjusted income to median adjusted income
(see text for explanation)

participation, the maturation of the public pension system, and the indexing provisions of cash transfers and personal income taxes under alternate economic growth assumptions.

Using a series of alternative scenarios, the major public-sector expenditure programs and taxes sensitive to these factors have been projected to 2011. These projections support the general view that the increasing proportion of the elderly has the potential to increase public-sector costs substantially. For example, taking account of population ageing and the maturation of the Canada and Quebec pension plans but no other factors, the costs of public pensions are projected to increase by about half as a proportion of aggregate wages.

However, these effects of ageing are substantially mitigated when account is taken of legislated indexing provisions, and a return to modest rates of economic growth is assumed. Depending on the economic scenario, it is possible that the effects of population ageing will be more than fully offset, so that with currently legislated indexing provisions, the total cost of public transfers to individuals and families will fall as a proportion of aggregate wages. These results underlie and help explain the possibly surprising result of a recent IMF study (Heller, Hemming, and Kohnert 1986). That study showed Canada facing the least public-sector cost pressures on account of population ageing of seven major industrial countries. However, these lower public-sector aggregate costs have their price: a considerable increase in the incidence of low income, including a tripling among the elderly, and a reduction in the size of the middle class. The current indexing provisions also result in about a 10 per cent increase (that is, of about 5 percentage points) in federal plus provincial income taxes as a share of aggregate wages, and more than a 90 per cent decrease in cash transfers in respect of children over the next two decades.

The net effect of the various factors analysed, including both demographic ageing and currently legislated indexing, is a substantial increase in the net fiscal balance – the surplus of personal income, payroll, and sales tax revenues over the costs of the public transfer programs analysed. These results apply both to Ontario residents and to all Canadians. The main differences are that the growth in the relative surplus of taxes over cash transfers will be smaller for Ontarians than for Canadians as a whole. However, the provincial share of this surplus will increase at the expense of the federal share.

Of course, the projections on which this analysis is based are somewhat mechanical. They simply extrapolate existing trends in demography, and draw out their implications for a set of tax and transfer program structures as they are defined by current legislation. They are certainly not forecasts. However, to the extent that the results of the projections appear unreasonable or unacceptable, it is an indication that substantial reforms will be forthcoming over coming decades. The projection scenarios suggest Canada and Ontario residents are on a track where deficits will decline substantially, notwithstanding the impacts of an ageing population. But at the same time, these scenarios suggest major increases in the incidence of low income among the future elderly. A new balance will likely have to be found.

Appendix A: Detailed Scenario Assumptions

TABLE A1

| | Base | | Population growth | | | | Results for 2011 | | | | | |
| | | | | | | | Labour force participation | | CPP | Legislated indexation and economic growth | | |
Program	1988 1	1993 2	Low 3	Ont 4	Mid 5	High 6	2000 7	2020 8	9	Low 10	Mid 11	High 12
Population assumptions												
Fertility rate	–	–	1.20	1.67	1.67	2.10	1.67	1.67	1.67	1.67	1.67	1.67
Net immigration (000)	–	–	140	140	200	200	200	200	200	200	200	200
Migration scenario	–	–	West	Ont	West	Trend	West	West	West	West	West	West
Statistics Canada projection number	–	–	1	2	3	4	3	3	3	3	3	3
Ontario population (millions)	9.5	9.5	11.1	11.8	11.8	12.2	11.8	11.8	11.8	11.8	11.8	11.8
Canada population (millions)	25.8	25.8	29.2	30.2	31.6	32.3	31.6	31.6	31.6	31.6	31.6	31.6
Economic growth rates												
Real per capita growth	–	0.3	–	–	–	–	–	–	–	1.0	1.3	1.5
CPI	–	3.9	–	–	–	–	–	–	–	2.0	3.5	5.0
Average nominal wage growth	–	4.2	–	–	–	–	–	–	–	3.0	4.8	6.5
Labour force participation rates	1988	1988	1988	1988	1988	1988	2000	2020	2000	2000	2000	2000
Legislative scenario												
CPP maturation	–	–	–	–	–	–	–	–	2011	2011	2011	2011
Indexation	–	–	–	–	–	–	–	–	–	2011	2011	2011

	Base		Population growth				Labour force participation			Legislated indexation and economic growth		
										Results for 2011		
Program	1988 1	1993 2	Low 3	Ont 4	Mid 5	High 6	2000 7	2020 8	CPP 9	Low 10	Mid 11	High 12
Aggregate wages[a]												
Ontario (billions)	131.3	132.5	160.7	166.5	166.6	168.8	167.0	166.5	215.8	206.1	215.7	223.5
Canada (billions)	301.3	304.0	359.9	360.7	376.8	376.9	379.4	378.3	490.5	468.6	490.5	508.1

[a] Aggregate wages are the total wages reported on the Survey of Consumer Finances plus the employer's contributions to payroll taxes (calculated as a percentage of employee contributions). Thus, the increase in aggregate wages between 1988 and 1993 is purely due to increases in the contribution rates on payroll taxes forcing an increase in employer's payroll tax contributions.

Appendix B: Supplementary Tax/Transfer Tables

TABLE B1

Cash Transfer Program Costs as Percentages of Aggregate Wages, for All Provincial Canada Residents[a]

	Base		Population growth				Results for 2011					
							Labour force participation			Legislated indexation and economic growth		
Program	1988	1993	Low	Ont	Mid	High	2000	2020	CPP	Low	Mid	High
	1	2	3	4	5	6	7	8	9	10	11	12
Total cash transfers	15.8	15.8	17.9	18.0	17.9	18.1	17.7	17.7	18.5	16.4	15.9	15.2
Federal transfers	14.4	14.3	16.3	16.5	16.4	16.5	16.2	16.2	17.1	15.2	14.7	14.1
Elderly	7.8	7.8	10.5	10.5	10.3	10.3	10.3	10.3	11.3	10.0	9.8	9.6
C/QPP	2.9	2.9	3.8	3.8	3.7	3.7	3.7	3.7	5.5	5.5	5.5	5.5
OAS	3.4	3.4	4.6	4.6	4.5	4.5	4.5	4.5	4.4	3.6	3.5	3.3
GIS/SPA	1.4	1.5	2.0	2.0	2.0	2.0	2.0	2.0	1.4	0.9	0.8	0.8
Child tax benefit	1.4	1.3	0.8	1.0	1.0	1.1	1.0	1.0	1.0	0.6	0.4	0.1
Sales tax credit	0.2	0.6	0.6	0.6	0.6	0.6	0.6	0.6	0.6	0.4	0.3	0.1
Other federal transfers	5.0	4.6	4.4	4.5	4.4	4.5	4.3	4.3	4.3	4.3	4.3	4.2
Unemployment insurance	3.3	3.1	2.8	2.8	2.8	2.9	2.7	2.7	2.7	2.7	2.7	2.7
Social assistance	0.9	0.8	0.8	0.8	0.8	0.8	0.7	0.7	0.7	0.7	0.7	0.7
Other	0.8	0.8	0.9	0.9	0.9	0.9	0.8	0.8	0.8	0.8	0.8	0.8
Provincial transfers	1.4	1.5	1.5	1.5	1.5	1.6	1.5	1.5	1.4	1.2	1.2	1.1
Social assistance	0.9	1.0	1.0	1.0	1.0	1.0	1.0	1.0	1.0	1.0	1.0	1.0
Other	0.5	0.5	0.5	0.5	0.5	0.5	0.5	0.5	0.4	0.2	0.2	0.1

[a]All ten Canadian provinces but excluding the Northwest Territories and the Yukon.

TABLE B2
Relative Program Costs for Ontario and Provincial Canada Residents (Table 2 entries as a percentage of Table B1 entries)

| | Base | | Population growth | | | | Results for 2011 | | | | | |
| | | | | | | | Labour force participation | | | Legislated indexation and economic growth | | |
Program	1988 1	1993 2	Low 3	Ont 4	Mid 5	High 6	2000 7	2020 8	CPP 9	Low 10	Mid 11	High 12
Total cash transfers	76	76	77	76	77	77	78	78	78	76	76	76
Federal transfers	74	74	76	75	76	75	77	77	77	77	76	76
Elderly	84	83	83	82	84	83	84	84	84	84	84	84
C/QPP	89	90	89	87	89	89	90	90	85	85	85	85
OAS	85	85	85	83	86	85	86	86	85	86	86	86
GIS/SPA	69	68	69	67	70	69	70	69	74	75	75	75
Child tax benefit	77	74	74	77	75	75	75	75	76	73	72	69
Sales tax credit	73	75	76	76	76	75	77	76	75	74	73	75
Other federal transfers	59	58	58	58	58	58	59	59	60	59	59	59
Unemployment insurance	50	52	51	52	51	52	53	53	52	52	52	53
Social assistance	64	47	42	43	43	43	45	44	44	44	44	44
Other	91	92	92	89	93	93	93	95	95	93	94	94
Provincial transfers	91	89	92	90	91	89	93	93	91	77	74	72
Social assistance	64	79	74	74	74	75	76	75	76	76	76	76
Other	137	113	131	124	126	117	126	126	126	85	63	43

TABLE B3
Major Tax Revenues as Percentages of Aggregate Wages, for All Provincial Canada Residents

| | Base | | Population growth | | | | Results for 2011 | | | | Legislated indexation and economic growth | | |
| | | | | | | | Labour force participation | | CPP | | | | |
Program	1988 1	1993 2	Low 3	Ont 4	Mid 5	High 6	2000 7	2020 8	9	Low 10	Mid 11	High 12
Federal/provincial taxes	40.8	46.2	47.9	48.0	47.8	47.9	47.7	47.6	49.3	52.5	54.1	59.4
Federal taxes	25.6	29.8	30.9	30.8	30.8	30.8	30.7	30.7	32.5	34.6	35.6	39.5
Payroll taxes	5.8	7.4	7.2	7.2	7.2	7.2	7.2	7.3	9.3	9.3	9.3	9.3
C/QPP	2.5	3.1	3.1	3.0	3.1	3.0	3.1	3.1	5.2	5.2	5.2	5.2
UI	3.3	4.3	4.2	4.2	4.2	4.2	4.2	4.2	4.1	4.1	4.1	4.1
Income taxes	14.8	15.8	16.7	16.7	16.7	16.6	16.6	16.5	16.4	18.8	19.9	24.3
Income taxes	14.8	15.7	16.6	16.6	16.5	16.5	16.5	16.4	16.3	18.7	19.8	23.9
OAS repayments	0.0	0.1	0.1	0.1	0.1	0.1	0.1	0.1	0.1	0.1	0.2	0.3
Commodity taxes	5.0	6.7	6.9	6.9	6.9	6.9	6.9	6.9	6.8	6.5	6.3	5.9
Provincial taxes	15.2	16.3	17.1	17.2	17.0	17.1	17.0	16.9	16.8	18.0	18.5	19.9
Income taxes	9.4	10.2	10.7	10.7	10.6	10.7	10.6	10.6	10.5	12.0	12.6	14.4
Commodity taxes	5.8	6.2	6.4	6.4	6.4	6.4	6.3	6.3	6.3	6.0	5.8	5.5

TABLE B4
Relative Tax Revenues for Ontario and Provincial Canada Residents (Table 3 entries as a percentage of Table B3 entries)

	Base		Population growth				Results for 2011					
							Labour force participation			Legislated indexation and economic growth		
Program	1988	1993	Low	Ont	Mid	High	2000	2020	CPP	Low	Mid	High
	1	2	3	4	5	6	7	8	9	10	11	12
Federal/provincial taxes	99	99	99	99	99	99	99	99	99	99	99	99
Federal taxes	103	102	102	101	102	102	102	102	101	101	101	101
Payroll taxes	96	96	96	96	96	95	95	96	96	96	96	96
C/QPP	96	95	95	95	95	95	95	95	95	95	95	95
UI	96	96	96	96	96	96	96	96	96	96	96	96
Income taxes	109	109	108	108	109	109	109	109	109	107	107	105
Income taxes	109	109	108	108	109	109	109	109	109	107	107	105
OAS repayments	0	129	120	120	120	120	133	133	133	115	120	106
Commodity taxes	92	92	91	91	91	91	92	92	91	92	92	91
Provincial taxes	91	94	94	93	94	94	94	94	94	94	94	96
Income taxes	86	93	93	92	93	93	93	93	93	92	93	96
Commodity taxes	99	96	96	95	96	96	97	96	96	96	97	96

TABLE B5
Net Fiscal Balances as Percentages of Aggregate Wages, for All Provincial Canada Residents and Ontario Residents as a Percentage of Canada

| | Base | | Population growth | | | | Results for 2011 | | | | | |
| | | | | | | | Labour force participation | | | Legislated indexation and economic growth | | |
Program	1988 1	1993 2	Low 3	Ont 4	Mid 5	High 6	2000 7	2020 8	CPP 9	Low 10	Mid 11	High 12
Canada (% Wages)												
Net fiscal balance	25.1	30.4	30.1	30.0	29.9	29.8	30.0	30.0	30.7	36.2	38.2	44.2
Federal (excl. C/QPP)	11.7	15.3	15.3	15.1	15.1	15.0	15.2	15.2	15.7	19.7	21.2	25.8
C/QPP	-0.5	0.2	-0.8	-0.8	-0.7	-0.7	-0.7	-0.7	-0.3	-0.3	-0.3	-0.3
Provincial	13.8	14.9	15.6	15.6	15.5	15.5	15.5	15.5	15.3	16.8	17.3	18.8
Ontario/Canada (%)												
Net fiscal balance	113	111	112	112	112	112	111	111	111	109	108	107
Federal	140	128	131	132	131	132	130	130	129	121	119	114
C/QPP	57	180	64	55	64	61	65	63	-85	-85	-85	-85
Provincial	91	94	94	94	95	94	94	94	94	95	95	98
Provincial	91.1	94.2	94.4	93.6	94.6	94.3	94.3	94.2	94.5	94.9	95.5	97.8

Appendix C: Distributional Tables

TABLE C1
Percentage distribution of Families and Unattached Individuals by Ratio of Family Income to Median Income, Selected Scenarios

Income to median ratio	Elderly families and unattached individuals			All census families and unattached individuals		
	Base 1993 (scenario 1)	CPP maturation (scenario 9)	Legislated indexation (scenario 11)	Base 1993 (scenario 9)	CPP maturation (scenario 9)	Legislated indexation (scenario 11)
0–.25	1.7	0.8	0.7	2.6	2.1	2.0
.26–.50	3.1	3.9	16.5	7.6	6.9	10.7
.51–.75	45.5	44.2	37.0	20.7	21.9	19.4
.76–1.0	19.3	21.3	18.2	19.1	19.1	17.9
1.01–1.25	11.7	12.1	10.4	17.2	16.4	15.3
1.26–1.5	6.8	6.3	6.3	11.3	10.8	10.9
1.51–1.75	4.6	4.6	4.2	7.7	7.8	7.9
1.76–2.0	2.1	1.6	1.6	4.9	5.0	5.3
2.01–2.5	2.3	2.5	2.3	4.4	4.8	4.9
2.5+	2.8	2.7	2.8	4.5	5.3	5.7

Notes

The authors accept full responsibility for any errors or omissions and for all views expressed herein. The analysis should not be taken as representing the views of Statistics Canada.

1 The fertility rate is the average number of births expected over a woman's lifetime.
2 For a discussion of this method see Lemaitre and Dufour 1987, and references included therein.
3 In his budget of 1985, the federal minister of finance stated that with respect to limited indexation of transfers "the government will review the adequacy of payments in light of future circumstances and will increase them as resources permit."
4 The analysis has not yet fully incorporated more recent population projections performed by the Ontario Ministry of Treasury and Economics in June 1991 (since renamed the Ministry of Finance). These projections reflect a fertility increase in the 1989–90 period and incorporate higher immigration assumptions. The projections result in roughly a 10 per cent increase in population over the appropriate Statistics Canada projection. It is not certain that the higher assumptions will be maintained throughout the projection period. New projections based on the 1991 census, corrected for undercount and transient populations, due later this year would serve as the basis for a more appropriate update. In any case, based on preliminary simulations not reported here, the Ontario projections produce burdens less than 1 per cent lower despite the difference in absolute populations.
5 A dependant, for purposes of the "labour force" dependency ratios, is either not in the 20–64 age range or is not in the labour force. We have not attempted to adjust for changes in retirement or education patterns.
6 The national accounts has always netted the child tax credit and refundable sales tax credit from total taxes. Beginning in 1990, the GST credit replaced the refundable sales tax credit and was treated as a transfer.
7 While these indexing assumptions may appear somewhat unrealistic over a two-decade period, note that the Ontario GAINS-A supplement for single pensioners has remained unchanged from 1984 to the present at $83 a month.

8 In the 1993 scenario, Ontario has 37 per cent of the population of Canada with 43 per cent of the employment income.

9 Scenario 2 reflects an increase in the UI contributions rate from 2.35 per cent to 3 per cent, while a corresponding increase in the payout of UI benefits refecting higher unemployment in 1993 is not simulated. As a result, this figure is overstated by roughly 1 per cent.

10 An equivalence scale accounts for economies of scale in the family. For a discussion see Wolfson and Evans 1990. In this study we adjusted family income by first setting the equivalent adult unit for each unattached individual to 1, and for each family to 1 plus 0.4 for each subsequent adult and 0.3 for each subsequent child (for example, a married couple with two children would have an EAU of $2.0 - 1 + 0.4 + 0.3 + 0.3$). The first child in a single-parent family is treated as an adult. Adjusted family income was then calculated as a family's disposable income divided by that family's EAU factor.

Bibliography

Beauchesne, E. 1993. "Alter Old-Age Pensions, Bureaucrat Warns." *The Ottawa Citizen*, May 6, 1993

Bordt, M., et al. 1990. "The Social Policy Simulation Database and Model: An Integrated Tool for Tax/Transfer Policy Analysis." 38 *Canadian Tax Journal*, 38: 48–65

Canada. 1988. *Canada Pension Plan Eleventh Statutory Actuarial Report*, Office of the Superintendent of Financial Institutions, December. Ottawa: Queen's Printer

- 1991. *Canada Pension Plan Twelfth Statutory Actuarial Report*, Office of the Superintendent of Financial Institutions, December. Ottawa: Queen's Printer

- 1992. *Canada Pension Plan Thirteenth Statutory Actuarial Report*, Office of the Superintendent of Financial Institutions, December. Ottawa: Queen's Printer

Conference Board of Canada. 1992. *Canadian Outlook Economic Forecast*, 8 (1) Autumn 1992. Conference Board of Canada

Falkingham, J. 1987. *Britain's Ageing Population: The Engine Behind Increased Dependency?* The Welfare State Programme, Discussion Paper No. 17. London: London School of Economics

Fellegi, I.P. 1988. "Can We Afford an Aging Society?" *Current Economic Observer*, 4.1–4.34. October 1988. Ottawa: Statistics Canada

Gault, V. 1993. "Pension, Health Systems in Peril." *The Globe and Mail*, April 8, 1993

Heller, P.S., R. Hemming, and P.W. Kohnert. 1986. "Aging and Social Expenditures in the Major Industrial Countries, 1980–2025." Occasional
Paper No. 47. International Monetary Fund, Washington DC, September
1986

Lemaitre, G., and J. Dufour. 1987. "An Integrated Method for Weighting
Persons and Families." *Survey Methodology*, 13 (2): 199–207

Murphy, B.B., and M.C. Wolfson. 1991. "When the Baby Boom Grows
Old: Impacts on Canada's Public Sector." *Statistical Journal of the United Nations Economic Commission for Europe*, 8 (1): 25–43

OECD. 1988. *Aging Populations: The Social Policy Implications*. OECD Manpower
and Social Affairs Committee Report, Paris

Statistics Canada. 1990. *Population Projections for Canada, Provinces and Territories*, Statistics Canada (Cat. No. 91-520), March 1990, Ottawa

Wolfson, M. 1989. *Inequality and Polarization: Is There a Disappearing Middle Class
in Canada?* Proceedings of the Statistics Canada Symposium on Analysis
of Data in Time, October 1989

Wolfson, M., et al. 1990. "The Social Policy Simulation Database and
Model: An Example of Survey and Administrative Data Integration." *69
Survey of Current Business*, May: 36–40

Wolfson, M., and J. Evans. 1990. "Statistics Canada's Low Income Cut-
Offs: Methodological Concerns and Possibilities." Statistics Canada Discussion Paper. Mimeo

Notes on Contributors

Bruce Campbell is research fellow and acting director for the Canadian Centre for Policy Alternatives, Ottawa.

David Conklin is research fellow, National Centre for Management Research and Development, Western Business School, University of Western Ontario.

Peter Dungan is adjunct associate professor of economics and associate director of the Policy and Economic Analysis program at the University of Toronto.

Brian Murphy is a senior researcher in the Analytical Studies Branch, Statistics Canada.

John Whalley is professor of economics, University of Western Ontario.

Michael Wolfson is director general of the Analytical Studies Branch, Statistics Canada.

Commission Organization

Chair*
Monica Townson

Vice-Chairs
Neiol Brooks**
Robert Couzin**

Commissioners
Jayne Berman
William Blundell
Susan Giampietri
Brigitte Kitchen**
Gérard Lafrenière
Fiona Nelson
Satya Poddar**

Executive Director
Hugh Mackenzie

Director of Research
Allan M. Maslove

Assistant Director of Research
Sheila Block

Executive Assistant to Research Program
Moira Hutchinson

Editorial Assistant
Marguerite Martindale

*Chair of the Research Subcommittee
**Member of the Research Subcommittee

Lightning Source UK Ltd.
Milton Keynes UK
UKHW010652160122
397192UK00001B/24